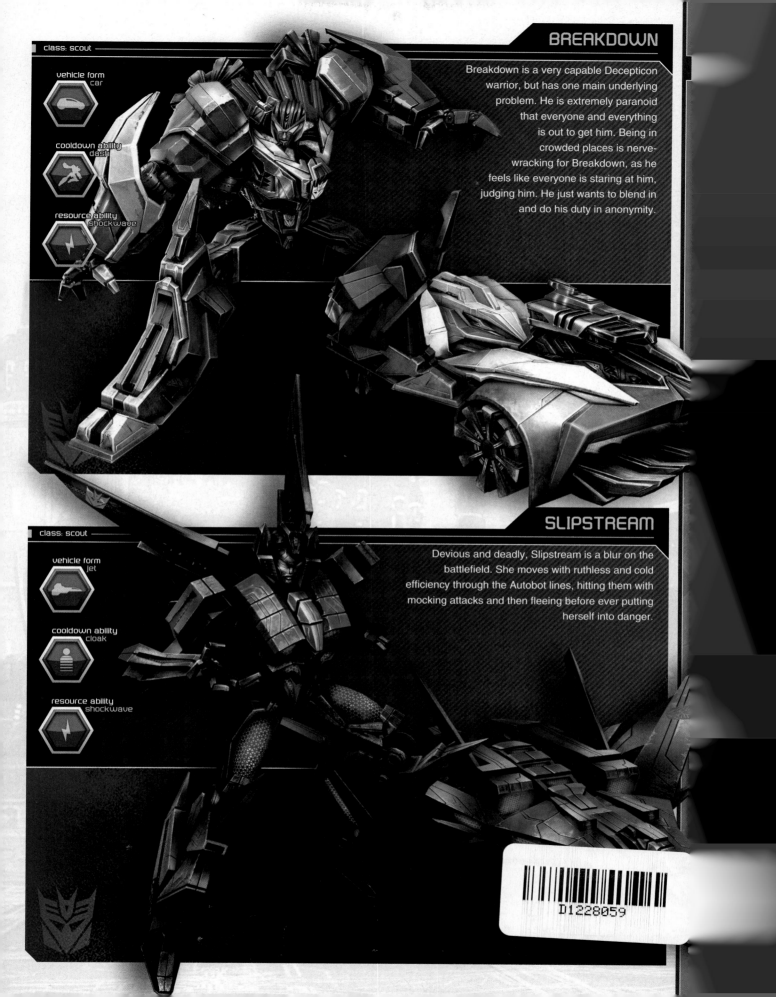

BREAKDOWN

class: scout

vehicle form
car

cooldown ability
dash

resource ability
shockwave

Breakdown is a very capable Decepticon warrior, but has one main underlying problem. He is extremely paranoid that everyone and everything is out to get him. Being in crowded places is nerve-wracking for Breakdown, as he feels like everyone is staring at him, judging him. He just wants to blend in and do his duty in anonymity.

SLIPSTREAM

class: scout

vehicle form
jet

cooldown ability
cloak

resource ability
shockwave

Devious and deadly, Slipstream is a blur on the battlefield. She moves with ruthless and cold efficiency through the Autobot lines, hitting them with mocking attacks and then fleeing before ever putting herself into danger.

ENEMIES

GENERAL ENEMIES

CAR SOLDIER

The Car Soldiers are the grunts in the war for Cybertron. Autobots and Decepticons both employ them, for they are plentiful. Car Soldiers carry basic weapons and do their best to lay down fire from a medium distance, using cover wherever possible. As their names imply, Car Soldiers can transform into cars when they want to zoom long distances.

- Their heads are small, but a headshot on a Car Soldier is an instant kill.
- Because their weapons are effective mainly at medium distance, Car Soldiers are easy pickings if you have a long-range weapon (e.g. Null Ray) or want to engage them at close range (e.g. EMP Shotgun, melee attacks).
- When you see a Car Soldier take cover, move around and flank to hit him from an unexpected angle

JET SOLDIER

Jet Soldiers are much like their Car Soldier counterparts in that they aren't very tough, and they prefer to engage enemies from medium distance. In robot form, Jet Soldiers hover above the ground via foot boosters. In vehicle form, Jet Soldiers are serious aerial threats. They lay down machinegun fire from high above, and they perform quick bombing runs to carpet the area with explosives.

- Target a Jet Soldier's foot boosters to send it flying.
- Jet Soldiers' bombing runs move in a straight line. When you see one coming, move to one side as quickly as possible.

ROCKET SOLDIER

Rocket Soldiers are upgraded versions of the regular troops, launching heat-seeking missiles from their Thermo Rocket Launchers. They prefer to stay at range, blasting you with their artillery, rather than move in for close-range combat.

- When a Rocket Soldier locks onto you, you see a "Missile Inbound" message on your HUD—this is a good time to take cover.
- The Rocket Soldier's preference for long distances can work to your advantage; the missiles they fire are avoidable if you pay attention and strafe to safety.

SHOTGUNNER

Masters of close-range combat, the Shotgunner is equipped with an EMP Shotgun, which deals massive damage at short range. As he approaches his enemies, the Shotgunner lobs a Flak Grenade right at them. As if that isn't bad enough, the Shotgunner also sports an Overshield, which he can regenerate. Be prepared to dump a lot of ammunition into this highly armored damage-dealing machine.

- Keep your distance from the Shotgunners whenever possible, as a shotgun blast at close range will shred your armor.
- When a Shotgunner's Overshield goes down, stay on him and follow up quickly with additional attacks before he can recharge his shield.
- Watch out for grenades—you'll see a small icon over live grenades that fall nearby.

CLOAKER

- If you see shimmering areas that look like heat distortion, you're most likely looking at a Cloaker.

- When a Cloaker charges its Plasma Cannon, you see the weapon start to glow—it looks like a floating ball of energy. That means the Cloaker is about to fire, so either attack the floating ball or get out of the way.

- Weapons that spray many bullets or create big explosions work great against Cloakers, because even a small amount of damage temporary disables their cloaking mechanisms.

The Cloaker is a prototype that has no vehicle mode. He is a master of stealth and misdirection—his strength lies in his ability to become nearly invisible. Cloakers use the Plasma Cannon in combat. They are very fast and very potent, so stay on your toes.

ROCKETEER

- Don't waste ammo on a Rocketeer's shield. Wait for it to drop—that's your chance to blast this enemy.

- When possible, a good flanking position works wonders against the Rocketeer, as the shield protects only the enemy's front side.

The Rocketeer functions almost like the Rocket Soldier. The main difference is that the Rocketeer generates a massive shield out from the ground, taking cover behind it. It's totally protected behind this shield, so shooting it does nothing. However, the Rocketeer is also immobile. Once it plants, it isn't going anywhere. When the Rocketeer has a good shot at an enemy, it rises up and the shield folds away, exposing the Rocketeer while it fires its rockets.

SNIPER

- Look for the Sniper's telltale laser sight as the enemy scans the area—sometimes you see the laser before you see the Sniper, giving you an idea of where it's located. Exploit this chance to attack the enemy before it attacks you.

- If the Sniper's laser locks onto you, quickly get behind cover to break the sightline.

- If you can, move around and take out Snipers from close range—they aren't very tough, and their attacks are much less effective.

The Sniper is a soldier variant that specializes in long-range combat, seeking out distant targets with its Null Ray. Snipers employ highly effective laser scanners. With enough time to calibrate sufficiently, these scanners pinpoint weak spots on a target in order to inflict maximum damage with each shot.

PROTECTOR

- Because the Protector usually assumes a more defensive posture, it's more vulnerable to long-range attacks.

This enemy has a load-out similar to the Car Soldier, but it employs unique battle tactics. When combat begins, the Protector stays in the back lines, firing from strategic defensive positions in order to stifle the advancing enemy.

SPIDERBOT

A mindless attacking drone, the Spiderbot has only one function: to seek you out and overwhelm you with numbers. Alone, the Spiderbot is virtually harmless… but they're rarely alone. If you see one, be prepared for many more. They're fast moving and fast attacking, so be wary when a mob of Spiderbots creeps your way.

- Weapons with splash damage work wonders against groups of Spiderbots.
- Avoid getting surrounded by multiple Spiderbots—a horde of these small machines can quickly chew through your armor.
- Low on ammo? If you time it right, you can melee stomp a Spiderbot without taking damage from its attacks.

BRUTE

The Brute is a hulking presence that wades into battle with a huge melee weapon and Energon shield. At medium range, the Brute attacks with a devastating EMP shockwave that temporarily scrambles your HUD and slows you down. Then, once you're unable to get away, the Brute rushes in to deliver powerful melee attacks. The Brute's armor is nearly impregnable, and its Energon shield can absorb unlimited amounts of fire. The only way to destroy a Brute is to destroy the Energon fuel tank on its back. This fuel tank becomes very unstable when sufficiently damaged, and when it explodes, the Brute is vaporized.

- With good timing, you can lure the Brute in to swing its melee weapon at you, then quickly sidestep its attack and shoot its energy pack.
- When the Brute whirls its hammer overhead, that means it's about to create an EMP blast—jump to avoid the blast wave and its slowing effects.
- If you move around the Brute's shield and inflict enough damage to its body, you can cause it to stumble, giving you a brief window to fire at the energy pack on its back.
- When the Brute's fuel tank is about to explode (you see lots of sparks, and the Brute stops and flails about), get out of there. The explosion damages anyone in the blast radius.
- When you play a Co-op Campaign or Escalation, work with your teammates to lure the Brute toward one player while other players focus fire on its back.

TITAN

Very similar to Brutes in size and strength, these hulking machines march into battle wielding tremendous Ion Displacers. Although Titans are slow-moving opponents, they can deliver a huge amount of damage and have very thick armor.

- Use speed and cover to stay out of an enemy Titan's line of fire.
- Be sure to pick up the Titan's big gun after you destroy the enemy. If you're in a fight against other opponents, it pays to pick off the Titan first, and then use its gun on the other enemies.

TANK (AUTOBOT DEFENDER, DECEPTICON DESTROYER)

This massive war machine can shred even the strongest opponents. It has two forms: vehicle and robot.

In its giant tank vehicle form, it possesses a massive cannon that fires high-impact explosive projectiles. If you get too close, the Tank unleashes an area-of-effect blast that pushes you back, scrambles your HUD, and slows you down for a short time. The vehicle is heavily armored, with only one vulnerable spot on its conversion cog, located on the back of the vehicle. If you destroy the Tank's conversion cog, it'll be forced to change to robot form.

The Tank has several powerful weapons at its disposal in robot form. First, it uses an amped-up Magma Frag Launcher to fire sticky grenades at targets. Second, the Tank has a mini-cannon, which can spray gunfire in a wide arc to hit multiple targets. And finally, if you get too close to the Tank, it performs an area-of-effect blast to push you away, similar to the one it uses in its vehicle form. The Tank is still very tough in robot form, but you can blast away the armored torso to reveal its vulnerable core.

- When you fight the Tank in vehicle form, avoid the main cannon at all costs. The cannon swivels slowly to track targets, so move fast to get behind it. Once you're behind it, blast away at the vulnerable back panel before the cannon can get a fix on you.
- Watch out for the Tank robot's sticky grenades—even if they don't hit you, they detonate after a few seconds and cause damage to anyone nearby.
- In robot form, the Tank stomps its foot just before firing a barrage from the mini-cannon—watch for this and take cover when it happens.
- You need to peel away only enough torso armor to expose the inner core. After knocking off a few pieces of armor (once you can see the glowing inner core), focus all your fire there until the Tank is destroyed.

SENTRIES

There are three types of automated sentries: Laser Sentries, Rocket Sentries, and Repair Sentries. All three can deploy from out of a wall, floor, or ceiling, depending on the environment. The Laser and Rocket Sentries fire at you until they are destroyed, or until you exit their field of fire. Neither of these sentries is particularly tough alone, though they can inflict a great deal of damage in numbers. Repair Sentries mend allied units until they are fully healed, or until the target is out of range.

- Sentries placed on walls or ceiling may be hard to spot at first—keep your eyes open for these threats. When all else fails, use your HUD's damage indicator to find them.
- If you see that enemies are being repaired during a fight, trace the beam back to the Repair Sentry and destroy that first. Any fight can seem next to impossible if your opponent is constantly being healed.

CYBERTRON SWEEPER

This floating maintenance unit is relatively harmless. When undisturbed, it conducts its scanning routines in peace. If you get too close to it or shoot it, it ceases its scan and pivots to blast you with its Energon beam. Once alerted, the Cybertron Sweeper does its best to track you, but it turns slowly as it does so.

- Use the Sweeper's reduced turning rate to your advantage by moving continually and attacking it from behind

WEAPONS

Weapon damage changes based on difficulty level. The numbers contained in this chapter reflect the Normal difficulty setting.

BASICS
CHARACTERS
WEAPONS
WALKTHROUGH
01
02
03
04
05
06
07
08
09
10
MULTIPLAYER
ACHIEVEMENTS

RANGED WEAPONS

NEUTRON ASSAULT RIFLE

Single Player/Multiplayer	
Damage	17
Rate of Fire	.095
Clip Size	32
Max Ammo	224
Reload Time	1.5s
Effective Range	Medium

This rapid-fire assault rifle has a high rate of fire, medium accuracy, and short reload time, making it a well-rounded weapon.

NULL RAY

Single Player/Multiplayer		
Damage	200	170
Rate of Fire	1.25	1.25
Clip Size	4	4
Max Ammo	20	16
Reload Time	2.5s	2.5s
Effective Range		Long

This sniper rifle with 10x scope is the best long-distance weapon in the arsenal. However, it is effective only in scope mode; accuracy from the hip is very low.

PHOTON BURST RIFLE

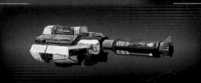

Single Player/Multiplayer	
Damage	29 (x3)
Rate of Fire	.3
Clip Size	24
Max Ammo	144
Reload Time	1.5s
Effective Range	Medium-Long

This scoped, semi-automatic rifle fires three-round bursts. The high damage per burst and its 2x Scope make the Photon Burst Rifle a highly accurate damage dealer. However, its slow rate of fire and its limited ammo capacity leave little room for error, so every shot counts.

ION BLASTER

Single Player/Multiplayer		
Damage	12	14
Rate of Fire	.065	.065
Clip Size	50	50
Max Ammo	300	300
Reload Time	1.5s	1.5s
Effective Range		Close

The Ion Blaster is a fully automatic SMG. In single-player, this weapon is exclusive to Optimus Prime. Its low damage and wide spread are balanced by having the highest rate of fire of any weapon and one of the biggest clips. It is very effective at close range.

ENERGON BATTLE PISTOL

Single Player/Multiplayer		
Damage	95	85
Rate of Fire	.5	.5
Clip Size	8	8
Max Ammo	40	24
Reload Time	1.5s	1.5ss
Effective Range		Medium-Long

This is a heavy pistol with a 5x Scope. The Energon Battle Pistol packs a punch with big damage and an even bigger kick. It has a slow rate of fire but fast reload time. Its scope gives each shot the potential for surgical precision.

ENERGON REPAIR RAY

Single Player/Multiplayer	
Damage	55
Rate of Fire	.1
Clip Size	100
Max Ammo	400
Reload Time	2.5s
Effective Range	Close

This beam weapon heals teammates and damages enemies. The Energon Repair Ray is a better defensive weapon than an offensive one, due to its healing capabilities and short range. Its beam locks onto any target at which it is aimed within its range.

FUSION CANNON

Single Player	Multiplayer
Damage	
125	95
Rate of Fire	
.8	.75
Clip Size	
5	5
Max Ammo	
20	15
Reload Time	
2.5s	2.5s
Effective Range	
Medium-Long	

The Fusion Cannon is a bazooka-like projectile launcher capable of large splash damage. In single-player, this weapon is exclusive to Megatron. Its automatic fire mode makes the Fusion Cannon unique. Its large splash damage radius means that misses can still deliver moderate damage.

PLASMA CANNON

Single Player	Multiplayer
Damage	
125/200/350	115/140/180
Rate of Fire	
.75/2/3.5	.75/2/3.5
Clip Size	
100	100
Max Ammo	
600	500
Reload Time	
2.5s	2.5s
Effective Range	
Medium-Long	

The Plasma Cannon is a powerful charge weapon with three levels of charge—the longer it's charged, the more deadly it becomes. Timing is everything with this weapon, as its ammo clip drains steadily when it reaches its final charge level.

SCATTER BLASTER

Single Player/Multiplayer
Damage
104
Rate of Fire
.4
Clip Size
6
Max Ammo
36
Reload Time
2.5s
Effective Range
Close

The Scatter Blaster is a full-auto shotgun, one of the most effective close range weapons in the arsenal. While its high rate of fire makes it powerful up close, its wide spread greatly reduces its effectiveness from medium and long range.

X12 SCRAPMAKER

Single Player/Multiplayer
Damage
30
Rate of Fire
.4-.09
Clip Size
60
Max Ammo
300
Reload Time
2.5s
Effective Range
Medium

The X12 Scrapmaker is a fully automatic mini-gun. Unlike its predecessor, the X11, the X12 Scrapmaker no longer overheats or misfires when it's down to its last clip. The X12 slowly winds up before unleashing its full power. It is the ultimate spray-bullets-everywhere weapon. Point the X12 in a general direction and ride its wave of awesomeness. You don't control it; the X12 controls you.

EMP SHOTGUN

Single Player/Multiplayer
Damage
169
Rate of Fire
.5
Clip Size
2
Max Ammo
20
Reload Time
2.5s
Effective Range
Short-Close

The EMP Shotgun is a semi-automatic combat shotgun. It holds only two shots per clip, but rest assured those two shots pack a mighty punch. It delivers double damage within short range, making it the ultimate close-quarters weapon and a strong counter to an impending melee attack.

MAGMA FRAG LAUNCHER

Single Player	Multiplayer
Damage	
250	145
Rate of Fire	
1.1	1.1
Clip Size	
3	3
Max Ammo	
15	12
Reload Time	
2.5s	2.5s
Effective Range	
Medium	

The Magma Frag Launcher fires sticky grenades that adhere to any surface, after which they can be detonated manually at any time.

THERMO ROCKET LAUNCHER

Single Player	Multiplayer
Damage	
185	135
Rate of Fire	
1.25	1.2
Clip Size	
4	4
Max Ammo	
16	12
Reload Time	
2.5s	2.5s
Effective Range	
Medium-Long	

This weapon is a rocket launcher with vehicle lock-on capabilities. The Thermo Rocket Launcher functions like a standard rocket launcher when aimed at robots. However, it truly shines against vehicles. By aiming at a vehicle, you can obtain a lock-on and fire heat-seeking missiles.

ION DISPLACER

Single Player	Multiplayer
Damage	
30	25
Rate of Fire	
.065	.065
Clip Size	
300	300
Max Ammo	
N/A	N/A
Reload Time	
N/A	N/A
Effective Range	
Medium-Long	

When mounted, this machinegun turret has unlimited ammo and delivers massive damage at a high rate of fire. But why stay in one place when you can rip it from its mount and go mobile? However, while you carry it, the Ion Displacer has limited ammo and it reduces your mobility.

NUCLEON SHOCK CANNON

Single Player/Multiplayer
Damage
400
Rate of Fire
1.75
Clip Size
10
Max Ammo
N/A
Reload Time
N/A
Effective Range
Medium-Long

When mounted, this rocket turret has unlimited ammo and causes huge damage but with a slow rate of fire. Like the Ion Displacer, it can be ripped from its mounting and carried. Likewise, in this configuration it has limited ammo and slows your movement.

BASICS
CHARACTERS
WEAPONS
WALKTHROUGH
MULTIPLAYER
ACHIEVEMENTS

MELEE

Each Autobot and Decepticon has access to powerful melee weapons, which can be used to dispatch enemies quickly at close range.

Single Player/Multiplayer

Damage
169

Effective Range
Short-Close

ENERGON BATTLE AXE

Melee weapon used by Autobot Leaders. A large-bladed axe used to chop through enemies.

ENERGON WAR AXE

A melee weapon used by Decepticon Leaders. Decepticons hack through foes with this large-bladed axe.

ENERGON BLADE

A melee weapon used by Autobot Scouts. A small and sharp sword used to slice enemies.

ENERGON SCIMITAR

A melee weapon used by Decepticon Scouts. Decepticons deliver a vicious cut to enemies using the Scimitar.

ENERGON CLUB

A melee weapon used by Autobot Scientists—they pummel their foes with this weapon.

ENERGON MACE

A melee weapon used by Decepticon Scientists. The Energon Mace smashes through enemies.

ENERGON HAMMER

A melee weapon used by Autobot Soldiers. Soldiers pound their enemies with this Energon Hammer.

ENERGON MAUL

A melee weapon used by Decepticon Soldiers. The Maul crushes anyone in the Soldier's way.

ENERGON DOUBLE AXE

A unique melee weapon used by Optimus Prime. It allows Prime to deliver resounding blows to the Decepticons.

ENERGON MORNINGSTAR

A unique melee weapon used by Megatron. This spiked cudgel allows Megatron to obliterate those who oppose him.

GRENADES

FLAK GRENADES

Single Player/Multiplayer

Damage	
450	325

Damage Radius	
200	200

Max Ammo	
3	1

These explosive grenades are great against a group of enemies, as they deliver high damage to a large radius.

THERMO MINES

Single Player/Multiplayer

Damage	
250	140

Max Ammo	
3	1

When in range, these heat-seeking mines hunt down their targets.

EMP GRENADES

EMP Grenades are like flash-bangs that blind and slow enemies. They're extremely useful if you want to stun a tough enemy and make it more vulnerable, or if you're taking heavy fire and just need a breather.

ENERGON GRENADES

Energon Grenades are explosives that create a temporary healing aura. The aura can heal multiple players, making them extremely effective if you throw them into a group of allies.

GENERAL GAMEPLAY TIPS

- In the Campaign, collect Energon Shards from fallen enemies to power your abilities.

- If an enemy gets too close for comfort, smash it with a melee attack.

- If you run out of ammo for your robot weapons, don't forget about your vehicle weapons.

- Remember to reload your weapon after every firefight.

- Firing in bursts helps maintain your accuracy. Be sure to spend your ammo on hurting your enemy, not the environment. Otherwise, you may find yourself out of ammo with an opponent on your heels.

- Remember to use your fine aim. It can come in very handy for long-range fights, and it helps you pick out enemies in Campaign and Escalation modes. Just be aware of your flanks.

- While jumping and shooting simultaneously may seem like a good avoidance tactic, remember that your accuracy decreases when you try to shoot while you're jumping. Try to use jumping for navigating the maps.

- It's easy to get caught up in the moment trying to destroy the enemy by just shooting. Don't forget about your abilities, which can be extremely useful. Keep an eye on your ability recharge, and plan for your next attack.

- Every weapon has an optimum engagement range. Using a given weapon can help or hinder you depending on the situation and the purpose for which the weapon is intended. Plan your load-out for each map to optimize your ability to destroy opponents.

- Use the boost ability in your vehicle form to jump gaps that you normally can't traverse in robot form.

- Using two abilities in conjunction with each other can help you eliminate opponents faster. In some cases, it enhances offensive and defensive traits.

- Some maps have setups, which allow for sneak attacks on your enemies from ledges, windows, behind boxes, etc.

CAMPAIGN GAMEPLAY TIPS

- Jets have infinite ammo in Campaign modes. Use this to your advantage.

- If all else fails, use splash damage to harm a Brutes' back.

- Rip turrets off their bases. This keeps you mobile with massive firepower.

- EMP Grenades freeze opponents in the Campaign. This is especially useful for Brutes and enemies with Overshields.

- Dash is an excellent evasion tool.

- Shockwave is the best area-of-effect ability.

- The Thermo Rocket Launcher is one of the best weapons in Campaign mode; it's great against every boss in the game. Its splash damage can help demolish multiple normal enemies at once, and it can lock onto Jet Soldier enemies.

- Recommended load-out: one machinegun, one heavy weapon.

- All of the "time trial" achievements/trophies are located at checkpoints that you can load into directly from the Chapter Select menu. If you don't get the achievement/trophy right away, simply go back to the Chapter Select and try again.

- In a Co-Op game, one player should always play as the healer.v

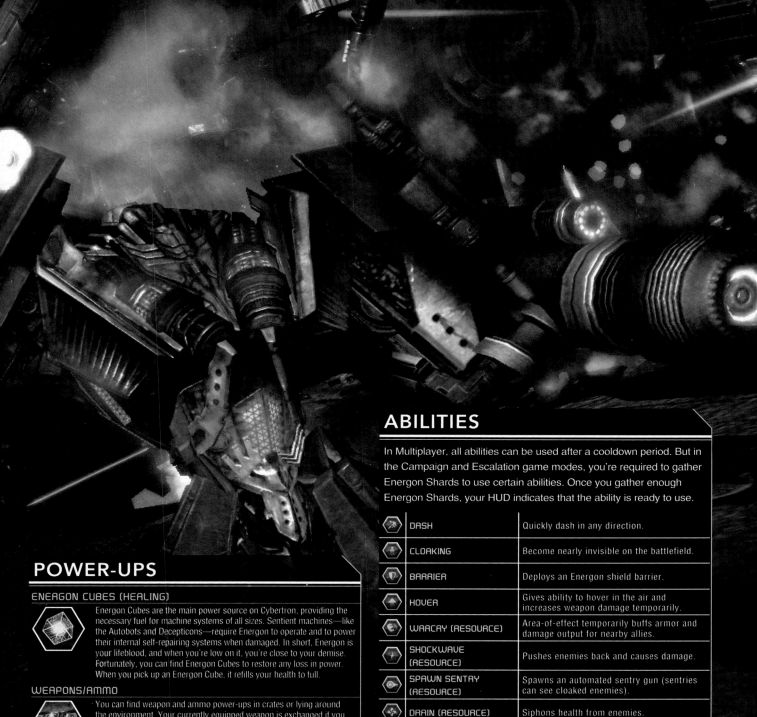

ABILITIES

In Multiplayer, all abilities can be used after a cooldown period. But in the Campaign and Escalation game modes, you're required to gather Energon Shards to use certain abilities. Once you gather enough Energon Shards, your HUD indicates that the ability is ready to use.

	DASH	Quickly dash in any direction.
	CLOAKING	Become nearly invisible on the battlefield.
	BARRIER	Deploys an Energon shield barrier.
	HOVER	Gives ability to hover in the air and increases weapon damage temporarily.
	WARCRY (RESOURCE)	Area-of-effect temporarily buffs armor and damage output for nearby allies.
	SHOCKWAVE (RESOURCE)	Pushes enemies back and causes damage.
	SPAWN SENTRY (RESOURCE)	Spawns an automated sentry gun (sentries can see cloaked enemies).
	DRAIN (RESOURCE)	Siphons health from enemies.
	WHIRLWIND (RESOURCE)	Provides the ability to perform a Whirlwind melee attack.
	MARK TARGET (MP ONLY)	Tags an enemy with an electromagnetic pulse, which weakens the target's armor and reveals its location.
	MOLECULON BOMB (MP ONLY)	Slows enemies who get near it, and causes damage when it explodes.
	DECOY TRAP (MP ONLY)	Spawns a decoy power-up, which stuns enemies when touched.
	DISGUISE (MP ONLY)	Allows the user to appear to the enemy as an ally.
	ENERGON SLING (MP ONLY)	Prevents or cancels the targeted enemy from using abilities.
	DISRUPTION (MP ONLY)	An area-of-effect ability that forces enemies to change form, locking them into that form for a brief time.
	AMMO BEACON (MP ONLY)	Deploys a beacon that automatically refills a teammate's ammo and infuses his or her weapons with Acid Rounds when near it.

POWER-UPS

ENERGON CUBES (HEALING)

Energon Cubes are the main power source on Cybertron, providing the necessary fuel for machine systems of all sizes. Sentient machines—like the Autobots and Decepticons—require Energon to operate and to power their internal self-repairing systems when damaged. In short, Energon is your lifeblood, and when you're low on it, you're close to your demise. Fortunately, you can find Energon Cubes to restore any loss in power. When you pick up an Energon Cube, it refills your health to full.

WEAPONS/AMMO

You can find weapon and ammo power-ups in crates or lying around the environment. Your currently equipped weapon is exchanged if you choose to pick up a new weapon. Weapons already in your inventory gain additional ammo when you walk or drive over them. Ammo power-ups fully refill ammunition for all of the weapons in your inventory.

OVERSHIELD

Equips you with temporary armor. While an Overshield is equipped, your health does not decrease as you take damage. However, the Overshield does not regenerate, and it depletes as you receive damage. Once the Overshield is gone, your health is vulnerable once again.

GRENADES

Similar to weapon and ammo power-ups, you can find grenade power-ups in their own special crate or lying around the environment. You can carry only one type of grenade. The grenade type that you have in your inventory automatically refills when you walk or drive over these power-ups.

ENERGON SHARDS

Energon Shards are small, unrefined bits of Energon that are released when Cybertron entities—robots, vehicles, sentries, and so forth—are destroyed. Although Energon Shards don't heal you, they provide the energy to enable certain powerful abilities (Campaign and Escalation game modes only).

DARK ENERGON

Civil War has ravaged Cybertron, which has been the Transformers' homeworld for millions of years. Megatron, the leader of the Decepticons, has recently discovered an ancient power that gives him the upper hand in the battle with the detested Autobots.

Called Dark Energon, this power remains locked away in an orbital station, under the protection of a Sky Commander named Starscream. Anxious to claim Dark Energon for himself, Megatron leads an all-out assault on the once forgotten station.

AVAILABLE CHARACTERS

MEGATRON

Pure power. His tank shell can crush enemies, and his Fusion Cannon, combined with the weapon-buffing Hover ability, blows away opponents.

BRAWL

The combination of his Dash ability and the power derived from his tank vehicle mode is devastating. This makes Brawl a well-balanced character and a smart pick for this level.

BARRICADE

Barricade can use his abilities to keep his enemies at bay. His Shockwave tears opponents apart while pushing them backward, and he can deploy a Barrier to shield himself from enemy fire. Barricade is a great defensive selection for this level.

CO-OP TIPS

If both players are tanks (Megatron and Brawl), stay in vehicle mode together; the combined might of two tanks shelling is unstoppable.

When you confront a battle with multiple lines, use Barricade's Energon Barrier to protect one of your sides.

If large numbers of enemies begin to swarm you, Megatron's Drain ability siphons life from them. This defeats multiple enemies simultaneously and keeps Megatron alive. Make sure Megatron stocks up on Energon Shards so he can unleash this Drain ability whenever necessary.

INTRODUCTION

Megatron, hell bent on acquiring Dark Energon, has crashed his War Cruiser into the Orbital Station. He begins to scour the facility in search of its location. With help from Soundwave, the Decepticons regroup and move forward.

SECTION 1 CRASH SITE

Stage Number

Door

Callout Number

Direction Arrow

Interact Switch

Weapon Pick-Up

Ammo Pick-Up

Energon Cube

Turret

Energon Shard Container

Shield

Grenade

Autobot Symbol

Decepticon Symbol

OBJECTIVE: ESCAPE THE CRASH SITE

STAGE 1

You begin this mission in the damaged cargo hold of your warship ①, which you just purposely crashed into the Orbital Station. Your wrecked ship's Energon core is unstable and threatens to explode.

DAMAGE INDICATOR

Notice the red damage indicator in the middle of the screen. It's designed to show you the direction from which incoming damage originates. The indicator's illuminated lower-middle portion tells you that fire at your back is damaging you; your controller also shakes as you suffer damage.

Your first priority is to get off your ship and traverse the crash site to safety. Things are burning, falling, and exploding all around you, but you're never in any real danger; this first stage gets you acquainted with the controls, movement, and power-ups.

Jump off the damaged warship. Then exit the crash site by performing a series of jumps along the room's left side ② to surmount the layers of debris. A short cinematic plays when you reach the brightly lit area at the top of the wreckage.

21

STAGE 2

Once you make it out of the crash site, the ship detonates, closing you and your companions into one room ③. As the explosion dissipates, a hologram appears! It's Starscream, the sky commander in charge of this Orbital Station. After he has a brief conversation with Megatron, sentry guns deploy from the walls and begin to fire on you.

CAMERA SHIFT

When key events occur, such as when the Decepticon reinforcements enter the room, you can press Down on the D-pad to shift the camera angle toward the key event's location. This can help you avoid missing any of the action.

An ammo crate is in the room, so you should have enough ammunition to liberally unleash your guns on the targets. Once all six sentry guns are destroyed, your Decepticon reinforcements break down the door to your left ④, enabling you to travel deeper into the space station in search of the Dark Energon.

SECTION 2 — ENTERING ORBITAL STATION

OBJECTIVE: SECURE THE STATION

STAGE 1

After you exit the hologram room, follow the corridors with your troops. You can find health and ammunition throughout this hallway. Round the next corner to the right, and you find more sentry guns shredding some of your troops. Large columns divide the hallway ⑤. Use the columns as cover from the sentry guns' fire. Destroy the guns from cover, and move up the hallway to the locked door at the end ⑥. To open the door, interact with the switch on its left side.

STAGE 2

As you enter the storage supply room, you witness troops running behind large windows, trying to get to you. Move farther into the room to greet your first mobile enemies. Car Soldiers drive down a ramp ⑦, convert into robots before your eyes, and prepare to shoot you where you stand! Plenty of storage crates in this room provide ample cover. Stay covered—the robots are much smarter than the sentry guns.

When you win this battle, Megatron instructs you to locate a switch that triggers lifting a box, moving it across the room, and dropping it. The switch is located on the second level. To find the switch, simply ascend the ramp ⑦ down which the soldiers drove. The dropped crate creates a step-like platform. This makeshift platform allows you to exit via the fiery hole ⑧ that your war cruiser created when it crashed into the Orbital Station. Before you go, a few more station defenders stream in from that direction, so take cover and eliminate them.

SECTION ③ THE AMBUSH

STAGE 1

Once you cross over the crate stack and reach the hole ⑧ that your kamikaze ship created, you must negotiate the flaming pathway. Two broken pipes shoot intermittent jets of fire, so pass each one just as it quits firing. You can find a Magma Frag Launcher (grenade launcher) at the end of the path, next to a soldier crushed under a large pillar. Because you currently have only one weapon, you can take the grenade launcher without replacing any other weapons. Once you possess two guns, any new weapon you pick up replaces your equipped weapon.

DECEPTICON COLLECTIBLE #1

The first Decepticon collectible is on the high beam above the ambush room. You can easily shoot the Autobot symbol from the ledge where the weapon power-up is located. You collect these icons by shooting them.

From the weapon power up, you look down into a large chamber and observe the ambushers that ran past you in the previous room. A holographic Starscream confers with his troops. They're under the impression that you're coming through the door they're guarding ⑨ and not the crash tunnel.

Get the drop on the troops waiting to ambush you by interacting with the switch to the left of the weapon. This drops an explosive on their heads, defeating several. Jump down into the chamber and use the storage crates for cover. You must endure several waves of station defenders, so stay stocked with the health and ammo distributed around the room. When you defeat the last wave, the door 🔟 leading out of the room opens, revealing

three more enemies. Blast them and move forward into the next room.

STAGE 2

Enter the horseshoe-shaped room 🔟, and walk around its glass-enclosed center. The room suddenly crackles to life as the holographic Starscream begins to harass Megatron. There is one health crate and one ammunition crate along your path. Proceed through the exit at the room's opposite end ⑪.

SECTION ④ MOVING FORWARD

OBJECTIVE:

MEET SOUNDWAVE AT THE FORWARD BASE

STAGE 1

Round the corner and confront the enemies at the end of the hallway. If you are playing as Megatron, then use the tank form to shoot long-range shells down the hallway ⑫. Otherwise, exploit some of the short cover; this small hallway can be deadly. Defeat the enemies and move up the hallway toward the debris. As you get closer, more enemies jump down toward you. Crush them!

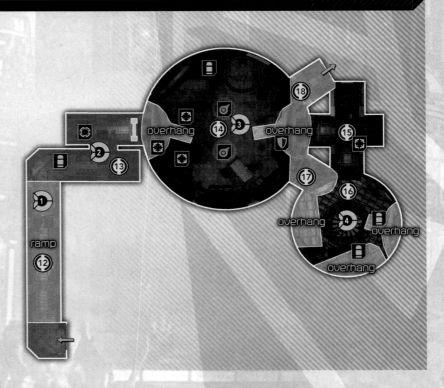

STAGE 2

Double-jump to the top of the debris ledges at the hallway's end, and then round the next corner. You can find ammunition in this area, if you need it. A sentry gun appears at the end of the next hallway ⑬. Take cover behind the large storage crate on your left, and take out the sentry. Two more station defenders blow open a hole in the wall to the left of the sentry gun. Remain behind cover and take them out. Once they're dead, step through the blast hole. An Energon Shard crate is to the left of the blast hole as you walk through it.

STAGE 3

Now step through the automatic shutter door, and move out onto the balcony overlooking a very large chamber ⑭. Find the ammo and health power-up on the same balcony.

OVERSHIELD

If you happen to be playing as Megatron or Brawl, you have the opportunity to grab an Overshield before you drop off the bridge. Run off the end of the bridge, and double-jump at the last second. At your jump's apex, activate either hover or dash, depending on your character. Reach the other side of the broken bridge, where the Overshield is located. Smash it and then jump to the bottom of the chamber.

Walk off the end of the broken bridge to drop down to the floor below. Don't worry; you won't take damage. The floor is littered with storage containers, two health crates, one ammunition crate, and two heavy Ion Displacers. Mount one of these bad boys and prepare to blast a slew of station defenders. Waves of Starscream's troops attempt to stop your progress. They start by entering via the balcony, and then though the doorway underneath—this provides you with an exit.

Once you're finished exploiting the turret's unlimited ammo, rip it from its mount and go mobile. At this point, the ammo is no longer unlimited—you have 250 rounds. Pick up the Energon Cubes at the back of the room if you need repairs. A hidden Energon Repair Ray is also on the room's right side, facing the enemy entry points.

STAGE 4

Enter the new hallway ⑮ and turn right at the intersection to find your enemies using a new weapon in the next chamber ⑯; they launch powerful missiles. These projectiles inflict much greater damage than anything you've dealt with so far, so avoid them. These enemies also have the advantage of higher ground. Use cover to take them out, and then find the stash of ammunition under the broken ramp. Jump up onto the broken ramp to reach the upper level.

Two more rocket soldiers engage you from the next exit as you make your way across the balconies. Deal with these pests in the same manner you eliminated the previous nuisances. Proceed forward into the next hallway ⑰ and neutralize one last station defender ⑱. Blast him in the back and make your way into the now Decepticon-controlled Command Center.

STAGE 1

Megatron is welcomed into his base of operations. The Decepticons have captured many of Starscream's soldiers. The more troublesome are properly silenced, while the others are left in their bonds.

"YOUR LUCKY DAY" ACHIEVEMENT/TROPHY

Destroying all but one of the captured soldiers, and then activating the lift unlocks the "Sole Survivor" achievement/trophy.

On the lift 19, you can see Jetfire hovering outside, imploring Megatron to give up the quest for Dark Energon. The substance is too dangerous, but that's exactly what Megatron is hoping. Approach the control panels when you reach the next floor.

Soundwave updates you on the status of your forces and provides the next objective: Secure the nearby data matrix center and download the station schematics to Soundwave for analysis. Before you leave via the next lift 20, collect the many ammo power-ups in the operations room.

OBJECTIVE: **SECURE THE STATION SCHEMATICS**

STAGE 2

The battle here isn't going as well for the Decepticons, and there are many wounded. Before you proceed though the newly opened doorway, notice a stash of Flak Grenades near it. Pick up a stack—you can put them to good use in the battles to come. As you move though the hallway 21, notice the other major pickup in this area: an EMP Shotgun. Activate the lift at the end of the hallway and proceed to the front lines.

STAGE 3

At the top of the lift (20), you find several wounded Decepticons, along with a few holding back Starscream's troopers. It's too late for these Decepticons. Exact Megatron's revenge by exterminating the two station defenders here. Try using your newly acquired EMP Shotgun for massive damage in these close quarters.

STAGE 4

As you continue toward the data matrix center, fight your way down a long hallway filled with Starscream's troops. The enemies continue to attack until you get far enough down the hallway (21) to disable their sentry defenses. Use the Flak Grenades and Shotgun to make short work of the enemies here. An Energon Cube is roughly halfway down the hall in case you take heavy fire.

STAGE 5

After you shoot the sentry guns off the walls, turn the corner and replenish your ammo and Energon. Open the door (22) by activating the switch. The Rocketeer is introduced in the next large chamber. These enemies have a transforming shield that protects them from frontal attacks. Occasionally, they lower their shields and release a barrage of rockets. When this happens, they're vulnerable to attack

However, there's a way to take them down even when their shields are active. Lob one or two Flak Grenades behind them to circumvent their defenses. Find a crate filled with grenades on the room's far side.

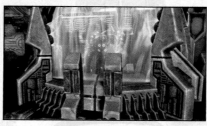

Taking out the Rocketeers and their buddies allows you move safely up the ramp to a switch (23). Activate the switch to create a bridge and to unlock the distant doorway. More of Starscream's soldiers pour out of this door (24). Destroy them.

SECTION 6 — TO THE DATA CENTER

STAGE 1

A hallway is across the bridge and through the open doorway. Turning left at this hallway's 'T' intersection gives you an opportunity to restock on ammo and health. Break open the weapon crate to get an additional EMP Shotgun for your co-op buddy.

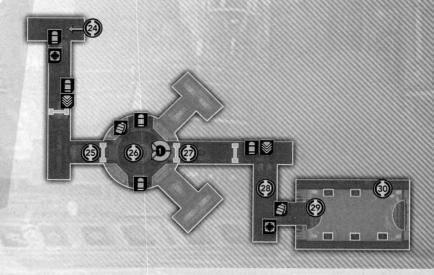

STAGE 2

Move to the hallway's end, and the door to the data matrix center (25) opens automatically. Several of Starscream's soldiers wait for you inside. Dispatch them and interact with the switch (26) in the room's center to send the data to Soundwave for processing.

Starscream notices your intrusion. After your conversation with his two holograms, two Rocketeers take up position at the holograms' former spots. Use the monitor stations as cover, and neutralize these enemies. After the battle, the monitors retract into the floor and Soundwave reports his findings. Move toward the exit (27) and expect a surprise.

STAGE 3

As you're about to exit the data center, you meet a new enemy: the Brute. Brutes carry a large shield and a hammer, which makes them tough to deal with in close-range combat. When you confront a Brute, try to get behind it to destroy its backpack—this is its only weakness.

OBJECTIVE: **SEIZE CONTROL OF DARK ENERGON**

STAGE 4

After you defeat the Brute and move through the next hallway (collecting power-ups along the way), you reach an electrical hazard (28). Destroying the marked targets shuts down the hazard and allows you to get through without taking damage.

STAGE 5

Past the electrical hazard, you enter a room with an impassible pool of Energon coolant. Be careful not to fall into the fluid; it damages your internal circuitry. Take down the Rocketeer firing at you from the other side of the room. Interact with the switch (29) to extend the bridge. Begin crossing the bridge but stop just before the end and look to your left. Destroy the marked vent shaft cover (30). Jump through the hole you created, down into the shaft.

SECTION (7) VENTILATION SHAFTS

Level 1

Level 2

Level 3

Level 4

STAGE 1

Avoid the jets of Energon flame that erupt randomly in the ventilation shaft (30). The center of the jet vent turns yellow-orange just before the flame erupts. Also avoid the fan blades—they can split even the strongest Decepticon in two. Aim toward the core to destroy them, and make your way to the end of the shaft (31).

STAGE 2

You reach a vertical vent shaft. Again, be careful of the fan blades. Aim to destroy the core of the blades just below the bridge on which you stand. Now, control your fall to the next bridge below 32. Find the power-ups in the adjacent shafts (dead-ends), and repeat the fan-destruction process as you work your way down the shaft 33 to the manufacturing plant 35.

DECEPTICON COLLECTIBLE #2

Between the third fan and the bottom of the ventilation shaft, you can find a horizontal offshoot 34 from the main shaft. Jump into this recess and destroy the second Autobot logo collectible that's inside. An Overshield is also located in this dead-end shaft.

OBJECTIVE: FIND AND SECURE DARK ENERGON
STAGE 3

You bend some pipes when you drop to the bottom of the ventilation shaft. Drop through the large hole in the pipes to reach the War Machine manufacturing plant below 35. Weapons are being constructed throughout this facility. As you progress up either of the side ramps, the power goes out and enemy Snipers take positions on the upper catwalks. Use the cover the room provides 36 to avoid the Snipers locking onto your position. Eliminate the enemies and progress forward.

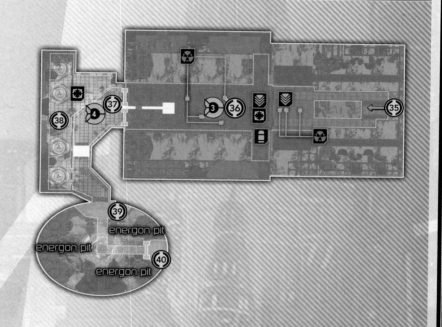

STAGE 4

The power is restored after you deal with the Snipers. Now you can move through a door into a smaller room 37. The room's back wall explodes, revealing a Brute. This room is much smaller than the site of your prior Brute encounter, so move back—into the previous room if you have to—and lock some shots onto its backpack until you defeat it. Find the Energon Cubes in the same room to recover lost health.

STAGE 5

With the Brute destroyed, make your way past the War Machine testing facility 38. Notice the circular pattern on the bluish-tinted floor; this is the edge of the pulse's area of effect. You can avoid the corruption blast if you time your movement by starting as soon as the test pulse triggers. Once you're safe, interact with the switch 39 on the balcony to extend the bridge that leads to a lift. Use the lift switch 40 to reach the laboratory above.

SECTION 8 LABORATORY

STAGE 1

Half of the orbital station laboratory ④ has been ripped away, exposing you to the vastness of space. As you explore the area, you discover Starscream has a surprise planned for you. Several Jet Soldiers fly into the room to keep you from your objective. Deal with the enemies appropriately. To assist you in this matter, find the Overshield in the room's back, right-hand corner, just above where you entered.

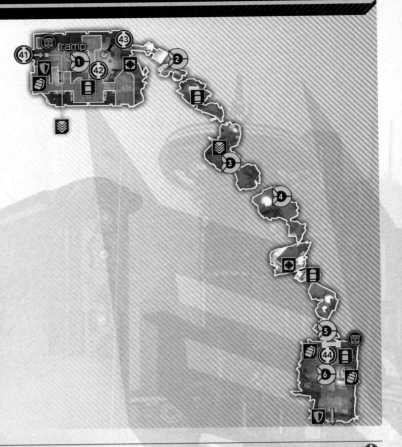

DECEPTICON COLLECTIBLE #3

The third Autobot logo is in this laboratory's back corner, above the entrance. It's on the ledge adjacent to the one with the Overshield. Destroy the Autobot logo.

STAGE 2

After you deal with the Jet Soldiers, you must find your way onto the debris through the gaping hole in the laboratory's side. A switch ④ is on the second-level catwalks. Activating it drops an arm and alerts a few remaining Jet Soldiers to your location. Once you destroy these enemies, use the lowered arm ④ to jump up to the hollow scaffold, the first hunk of debris in space outside the hole's upper-left corner. Proceed out into the rubble.

STAGE 3

Jet Soldiers continually harass you out on the rubble; this persists until you reach the central building ④. Be careful of your footing on the rubble pieces—one false step can send you over the edge into oblivion.

DECEPTICON COLLECTIBLE #4

Look toward the central building entrance's upper-left corner. The Autobot logo is hidden among the ruins. Lay waste to their token.

STAGE 1

As you enter the central building (44), two Rocket Sentries open fire on you. Use the crates for cover, and take them down before you proceed further. After you destroy them, remain behind cover—Snipers have taken up positions on the upper balcony.

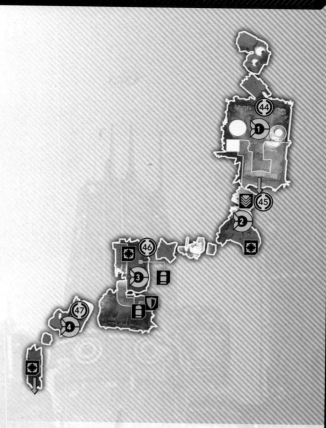

A squad of car soldiers and a single Brute reinforce the Snipers. Try to take out the Snipers as quickly as possible so you can engage the Brute without getting sniped. Once all the enemies are destroyed, use the crates to reach a platform that grants you access to the upper balcony. From there, use the doorway and jump down to continue along the floating debris.

STAGE 2

After you leap down from the central building, notice the crashed Jet Soldier (45). A Thermo Rocket Launcher pickup is next to it. This weapon can lock onto and launch a homing rocket at enemies that are in vehicle form. This is quite handy, considering the squadron of flyers heading toward you. Take out the Jet Soldiers and continue toward your objective. You reach a platform that breaks under your weight. Quickly jump from each of the debris pieces to safe ground before they separate too far from each other.

STAGE 3

As you land on solid ground (46), watch out for enemies that come over the left wall. Use the Thermo Rocket Launcher to make quick work of the Jet Soldier, and then deal with the Rocket Soldiers. Two more Jet Soldiers attack as you near the next debris piece—don't let them catch you off guard.

An alternate path leads on top of the ruined scaffolding and across some debris chunks. Choosing this path leads to an Overshield, along with a chance to ambush the Rocket Soldier below. Use a stack of crates in the area's right corner to reach this upper pathway. Jump across the remaining floating debris (47) to make it back to the station. Destroy the flying station defenders along the way.

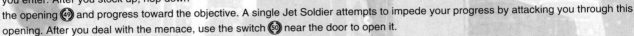

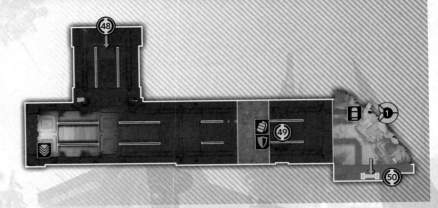

STAGE 1

When you reenter the station (48), you find plenty of weapons and ammo power-ups. A weapon crate is located to the right as you enter. After you stock up, hop down the opening (49) and progress toward the objective. A single Jet Soldier attempts to impede your progress by attacking you through this opening. After you deal with the menace, use the switch (50) near the door to open it.

STAGE 2

The doorway opens to reveal a ruined room. The floor is cracked and spraying steam. Walking onto the floor is too much stress for the floor to take, and it breaks apart,

scattering pieces of the room outward. Quickly hop from platform to platform toward your objective point. Be quick, or you'll end up drifting into the cold darkness of space.

After you land safely on the opposite side, proceed though the doorway (51). Find the EMP Shotgun as you enter the Dark Energon containment area (52). The rooms ahead are narrow, and this shotgun works well in close-quarters fighting.

DECEPTICON COLLECTIBLE #5

After you cross the floating debris, look to the right of the next doorway. Find the Autobot logo among some debris behind a column. Destroy the fifth and final icon in this chapter.

OBJECTIVE:

DESTROY THE DARK ENERGON CONTAINMENT

STAGE 3

While Starscream attempts to destroy the final quantities of Dark Energon, he sends in his troops to stop you. Move though the doorway and engage the enemy. Be aware that Starscream has also activated the auto defenses. Four rocket turrets are in the next room, along with a single trooper. Gear up before you drop down into the next area (53).

STAGE 4

Watch out for automated sentries and Rocket Soldiers after you drop down into the new area below (54).

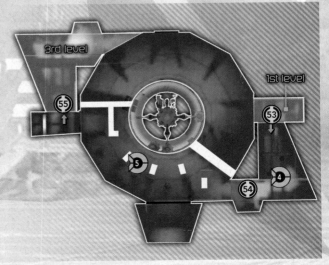

STAGE 5

Use the pillars between you and the enemy for cover as you take down the sentry guns. Then destroy the Rocket Soldiers. The final two station defenders fire at you for a moment, retreat though the doorway, and then jump down into the next lower floor (55).

Gear up before you make the next jump; you can't return once you make the jump. Follow the retreating enemies and eliminate them. Round the next corner and defeat the single sentry, as well as the waves of Starscream's troops to follow. Continue using the pillars for cover as you engage these enemies.

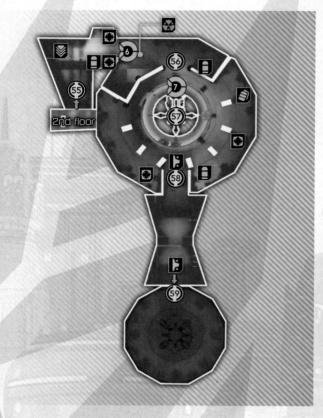

STAGE 6

Once you reach the Dark Energon Chamber (56), you face the biggest threat yet: two Titans. These enemies move slowly, and you have to dish out a lot of damage to take them down. To make the most of your effort, focus your fire on one of them. If you can neutralize one, you can pick up its Ion Displacer. The Displacer makes short work of the remaining Titan.

Starscream tells you you're too late and unleashes his final wave of enemies. Two sentries deploy out of the containment chamber, and waves of enemies drop down into the arena. Lay waste to all of them. With the final Decepticon down, the Dark Energon Chamber becomes vulnerable. Shoot open the containment chamber (57), and Megatron infuses himself with Dark Energon.

OBJECTIVE:

DESTROY THE DARK ENERGON CONTAINMENT
STAGE 7

Megatron then demonstrates his newfound abilities by destroying hordes of Starscream's forces. If you're playing as Megatron, you'll see a purple icon appear. Walk up to the marker (58) and use your abilities to unleash Dark Energon onto the troopers. Do this once more at the end of the hallway (59) to finally confront Starscream.

CONCLUSION

Megatron has claimed the Orbital Station for his own and captured Dark Energon, but at what cost? Starscream's battle with Megatron exhausted the supply of the precious substance and nearly destroyed the space station in the process. But all is not lost for Lord Megatron. In exchange for his life, Starscream informs Megatron of an Energon Bridge that could restore power to the battered Orbital Station and breathe life back into the production of Dark Energon. Megatron orders Starscream to activate this Energon Bridge while he remains aboard the station to oversee repairs.

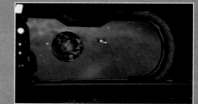

FUEL OF WAR

Anxious to prove themselves worthy of the Decepticon name. Starscream and his minions fly to Cybertron. There, they must reconnect the Energon Bridge that will enable Megatron to manufacture more Dark Energon and conquer the Autobots once and for all.

AVAILABLE CHARACTERS

STARSCREAM

The best all-around fighter of the group, Starscream's Null Ray allows him to pick off enemies before they are ever alerted to his presence. His powerful Scatter Blaster and Shockwave combo ensures that enemies moving in close don't last for long.

THUNDERCRACKER

Thundercracker serves a support role in the group. His ability to spawn sentries let him focus on using his Energon Repair Ray to heal his teammates.

SKYWARP

Loves to get in close and cause maximum damage. His cloaking ability allows him to infiltrate squads of enemies. Once he's in close, his Scatter Blaster and Whirlwind allow him to eliminate all opposition.

CO-OP TIPS

If you ever get low on ammo, switch to vehicle form. Jet form equips each character with an infinite machine gun and homing rocket clip.

In many of the larger arena battles, have Starscream hang back and use his Null Ray to pick off pesky Rocket and Jet Soldiers.

The player controlling Thundercracker should focus on using the Energon Repair Ray to support the others during heavy firefights.

If you're playing a competitive co-op game, use the environments' many destructible Energon batteries to keep your multiplier high between battles.

BASICS
CHARACTERS
WEAPONS
WALKTHROUGH
01 DARK ENERGON
02
FUEL OF WAR
03
04
05
06
07
08
09
10
MULTIPLAYER
ACHIEVEMENTS

INTRODUCTION

Megatron commands his newest recruit, Starscream, to activate the long dormant Energon Bridge on Cycbertron. Once the bridge is activated, Megatron will create more Dark Energon to fuel his war. Megatron orders Starscream, Skywarp, and Thundercracker to complete this important task.

SECTION 1 KAON CLIFFS

OBJECTIVE:

FIND THE HIDDEN UNDERGROUND ENTRANCE
STAGE 1

The opening cinematic flies your squad into a deep canyon (1). Use this safe area to learn the jet controls. Try flying around some of the pillars and pipes to master maneuvers that come in handy during the level's dogfights.

DECEPTICON COLLECTIBLE #6

 The sixth Decepticon collectible is on the high earthen bridge at the beginning of the level.

For anyone seeking a little extra firepower, several weapon and grenade pickups are at the canyon's far end (2).

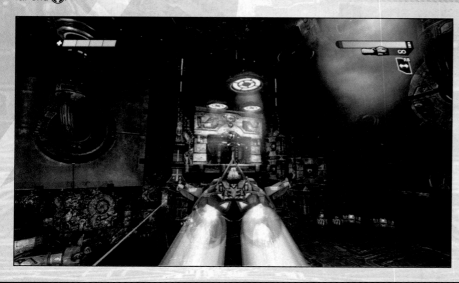

STAGE 2

You are alerted to the presence of a Cybertron Sweeper when you enter the first cave ③. These drones follow you and attack with deadly Energon beams. Either attacking them or entering their zone of awareness alerts these security probes to your presence. The best strategy is to attack them from a distance and take them down before they have time to lock onto you and attack. Jet rockets are highly effective against these enemies. If a Cybertron Sweeper manages to get close to you, quickly use your boost mode to move to the probe's back. This buys you a free moment to attack while the probe slowly turns to resume its beam attack.

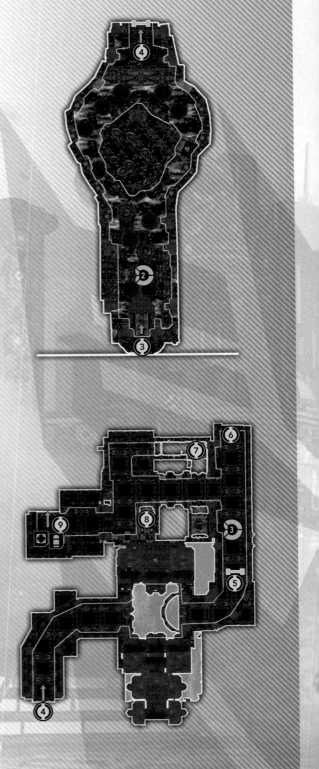

STAGE 3

As you progress deeper into the cave, you come to a locked door ④. Activate the switch to open the door ⑤. An Autobot enemy detection barrier is beyond the door. Crossing the enemy detection barrier without first disabling the unit triggers an alarm that calls in Autobot reinforcements. Once the reinforcements are called, you have to eliminate all threats before you can proceed to the next area. Each time you encounter a barrier, you must disable its power source to progress safely beyond it. You can find a barrier's power source by tracing the glowing red power conduit connected to its distant base. The power source ⑥ for the first barrier is located at the end of the hallway, directly in front of you. Shoot it through the barrier.

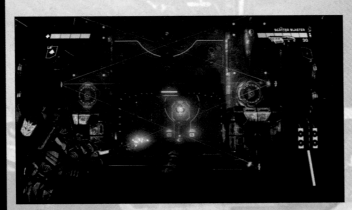

The power source for the second barrier is a little trickier. Notice that the power conduit flows off to the left and out of sight. A small hallway ⑦ with a deadly Energon floor is to the right of this entrance. Change into jet form and fly through this narrow opening to land safely behind another detection barrier. From this vantage point, you can see the power source ⑧ for both barriers. Destroy the power source through the barrier.

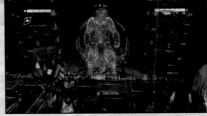

Round the next corner, and the seeker squad can eavesdrop on Zeta Prime's plan to squash the Decepticon threat. Flak Grenades lie on the left of the ledge. Feel free to pick up and toss a Flak Grenade or two into the room below ⑨. This interrupts Zeta's monologue and lets you launch a surprise attack on the Autobots. During the battle, avoid breaching the next enemy detection barrier, lest additional reinforcements arrive and trap the squad.

STAGE 4

Once you quash the Autobot presence, destroy the detection barrier. Investigation reveals that the power source for this room ⑩ is hidden better than most. The power conduit looks to flow upward and disappear into the ceiling. Change into jet form and hover up to the top of the room. Find the hidden door at the top of the room. Destroy the locks on the door and then the power cell. You can also find power-ups inside this small chamber. One of these power-ups is an Energon Shard Container.

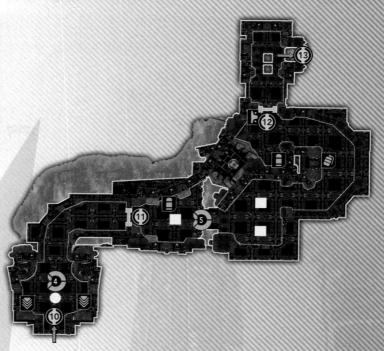

STAGE 5

Once you disable the third detection barrier and enter the next room ⑪, you face a squad of Autobots defending the entrance into the next canyon. Starscream can use his Null Ray from behind the pillar on the starting platform to pick off the first few enemies. He can also take down the Rocket Soldier off to the left. As you progress through the fight, be sure to use the explosive Energon containers and Flak Grenades to eliminate enemy groups quickly.

After you eliminate all Autobot resistance, interact with the switch ⑫ to open the door. An Autobot Shotgunner, the most powerful foe you've faced so far, is behind the door. The Shotgunner is devastating at close range, so keep your distance. At long-range, it tosses Flak Grenades, but you can dodge those easily. Try to keep one Flak Grenade handy to take out the Shotgunner's Overshield. Once you get the Overshield out of the way, a few well-placed shots to the head end the encounter.

With the Shotgunner destroyed, the squad realizes that the Autobots have locked the door. You need to find a new way to the next canyon. Jump down the elevator shaft to the right ⑬ to enter the Energon reservoir below.

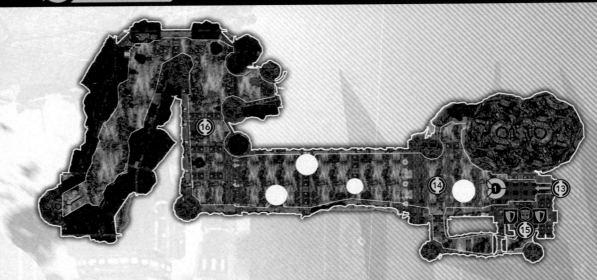

STAGE 1

Thundercracker informs the group that crude Energon is highly volatile and flying close to it is very dangerous. Heed the warning as you fly through the cave ⑭; avoid contact with any of the Energon lakes.

DECEPTICON COLLECTIBLE #7

The Autobot symbol is hidden in a room ⑮ to the left of the Energon Reservoir's starting platform. Pivot and shoot it through the bars from your starting position.

OVERSHIELDS

Flying through the Energon Reservoir waterfall to the left of your starting position allows you to access the hidden room that holds Decepticon Collectible #7. From there, fly through a hidden tunnel that leads to two Overshield pickups ⑮.

To stay healthy as you continue toward the objective, maneuver the jet between the waterfall-like Energon and the adjacent walls. Partway through the cave, you must avoid a gauntlet of dangerous Energon vents ⑯. Explore the far side of the Energon gauntlet to find a set of Flak Grenades ⑰.

Your squad approaches a group of Autobot Rocket Soldiers at the Energon Reservoir cave's end (18). Try using the jet's machineguns from behind a large metal pillar near the back of

the cave. Once you neutralize the Soldiers, lock your homing rockets onto the two Rocket Sentries posted on the side of the walls.

With the first wave of defenses eliminated, it's time to advance and take the platform. When you move in close to the platform, a second team of Rocket Soldiers appears. Land on the platform (20), use the cover in the center to flank your enemies, and take them down from behind. Now destroy the fan on the room's far end to progress safely to the next canyon.

DECEPTICON COLLECTIBLE #8

Find the eighth Autobot symbol by retreating back toward the waterfall and entering the hidden tunnel (19). The Autobot symbol is on a high ledge at this tunnel's end.

SECTION 3 — CANYON CRUISER

OBJECTIVE: DESTROY THE SHIELD GENERATOR

STAGE 1

The squad's mission to find the hidden underground entrance is quickly interrupted as you enter the next canyon (21). A large Autobot dropship (22) moves in from over the canyon wall and throws a force field over the only exit from the canyon. Your team must destroy the ship and drop the force field for any hope of awakening the Energon Bridge.

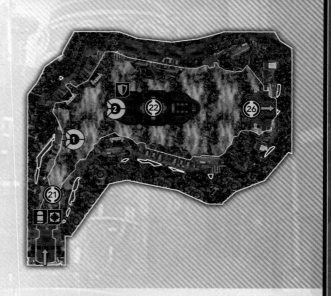

The first step is to destroy the ship's outer mortar defenses. The mortars fire a flurry of homing missiles into the air. As the mortars charge, hover, and deplete their health by using the jet's machineguns. Then quickly transition into boost mode and use the jet's barrel roll to break the homing mortar's lock on you. If you prefer to stand on the ship and shoot the mortars with a shotgun

at close range, be aware that their shockwave sends anything in the vicinity flying backward. Jump into the air to regain control when this happens.

After you take the first three mortars offline, four more appear: two on each end of the ship. The same basic strategy applies.

Just remember to listen for the mortar blast audio queue, because this time you can't keep all the mortars in your field of view at the same time.

During the mortar attack, Autobot Jet Soldiers sporadically emerge from the ship's back end to try to stop you. On higher difficulties, it is very important to take down these enemies quickly, as their machinegun blasts and bombing runs can be devastating. As soon as you see the Autobot Jet Soldier, switch to your jet rockets, obtain a homing lock, and blast it out of the sky.

STAGE 2

After you destroy all the mortars, the Autobots open up the ship's back end ㉓ and send out a large squadron of Autobot Jet Soldiers. Switch to your homing rockets and try your best to eliminate them from a distance. Avoid getting surrounded, as that is the quickest way to expire. Once you destroy some of the Jet Soldiers, two smaller reinforcement waves emerge.

At this point in the battle, you might be getting a little low on health. If you feel overwhelmed, try retreating to the previous area. Find a health and ammo pickup on the ledge just past the large fan ㉑. You can also find four health power-ups in the dropship's side ledges. To stay mobile, try dive-bombing the ledges to get a quick pick-me-up, and get right back into the battle.

STAGE 3

After you eliminate most of the Autobot Jet Soldiers and only a few stragglers remain, the Autobots open up the ship and attack with Rocket Soldiers. Starscream commands the team to take down the ship by fighting inside and destroying the ship's power core. You can approach this battle from the ship's upper or lower levels.

Lower Level

Upper Level

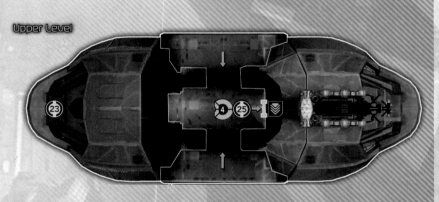

CO-OP TIP

If you're playing co-op and need more healing support, choose the upper path. After you clear out the upper deck, locate the interactive panel. The panel opens a door on the upper deck, revealing an Energon Repair Ray power-up.

ENERGON REPAIR RAY

You can find the Repair Ray on the dropship's upper level, behind the sealed door.

If you're low on health, we suggest attacking from the lower levels ㉓. Take out the two Rocket Soldiers protecting the lower entrance. Eventually, the path you choose converges in the ship's lower-level interior. The Autobots shout, "Close the blast doors and seal the ship," making a move to trap the squad inside and eliminate them.

Continue fighting your way to the back of the ship. Watch out for the three Autobot Shotgunners that emerge from the back of the ship. Once you fight your way to the power core, activate the switch (24) a few yards away from the door to set the ship to blow up from the inside out.

OBJECTIVE: **ESCAPE THE AUTOBOT DROPSHIP**

STAGE 4

Once the detpack explodes, the dropship's destruct sequence commences. Starscream orders the team to quickly head to the upper deck and look for an escape route. Up top, the squad discovers that all of the doors are locked down. Moments later, a large explosion rips off the front of the ship, creating a perfect escape hatch (25). Quickly fly out of the ship and head for the newly cleared canyon entrance. Don't stick around in the ship any longer than you have to; once the ship crashes into the Energon below, anything still inside is instantly destroyed.

SECTION 4 **AUTOBOT MENACE**

OBJECTIVE:

CONTINUE YOUR SEARCH FOR THE UNDERGROUND

STAGE 1

Stock up on ammo and grab the pair of EMP Grenades after you land at the canyon entrance (26). Further into the canyon interior, your squad briefly catches a glimpse of a new, cloaked Autobot threat. After the cinematic plays, grab the Plasma Cannon tucked into a nook to the left (27). The Plasma Cannon and EMP Grenade combo is your best offense against your next challenge…

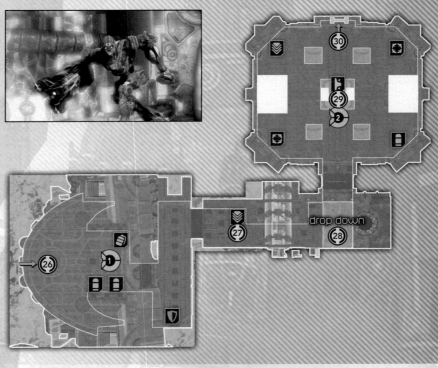

drop down

STAGE 2

Drop down to the lower floor in the next room (28). Below, a cloaked enemy traps your squad and turns off the power to the room. In this low-light setting, a group of Autobot Cloakers attacks your squad. The Cloakers are almost invisible to the naked eye. Watch for the red glow from the charge of their Plasma Cannon. When you see the glow, toss an EMP Grenade. The blast permanently de-cloaks the enemy and leaves it temporarily vulnerable to all attacks. Wipe out large groups of Cloakers simultaneously with a fully charged Plasma Cannon blast. Once you destroy the Cloakers, find the controls (29) to restore power, and then proceed into the next area (30).

OBJECTIVE: DEACTIVATE THE FORCEFIELD

In the next canyon (30), the squad finds what it has been searching for: the entrance to the underground. Unfortunately, it is heavily defended. A battalion of Autobot Snipers, Rocket Soldiers, and Jet Soldiers guard an already shielded entrance (33). You can approach this encounter in a number of ways. You can try flanking from either side, sniping from a distance using the Null Ray located near the entryway, or attacking the enemy head-on. The squad's goal is to clear the area of all Autobot threats and use the side terminals to open the shield's battery housings. Once the batteries (32) are destroyed, you can open the door and gain entrance to the Cybertron underground.

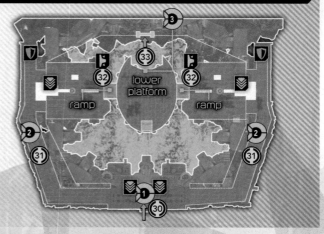

STAGE 1

As you enter the next canyon, the squad can choose to equip a Null Ray (sniper rifle) or a Rocket Launcher. Ammo for these weapons is limited in this area, so choose your shots wisely. First, focus fire on the Autobot Snipers. Without eliminating the Sniper threat, the squad has a very low chance of survival as it enters the canyon. Use your remaining ammo to tear the Autobot Jet Soldiers out of the sky. Once you thin the Autobot defenses, it's time to push forward.

STAGE 2

The safest path is to flank the base from one of the side tunnels (31). Decide whether to move left or right from the squad's sniping location. Around each turn, the squad must disable an enemy detection barrier unless it wants to face off against a wall of homing-rocket sentries. Disable the barriers, use the base's back door to sneak in, and quickly take out any remaining Autobot Soldiers. These covered locations are great places to pick up new weapons and take out remaining Autobots from a shielded position. There are also Overshields at the end of the halls past both detection barriers.

STAGE 3

Once you wipe the area clean, use one of the two switches (32) to open the battery housing. With the Energon Batteries fully exposed, focus fire on them to begin lowering the shield. Once you complete a side, convert back into jet form, and quickly boost over to the opposite platform to repeat the process. Upon lowering different parts of the shield defenses, Autobot reinforcements are called in to stop you from gaining access to the underground.

If you have already eliminated all of the Autobot Snipers from the area, you should be safe to change into jet form and blast these enemies with your jet rockets. If your health gets low during these dogfights, you can find health near the back wall on each of the upper platforms.

OBJECTIVE: DESTROY THE ARMOR PLATING

Once you destroy both sets of shield batteries, the shield lowers. Finally, you must destroy one last layer of high-density shielding. Watch out for the sentries that pop up from the shield battery platforms. Switch to your jet rockets and pelt the door (33) to break off the shield and gain entrance to Cybertron's underground.

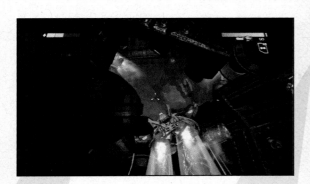

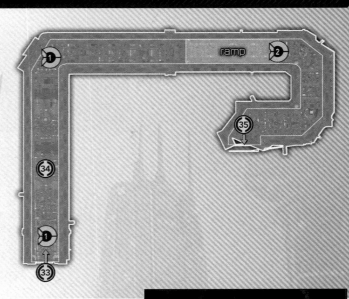

OBJECTIVE:

RE-ROUTE POWER TO THE ENERGON BRIDGE

STAGE 1

Cybertron's underground ㉞ is a much more cramped and dangerous environment than anything you've flown in so far. Luckily, this first stretch of tunnel was decommissioned long ago. The squad must find the power terminals to get the stations back online and successfully route power down to the Energon Bridge. Use this first stretch of tunnel to adjust to flying through such tight quarters.

A little way into the tunnel, the team comes to some large life forms, unknown even to Thundercracker. Not knowing what their intentions are, Starscream gives the order to blast them if they get in the way.

STAGE 2

The next section of tunnel ㉟ is mined with these Energon Jellyfish. When the Jellyfish appear, make sure you destroy them before they can collide into you. These enemies explode on contact, inflicting massive damage and temporarily disorienting the squad's head-up display. Destroy or avoid all of the Energon Jellyfish to reach the next area ㊱.

STAGE 1

The first tunnel section ㊱ opens up to reveal the first Energon Bridge Power Routing Station. Your squad must move inside and activate the station to send power from the surface of Cybertron down to the long-dormant Energon Bridge. Unfortunately, this station is not as dormant as Starscream had hoped. Rocket sentries line the opening to each of the station's side entrance gates ㊲.

Try to destroy the sentries from a distance with your jet rockets. Use your barrel roll to avoid rocket fire, or snipe them from a nearby platform, using the walls' edges for cover.

Along with the rocket sentries, a pair of Cybertron Sweepers emerges from the station to attack unless you infiltrate and find them inside. Once you eliminate the rocket sentries, move behind the security drones and neutralize them with your jet rockets. When the area is clear, move inside the power routing terminal.

STAGE 2

Inside, the squad meets another group of Cloakers on the lower level, which is accessible via the ramp (38). This group is far larger than the previous encounter. On your way into the station, you passed a set of EMP Grenades and a Plasma Cannon. Employ the same tactics you used during the previous encounter. Toss an EMP Grenade into the group to permanently de-cloak the enemies and leave them temporarily vulnerable. Use the Energon canisters along the walls to dispatch large groups of immobilized Cloakers with a single blast. Use your Plasma Cannon to take out the remaining stragglers.

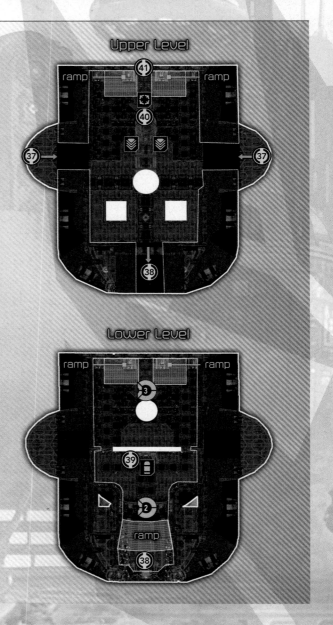

Upper Level

Lower Level

Once you eliminate the Cloakers, use the terminal controls (39) to restore power to the station.

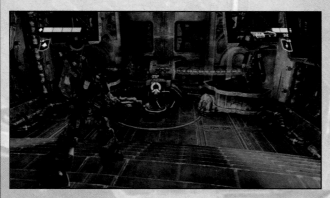

STAGE 3

A squadron of Autobots storms the station. You can see them moving through the travel tube above the power switch. Press down on the D-pad to focus on them after you throw the switch.

Use the nearby power-ups to restock on ammo, and start making your way back to the Power Routing Station's upper level. Fight from the doorway to eliminate the Jet and Rocket Soldiers on the bottom level. From there, fly up top and take out the Autobots guarding the exit controls (41). This group of enemies presents a great opportunity to use Starscream's Shockwave or Skywarp's Whirlwind abilities to clear the area quickly. When all the Autobots are destroyed, activate the exit controls and pass through the glowing tunnel (41) beyond the switch.

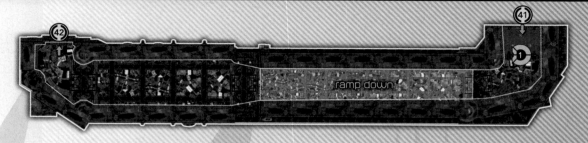

STAGE 1

The next section of tunnel ④① is restored to 50 percent of its full power. The tunnel is starting to come to life, and the squad must now dodge between dangerous laser-shooting pistons and welding arms. After you successfully navigate the first stretch of tunnel, watch for more Energon Jellyfish to attack from the tunnel walls.

STAGE 2

At the bottom of the Jellyfish tunnel, your squad reaches a highly defended area ④②. Snipers scan the tunnel from perches. Autobot Rocketeers volley groups of homing missiles toward you from the tunnel's base. The large, moving pistons cutting through the area's center prevent you from getting a clear line of sight on every enemy from any single location. Your best strategy in this situation is to work your way slowly up through the tunnel. Grab the Null Ray on the starting platform, and pick off the first Sniper safely from cover. Use jet boost mode to push quickly up through the tunnel, sniping enemies as you go.

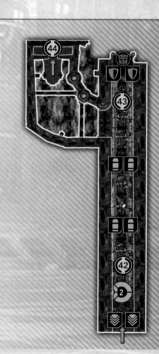

Partially down the tunnel, a group of Jet Soldiers enters, performing bombing runs on the platforms. After you eliminate the Snipers and Rocketeers, take to the sky and use your rockets to nail these Jet Soldiers.

DECEPTICON COLLECTIBLE #9

 A large Energon waterfall ④③ is at the end of the Sniper tunnel. Fly behind the waterfall to find a secret room housing a Decepticon Collectible and a couple of Overshields.

The second Power Routing Station is just ahead (44). Your team must get inside and finish sending power down to the Energon Bridge.

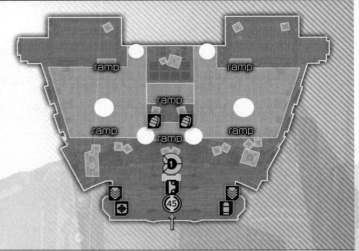

STAGE 1

Land on the platform rising out of the Energon, and approach the door controls (45). Take this moment to refuel on health and ammo via the many power-ups in the nooks to the left and right of the switch. When you activate the door controls, you surprise an unaware Protector Autobot. Quickly terminate him with a well-placed melee strike, and take cover behind the crates.

Now fully alerted, the Routing Station goes into full battle mode. Two Soldiers man Ion Displacers and shoot at your group from the station's second story. After you eliminate the turret Soldiers, Protectors emerge to guard the lower doorway. Defeat these Protectors by flanking around the pillars and attacking them from behind.

With the Protectors destroyed, the doors into the station open. More Autobot resistance waits inside, so take a moment to refuel on health and ammo, and grab a set of Flak Grenades from the arena's center.

STAGE 2

Fully equipped, it's now time to move inside and take over the power terminal. You can choose to enter through the left or the right doors (46). In co-op, a good strategy is to have each player take a side. This allows you to surround the final encounter in the upper command station. Fight through the base until you reach a closed door (46). The fight behind the door can be very challenging if you are ill equipped and unprepared. Again, stock up on health and ammo, and either grab the Flash Grenades or rip one of the Ion Displacers.

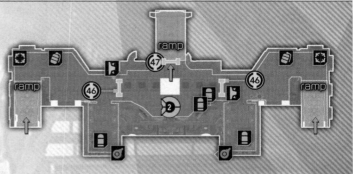

A group of three Shotgunners is behind the door. At close range, they can be very deadly. Immediately toss in a Flak Grenade to lower their Overshield. Then target the Energon canisters on the side of the room. This should allow you to take out most of the group with a single shot. Once you quash the Shotgunners, blast the door lock (47) and proceed into the Power Routing Station.

The Power Routing Station presents a slightly different challenge. There are no enemies to blast in this room. Instead, the team must figure out how to restore power to the Energon Bridge. After the central switch is flipped (48), Starscream learns that to restore power he needs to move the station's power cells into position.

Move to the power cells and flip their switch (49) to activate them. It looks like the Autobots have locked down the power cells. Shoot the locks on the power cells to release them from their bonds. Activate the battery terminal again to trigger a cinematic of the power cells starting to move into position.

Unfortunately, it looks like the Autobots have booby trapped the room. They will stop at nothing to keep you from activating the Energon Bridge. Your squad must disable three trip wires that are causing the power cells to explode on contact. Trace the glowing red power conduits along the floor and destroy the power source. The first power source (50) is located on ground level, to the right of the power cell station. The next two power sources are more hidden. They are located above the second-story shelving ((51) and (52)), hidden behind boxes and wires. Follow the power conduit, and you should have no trouble finding them.

Return to the power cell station and activate the controls (49). The power cells start moving along the floor and into position. You can use this time to explore the room and collect the hidden Overshield and Decepticon Collectible. When the power cells are fully in position, head back and activate the first switch (which rises out of the floor) (48) to finally route power down to the Energon Bridge.

DECEPTICON COLLECTIBLE #10

The Decepticon Collectible is hidden on the second-story shelving, to the right of the power cell station.

STAGE 4

Now that power is restored, fly through the next tunnel (53). Power in this tunnel is at 100% efficiency. Fly through the tunnel to reach the Energon Bridge Chamber (54).

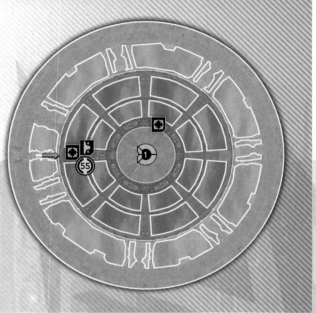

OBJECTIVE: ACTIVATE THE ENERGON BRIDGE

Lying before the squad is the object of Megatron's desire: the Energon Bridge. Against Thundercracker's warning, Starscream orders the squad to plant a Dark Energon detpack on the power cable to corrupt the machine. Activate the interact point (55). Planting the detpack triggers a cinematic in which the Energon Bridge Guardian awakens and begins its assault on your squad.

After you survive both first-wave attacks, the boss opens his core to recharge. When this happens, focus fire on the core. When you deliver enough damage, one core control ring snaps off, and the boss closes up to begin its next assault.

OBJECTIVE:

DESTROY THE ENERGON BRIDGE GUARDIAN
STAGE 1

The boss's first attack wave consists of a rocket barrage and a devastating beam attack. During the rocket wave, stay in boost form as much as possible. If you are up to it, you can focus fire on the boss's gun arms. Destroy them to reduce the number of homing rockets he can fire simultaneously. If one of his homing shots gets close, use the jet barrel roll to evade the blast. During the beam attack, he shoots four beam sheets and sweeps the room. Stay in boost mode and run from the beams. Getting struck by either of these attacks causes major damage.

ENERGON CANISTERS

Between each attack wave, Energon Canisters rise into position around the Guardian. Destroy these canisters to spawn health power-ups.

STAGE 2

For the second attack wave, the boss employs amped-up versions of his first attacks. Instead of a single rocket, his cannons now fire a three-rocket burst per shot. Your strategy remains the same, but the penalty for getting hit increases substantially. Boost and barrel roll to avoid his attacks. The Guardian's beam attack now fires eight beams. Avoid getting hit from behind. The screen turning red indicates that a beam is hot on your trail. Quickly switch altitude and direction to outmaneuver the attack.

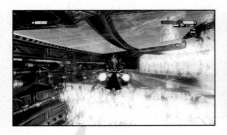

After both second-wave attacks, the boss again opens its core to recharge. Focus fire on the core to destroy the second core control ring, blasting him into his third and final stage.

STAGE 3

For its final wave, the boss goes into berserker mode. He summons a pool of deadly Energon up from the pit below, devastating the room's foundation and destroying all safe landing zones. When the floor is completely destroyed, the boss fires homing Energon balls out of the pool. Stay in boost mode as much as you can, and barrel roll when you see the fireballs getting close.

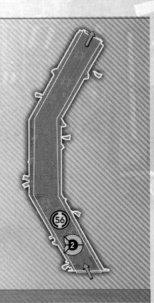

Once you survive a few waves of the deadly Energon balls, you hear the boss change back into his beam phase. Be prepared, because the Guardian changes tactics from the prior two waves.

With the Energon balls still pelting you, the Guardian extends its beams but does not instantly sweep the room. When you see the beams appear, be sure to suppress your instinct to boost instantly. The Guardian keeps the squad trapped for a few moments, and then the beams start to sweep the room. To throw another kink into the proceedings, the boss also randomly switches the beams' directions. Pay close attention as the beams become stationary and then spin. This tips off the direction in which the beams will sweep next.

After the final beam phase, the boss opens up to recharge one last time. Focus fire on the core to destroy the final core control ring.

OBJECTIVE: ESCAPE TO THE SURFACE
STAGE 1

With the Guardian's power core completely destroyed, the machine makes a final attempt to change form and attack you. Before it can get into battle position, something begins to destroy the Guardian from the inside out. The now corrupted Energon Bridge power cable bursts out, ripping the Guardian to pieces. Sprouting out, the cable rips a hole in the roof, exposing the Energon Bridge power shaft (56). The squad flies up through the shaft as the unrestrained power cable bursts in and out of the wall, destroying anything it touches as it moves toward the surface. Continue flying through the tunnel to escape.

CONCLUSION

Reaching the surface, Starscream and his minions watch as the long dormant Energon Bridge is finally activated. After it transitions up into position, the bridge fires a powerful beam of corrupted Energon into space to connect with Megatron's Orbital Base. Having completed their task, the squad fly up with the beam to join Megatron and continue the Decepticon takeover of Cybertron.

03 IACON DESTROYED

Hungry for more power. Megatron plans to corrupt the very core of Cybertron itself with Dark Energon. But to do so. he must first find the Omega Key. which unlocks the gateway to the core. Megatron launches a full-scale assault on Iacon. capital city of the Autobots. where the key is protected by Zeta Prime—leader of the Autobots.

AVAILABLE CHARACTERS

MEGATRON

The heavy hitter of the group. Both his Fusion Cannon and his tank cannon deal tremendous damage and have a decent blast radius, making them especially powerful against enemy clusters.

SOUNDWAVE

In robot form, Soundwave performs exceedingly well in a support role—he can use his Energon Repair Ray to heal the other two Decepticons. In truck form, Soundwave can move swiftly and has the added ability to ram enemies.

BREAKDOWN

His Dash skill, combined with his ability to transform into a speedy little car, makes Breakdown extremely fast and maneuverable.

CO-OP TIPS

The person who plays as Soundwave should focus on using the Energon Repair Ray to support the squad during heavy firefights.

Once Energon Grenades become available in this level, at least one member of the squad should always carry some. Thus, he or she can drop one near the squad for a quick group-heal effect.

INTRODUCTION

Megatron's elite squad flies into the heart of the city, while Starscream leads the main Decepticon armies in an attack on the Autobot city of Iacon. Megatron expects to find the Omega Key here at the Stellar Galleries, which gives him access to Cybertron's core.

SECTION **1** INFILTRATING IACON

OBJECTIVE:

ENTER THE STELLAR GALLERIES

STAGE 1

A squad of Autobots defending the route to the Stellar Galleries attacks the moment you deploy from the Decepticon dropship ①. Autobot Car Soldiers, Protectors, and Rocketeers protect the route. Use the nearby fountains and columns as cover as you advance to the other side of the courtyard. Weapon power-ups along the way present more attacking options.

STAGE 2

After you clear the first courtyard, proceed through the small passageway ②, where you can restock on ammo and health. In the next courtyard ③, you spot more Decepticons getting ambushed by Autobot Cloakers. EMP Grenades, which are located at the central statue's base, are extremely effective against these enemies.

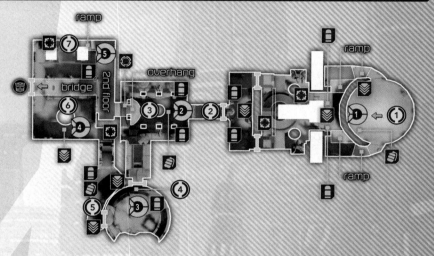

STAGE 3

A doorway on the courtyard's left side leads to a terrace ④ overlooking the city. The aerial battle progresses pleasingly here, as Starscream's squadron destroys a large Autobot ship. Press Down on the D-pad to focus on it as it collides with a nearby spire.

STAGE 4

Continue toward the fallen drop ship to find a hallway leading from the terrace. In this hallway ⑤, you find ammo and weapons—mostly long-range guns useful for the next encounter. Stop short of the next courtyard ⑥ so you can use the hallway's edge as cover while you snipe. The bridge in the courtyard leads to the Stellar Galleries. Snipers are posted on the bridge, and Autobot Soldiers fire from underneath. Snipe the snipers on the bridge first. You can also take cover and snipe from the nearby fountain.

DECEPTICON COLLECTIBLE #11

Snipe the Autobot icon framed in the glowing orange emblem. directly above the doorway to the Stellar Galleries.

STAGE 5

Once you clear the bridge, pass under it and continue between the Energon pools. As you ascend the ramp ⑦ on the right, more Snipers appear on the Stellar Galleries' ledges. Additional Protectors leap down to the bridge to guard the door ⑧. Use

cover and long-range weaponry to destroy these enemies. When you clear the way, Megatron must use Dark Energon to breach the locked door ⑧ leading into the Stellar Galleries. Load up on the power-ups scattered throughout the entry hallway.

SECTION ② SECURITY STATION

OBJECTIVE: **DISABLE THE SECURITY SYSTEM**

STAGE 1

As soon as you step inside the Stellar Galleries security station ⑨, the automated defense systems unleash a grid of deadly, spinning lasers that can annihilate you. Avoid the lasers by jumping, being careful not to land on the electrified floor below.

As you avoid the deadly beams, jump down from one raised platform to another in order to use Dark Energon on the three key terminals inside the room. One terminal is on the left; one is on the right; and one is on the room's opposite side, on the highest platform. As you begin to corrupt the terminals, sentry guns activate along the walls, peppering you with additional fire. Don't let these distract you, as their weapons deliver only light damage (and you can easily get blindsided by the bigger lasers while you're fighting). Focus on corrupting the terminals. When you corrupt all the terminals, the lasers shut off, the sentries deactivate, the exit doors open, and you can safely move deeper into the structure.

OBJECTIVE: **FIND THE OMEGA KEY**

STAGE 2

After you disable the security system's first level, enter the wide passageway ⑩ accessible from the floor level. Just inside and to the left, three Rocket Sentries on the back wall fire at you. Autobot Shotgunners guard them. Exploit the cover in the center and along the sides, avoiding the rockets as you deal with the Shotgunners at close range. You can find more health and ammo power-ups at the passageway's other end. When you eliminate the preceding threats and Megatron uses Dark Energon on the final door ⑪, the way into the Stellar Galleries is mostly clear. Proceed to the chamber that holds the Omega Key.

CHAOS BRINGER ACHIEVEMENT/TROPHY

Shoot all the planets orbiting the Cybertron model to corrupt the planet and to unlock the Chaos Bringer achievement/trophy.

SECTION ③ **THE STELLAR GALLERIES**

STAGE 1

Enter the Stellar Galleries ⑫ and climb the ramps along the sides to the raised platform. Then interact with the terminal ⑬ in order to access the Omega Key chamber. This triggers a cutscene. Megatron opens the chamber containing the Omega Key only to find it is empty. A hologram appears. It's the Autobot leader, Zeta Prime. He has taken the key and has left a host of Autobot enemies to ambush you.

OBJECTIVE: **DEFEAT AUTOBOT AMBUSHERS**

The Autobot ambush inside the Stellar Galleries consists mainly of Jet Soldiers and Car Soldiers. The Jet Soldiers attack from above, while the others fire from the ground and the ramps. The Thermo Rocket Launcher is effective against Jet Soldiers, while the nearby Thermo Mines work well against the enemies attacking on foot.

STAGE 2

When you dispatch all the enemies, approach the exit ⑭ doors on the room's ground level. But use caution—as soon as you get near the doors, Autobot Titans burst through and stomp into the room. Back off and use cover to avoid their fire. If any of the explosive containers remain from the previous battle, you can lure a Titan near one and blast it to inflict a lot of damage.

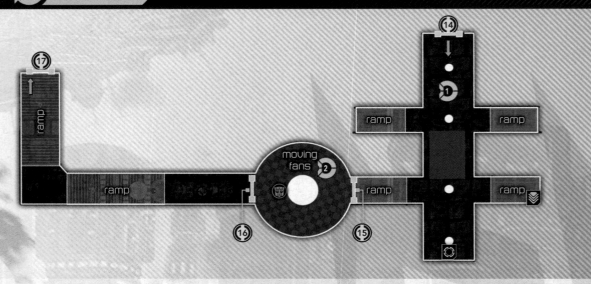

OBJECTIVE: PROCEED TO THE LOWER CITY

STAGE 1

Defeat the Autobots in the Stellar Galleries chamber, and Soundwave traces Zeta Prime's signal. He discovers a shortcut through the maintenance tunnels that run underneath the Stellar Galleries. Blast open an access hatch to enter the first passageway (15). Look for ammo and health containers in the side passages. The furthest passage on the right leads to another destructible access hatch—this one has two locking mechanisms that you must destroy.

STAGE 2

Pass through this hatch into a huge ventilation shaft (15). Use the slowly spinning fan blades as platforms to drop down two levels. You only want to drop down two levels—any further and you'll fall to your death. On the lowest fan blade level, look for another access hatch (16) to blast open.

DECEPTICON COLLECTIBLE #12

Ride the top set of rotating fan blades 180 degrees around the center. Do not drop down to another level. The Autobot symbol is located on the central shaft—shoot it.

STAGE 3

Follow the stairs in the ventilation shaft through a door ⑰ to reach the train tunnels. You catch a lone Autobot Soldier by surprise at the top of the steps. This is an easy kill, but its last act is triggering the defensive systems in the tunnels.

STAGE 4

Using your vehicle form, make your way down the train tunnel. Soundwave and Breakdown can move extremely fast. Megatron is slower, but he can use his tank cannon to blast any threats along the way. Rolling mines spawn from the illuminated red tubes along the sides. Hitting any of the tripwires activates Rocket Sentries along the walls and ceiling. Shoot the Rocket Sentries to allow safe passage.

The first downhill track ends at an intersection ⑱. Turn right at the intersection, and then make a quick left into the doorway ⑲, but look out for oncoming trains. Flashing red lights and warning klaxons signal when one is coming.

STAGE 5

This passage ⑲ immediately forks left and right. At the fork, you see EMP grenades, which are useful for the next fight. A locked maintenance hatch is to the right, but the locks aren't visible from that side. So, go left from the fork, down the left-hand passage. Here you find the same maintenance hatch ⑳ but from the other side and with visible locks. Blast them through a gap in the thick cable snakes. Blow off the locks and then destroy the maintenance hatch itself. Return to your squad on the other side of the door and proceed through. You drop down to a lower level ㉑.

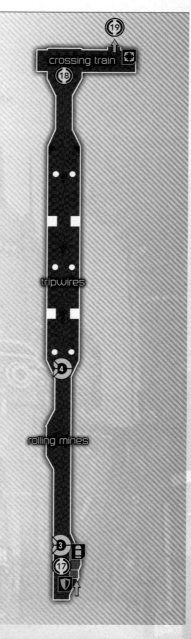

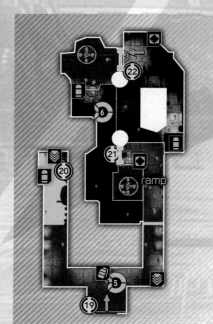

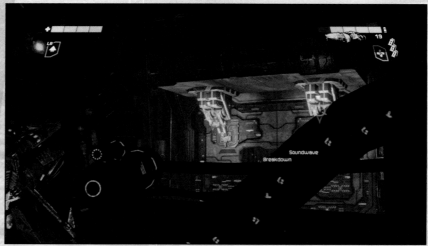

STAGE 8

Autobot Cloakers ambush you as soon as you drop down into the maintenance area. The Cloakers drop through the ventilation shafts in the ceiling. They don't stop appearing until you use Dark Energon on the two consoles in the room. This corrupts the system.

Dark Energon crystals clog the nearby ventilation shaft each time you corrupt a console. Once both consoles are disabled, defeat all remaining Cloakers. Then interact with the switch (22) at the

room's far end to open the exit door. A short passageway leads to the next section of descending tracks.

STAGE 7

As you race down the second section of downhill tracks (23), you face more tripwires, rolling mines, and train crossings. Once again, watch out for crossing

trains—listen for warning klaxons and watch for flashing red lights as you approach the intersections. In vehicle form, Megatron can race up ramps to leap over train intersections.

A train wreck (24) at the bottom marks the end of this segment. If you need health, ammo, or weapons, you can find some on the left side of the train wreck. If you climb over the wrecked train, you can find an Energon Repair Ray on the tracks. A vending machine on the right-hand platform dispenses an Energon power-up if you press the button. Follow the walkway to the right to exit (25) the train tunnel.

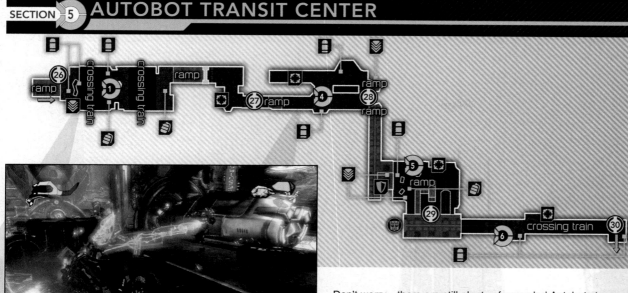

OBJECTIVE: PASS THROUGH THE LOWER CITY

STAGE 1

When you climb the ramp to the train station, you see trains crossing the area 26 on two tracks. The train on the far track stops and deploys Autobot Soldiers. Use nearby cover to avoid their attacks, and eliminate them quickly. Explosive tanks are scattered throughout the area. You can blast them to trigger explosions that take down anything within their radii. You can also try to lure the Soldiers onto the train tracks, where speeding trains can plaster them.

STAGE 2

When you clear the initial group of Soldiers, Autobot Shotgunners drop from ledges above. Use cover, lure them into trains, and

target explosive barrels to take out the Shotgunners. They try to close the distance, so be careful that you don't fall victim to the same traps you employ.

STAGE 3

After you deal with the Shotgunners, a final wave of Protector Autobots enters from the train station's far end, intending to defend the exit. Destroy them and exit the train station by moving up the ramp, into the main portion of the lower city.

STAGE 4

In the halls 27 above the train station, you find signs of battle and destruction in Iacon's lower city sector. Enter the city through the automatic doors down the far left tunnel. Autobots and Decepticons are fighting in the streets. Take care not to rush forward, as a huge building soon collapses thanks to Megatron's Dark Energon bombers.

Don't worry—there are still plenty of wounded Autobots to smash. When the building falls completely, traverse the debris and access the broken train bridge 28. Proceed right down the tunnel to reach the train yard.

STAGE 5

Soon after you approach the ledge overlooking the train yard, two trains pull in and deploy troops. The train at ground level deploys Car Soldiers, and the one on the opposite elevated track deploys Rocket Soldiers. Grab the Photon Burst Rifle on this entry ledge; it's excellent for dealing with enemies at long-range. As you start to clear out these enemies, Autobot Jet Soldiers reinforce the Autobots from above. A Thermo Rocket Launcher is on the ground directly below the ledge where you entered. This is very effective at taking down these Jet Soldiers.

OVERSHIELD

A destructible maintenance hatch similar to the others you've seen is just below the ledge where you enter the train yard. Blow this open to find an Overshield power-up.

STAGE 8

When you clear all the enemies in the train yard, use the scaffolding at the nearest train to jump to the elevated track. Move left down the train tracks ㉙, being careful to avoid the oncoming trains—use the side alcoves to dodge them. You find a maintenance hatch ㉚ on the ground to the right, at the end of the train tunnel. Blast this open and drop through the opening.

DECEPTICON COLLECTIBLE #13

When you climb to the elevated train track, move to your right (instead of left ㉚ toward your destination). Look through the force field—an Autobot symbol is on the train tunnel's inside roof. You can't pass through the force field, but you can shoot through it to destroy the Autobot symbol.

SECTION 6 WAR IN THE STREETS

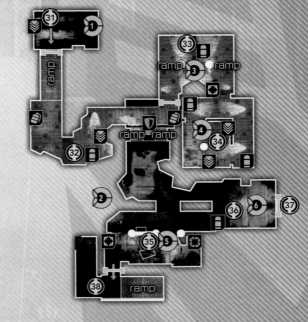

STAGE 1

You drop into a small room ㉛ below the rails. Stock up on the weapons here. Interact with the wall console to open the exit. You soon hear radio chatter from a nearby Decepticon squad that's fighting Autobots near the Autobot Vaults, which is your next destination.

OBJECTIVE: APPROACH THE IACON VAULTS

STAGE 2

Climb the ramp to see a group of Autobot Soldiers to your left firing through the windows at Decepticons in the street below ㉜. Take out these Soldiers, and a cutscene plays… Megatron's squad watches the scene unfold in the street below. Large numbers of Autobots rush Brawl. The Autobots pile onto Brawl, but he blasts them away and continues to fight against a growing number of Autobot enemies.

STAGE 3

Move down the corridor, past the windows overlooking the street, and go left. Make sure you pick up the EMP Grenades at the end of the corridor. You face an Autobot Brute and two Shotgunners inside this small room ㉝. This is a tough fight in close quarters. The EMP Grenades are extremely useful here. They strip the Shotgunners of their Overshield, and they slow down the Brute.

STAGE 4

Continue through the door at the room's far end, to a T-shaped corridor. As soon as you reach the fork, the wall ahead blows open and more Shotgunners assault you from inside the next room ㉞. You can return fire through the hole, or you can flank left or right to enter the room and take on the Shotgunners. A final Rocket Soldier guards this room near a gap in the wall. This gap leads to the street outside where Brawl and his soldiers are fighting the Autobots.

STAGE 5

Autobot Snipers take up positions on the opposite roof ㉟. Another Photon Burst Rifle is here to help you destroy the Snipers from long range—shoot the explosive canisters that are close to them. A few scattered Autobot Soldiers are on the street below. Snipe them from above, or drop down and dispatch them from ground level. Once you eliminate all the Autobots, drop down to the street and proceed left to rendezvous with Brawl ㊱.

STAGE 6

After Megatron has a short conversation with Brawl, he uses Dark Energon to try to open the nearby Vaults ㊲. But, surprise! It doesn't work this time. The hologram of Zeta Prime taunts Megatron, so Megatron orders Brawl to call in a bombing strike. Everyone needs to clear the street.

STAGE 7

Enter the building ㊳ on the left. Health is in here if you need it. An Energon Shard Container is to the left around the crates. Use the button at the room's far end to open the door. Once you pass through the door, a cutscene plays…

The Dark Energon bombers fly low over the city, approaching the coordinates of the Iacon Vaults. Before they can release their payload, huge Autobot anti-aircraft guns unfold from the rooftops and shoot them down. One of the bombers crashes into the building across the street from where Megatron and his squad are watching.

OBJECTIVE:

DISABLE THE ANTI-AIRCRAFT GUNS

STAGE 1

Megatron ㊳ gives the order to take out the anti-aircraft guns at the end of the street. You can follow Brawl down the ramp, but the better route is to move right, staying on the rooftop. If you don't have a scoped weapon handy, a Scoped Weapon Crate is on the rooftop; it provides useful long-range guns. You can also pick up Energon Grenades. These are extremely helpful during the assault, as they let you heal yourself or your teammates in a tight spot.

When you reach the rooftop's edge ㊵, Autobot Snipers and Rocket Soldiers take up positions in the buildings and on the bridge ahead ㊷. Use your position to counter-snipe them. If you get into trouble, fall back along the roof, or move forward, drop down to the street level, and use the cover of the building to your right ㊶.

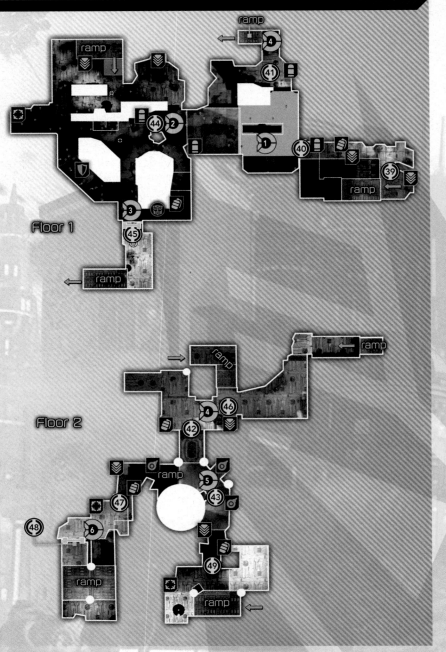

Floor 1

Floor 2

After you deal with the Snipers and Rocket Soldiers, you have to get to that AA Gun Platform ㊸. The Autobots defend their position there with turrets, including the heavy Nucleon Shock Cannon. You have two viable options for assaulting the AA Gun Platform.

STAGE 2: OPTION 1

Your first option is to head directly down the street ㊹, using cover and staying close to the big Decepticon Titan. When the Titan drops, pick up its Ion Displacer and return fire. Clearing the enemies in the turrets only gives you a brief pause—they respawn. Focus on the street enemies, and continue forward until you reach the platform—the closer you are, the less likely the turrets will hit you. Then turn left toward the two Decepticons working on the door ㊺.

STAGE 3

As soon as you approach these Decepticons, the door  45 blows open and an Autobot Brute charges through. Lure it out, and blast it when it lowers its shield. If you still have ammo for the Ion Displacer, you should be able to make the Brute stumble so that you can shoot its vulnerable backpack. Remember to avoid backing up too far, or the turrets will hit you from above. When you finish off the Brute, enter the building. Get more Energon Grenades just inside if you need them, and climb the stairwell to the platform.

OVERSHIELD

A passageway is at the AA Gun Platform's base (directly underneath the turrets). Inside, you can claim an Overshield.

DECEPTICON COLLECTIBLE #14

Stay to the street's left side as you approach the AA Gun Platform 43. You encounter a half-destroyed building leaning against another. Move around the leaning building and look behind it to see an Autobot symbol—destroy it.

STAGE 4: OPTION 2

Your second option is to take the high path to the AA Gun Platform, through the buildings. There are several entrances, the easiest one being 41 at street level when you engage the Snipers and Rocket Soldiers. Just cross the street and move through the buildings.  You're protected from most of the turret fire, and you can pick up ammo, health, or weapons along the way.

STAGE 5

Continue through the buildings until you reach the windowed space opposite 46 the AA Gun Platform. You can find more Energon Grenades at the room's far end. The turrets can fire through the windows here, so be careful. You'll see a bridge 42 that you can cross in order to reach the platform, but don't rush out. As soon as you approach, Autobot Snipers scan the area from high vantage points. Clear out the Snipers; they eventually respawn, so you have to move quickly. Then charge across the bridge to the AA Gun Platform.

STAGE 6

Whether you're coming across the bridge or up the stairwell, you have to deal with the Autobots on the AA Gun Platform 43. These are just regular soldiers, and their attention may be directed toward the enemies on the ground—it's easy enough to massacre them while they're distracted. More Energon Grenades are also here if you need healing.

STAGE 7

With the platform clear, quickly move toward the doorway underneath the Sniper 47 in the control room (left if you came up the stairwell, right if you came across the bridge). Climb the stairs and press the button to open the door 48 to the control room. Now you can safely shoot the Sniper in the back.

After you clear the AA Gun Platform and control room, use a Dark Energon detpack on the nearby console 47. This destroys both anti-aircraft guns and causes a chain reaction in the control room, which soon ends with a big explosion. Once you place the detpack, get out of there quickly. Jumping directly through the opening in the wall is the quickest way down.

OBJECTIVE: **DEFEND THE ANTI-AIRCRAFT GUNS**

STAGE 1

After disabling the Autobot AA guns, the Decepticons must ensure they stay offline long enough for their bombers to fly over. Unfortunately, this takes a while, and more Autobots are coming. You're locked into the platform area ⓸③, charged with defending that position. Before the Autobots come, be sure to grab the Energon Grenades on the platform, and feel free to mount or rip up one of the turrets.

STAGE 2

The first Autobot wave comes directly down the street. The Nucleon Shock Cannon on the platform's corner is great against these enemies. It can take out groups with massive explosions. Soon, Snipers positioned on the bridge reinforce the enemy. Blast them before

they get a bead on you. Note that if you miss one of the enemies in the street, it'll come up through the door to your right and hit you from your flank. If this happens, you'll have to detach the turret—it can't aim that far to the extreme right.

STAGE 3

The second Autobot wave comes from the building to your left: Snipers on the rooftop, then Soldiers inside the building. The Soldiers attempt to charge directly across the bridge and engage you from the platform itself. To deal with these enemies, you can stick with the Nucleon Shock Cannon, but it's definitely better to rip it from its mount to gain mobility and new firing angles. You can also use the Ion Displacer on the platform's far left side, which provides a very good angle on all of this side's threats.

STAGE 4

The third Autobot wave comes down the street again. This wave begins with Jet Soldiers and foot Soldiers. The Jet Soldiers are fairly easy to pick out of the air by using the Ion

Displacers (a Thermo Rocket Launcher also works well, if you have one). While you look up at the Jet Soldiers, it's easy for the other Soldiers to flank you. Be sure to keep an eye on the doorways (⓸⑨ and

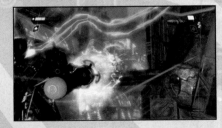

⓸②). After a little while, two Titans take up positions on the bridge. You can use the Ion Displacers to go toe-to-toe with these enemies, or you can switch to the Nucleon Shock Cannon. Either way, your best bet is to rip the turret from its mount and stay mobile to avoid the Titans' fire.

STAGE 5

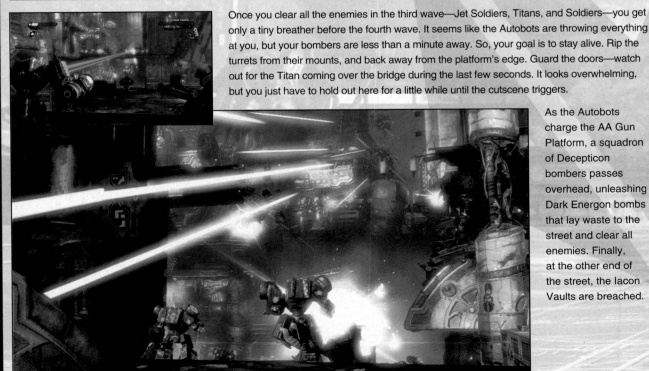

Once you clear all the enemies in the third wave—Jet Soldiers, Titans, and Soldiers—you get only a tiny breather before the fourth wave. It seems like the Autobots are throwing everything at you, but your bombers are less than a minute away. So, your goal is to stay alive. Rip the turrets from their mounts, and back away from the platform's edge. Guard the doors—watch out for the Titan coming over the bridge during the last few seconds. It looks overwhelming, but you just have to hold out here for a little while until the cutscene triggers.

As the Autobots charge the AA Gun Platform, a squadron of Decepticon bombers passes overhead, unleashing Dark Energon bombs that lay waste to the street and clear all enemies. Finally, at the other end of the street, the Iacon Vaults are breached.

STAGE 1

Move down the ruined and corrupted street, passing wounded Autobots on the way back to the Vaults. If you're low on anything, this is a good time to explore the various building interiors for useful power-ups and restock on Energon Grenades if you're out. You can even rip loose one of the turrets and carry it with you. When you get to the middle of the street, another cutscene plays.

A giant Autobot Tank bursts through a wall of debris, crushing a Decepticon soldier just before it transitions into its vehicle form and fires at you.

OBJECTIVE: DEFEAT THE AUTOBOT TANK

STAGE 2: VEHICLE FORM

You must defeat the Tank (36) in order to advance. First, you face the Tank in vehicle form. During this stage, use the cover that the ruined buildings and Dark Energon spikes provide as you move around to get behind the Tank. Avoid its cannon fire as you do this. Don't get too close to the Tank, or it'll unleash a large-radius shockwave that throws you back. Once you're in position, blast away at the vulnerable spot on the Tank's back. Once you destroy this panel completely, the Tank changes back to its robot form.

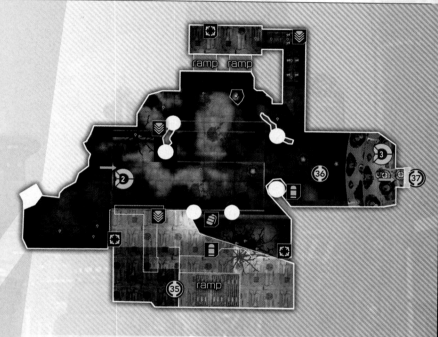

ROBOT FORM

In robot form, the Tank is terrifying. Again, exploit the cover along the sides—the building on the arena's right side (35) is a good choice. Enter this structure and ascend to the second floor, where you find additional power-ups. You can use the elevation advantage to fire down at the Tank, avoiding its counter fire by ducking behind cover or simply backing up a bit. Blast away at the Tank's torso armor until it breaks off. Then continue to damage the glowing portion of its chest until the enemy falls.

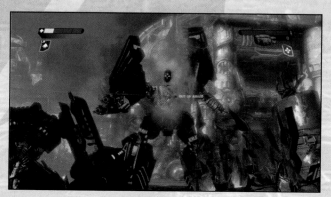

STAGE 3

With the Tank defeated, feel free to explore this area to gather additional power-ups. Proceed down to the end of the street, back to the Vaults' entryway (37). To enter, use a Dark Energon detpack on the debris blocking the way into the Vaults.

OBJECTIVE: FIND THE OMEGA KEY

STAGE 1

Zeta Prime greets you in hologram form when you enter the broken wall in the Vaults. He warns you to stay away. Power-ups are scattered in these first few calm areas. Gear up before you progress further. Near Zeta Prime's hologram, a damaged support strut (50) hangs over the floor near the central force shield. Shoot it to create a hole in the floor. Drop down through the hole to the level below.

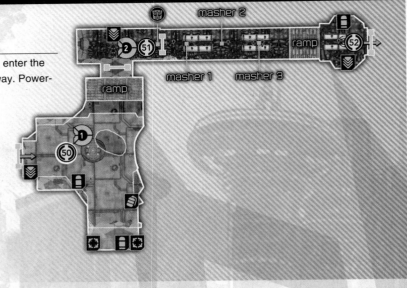

STAGE 2

Below, you find yet another Zeta Prime hologram. It demonstrates the transforming defenses of the Vaults. In the next room, you witness a hapless Decepticon soldier crushed under a giant pillar.

Immediately following this scene, you arrive at a hallway (51) that contains three similar pillars. Watch the floor—glowing areas indicate that a mashing pillar is about to descend on that spot. Move forward down the hallway, and avoid getting crushed. If you time your attempt properly, you can boost forward in vehicle form, slipping under all of the mashing pillars in one quick sprint.

Megatron approaches the Omega Key hovering just inside the room. As he attempts to grab it, the Key floats away into the waiting hand of Zeta Prime, who stands on a pedestal in the room's center (52). Surrounding himself with a protective force shield, Zeta Prime projects an enormous hologram of himself and starts to convert the room in preparation for battle.

OBJECTIVE: DEFEAT ZETA PRIME

STAGE 1

The fight against Zeta Prime consists of three stages broken down into a pattern of attacks. First, Zeta Prime attempts to use the mashers against you. Watch out for glowing areas on the floor, which precede masher attacks in those spots. In the first phase, the mashers follow a simple pattern around the room. You can easily avoid them by circling the room in one direction.

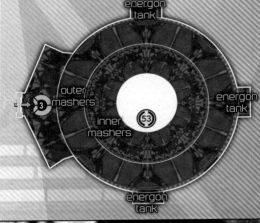

DECEPTICON COLLECTIBLE #15

As you move through the hallway of crushing pillars (51), look back at the door through which you came. An Autobot symbol is just above the door. Take care not to linger too long here, or you'll get smashed.

At the end of the hall, Megatron must use Dark Energon to break through the final doorway (52) into the central chamber. This triggers a cutscene.

This stage's second phase involves Zeta Prime spawning small, holographic copies of himself. These copies behave very much like Brutes, rushing to get close to you for melee attacks. Fortunately, they're much easier to destroy than Brutes are. Try to blast them as quickly as you can, and avoid getting mobbed from multiple sides. Watch out for mashers as you fight the holograms as well.

When you clear the holograms, Zeta Prime recharges his machinery and opens his vulnerable core. Shoot at the glowing white core, timing your shots to bypass the spinning shields attempting to protect it. You have a narrow window of opportunity, so act quickly and make your shots count. If you're badly damaged, gather Energon by shooting the tanks that pop out of the walls. If you don't inflict enough damage to Zeta's vulnerable core within the allotted time, the core closes and you have to

repeat stage one. If you deliver enough damage, you trigger a small explosion in the core before it closes and stage two begins.

STAGE 2

Stage two begins with a masher attack. This time, the pattern moves in a very quick spiral, first the outer ring, then the inner ring. The best strategy is to stay within the inner ring, and then wait while the outer mashers hit the ground. Avoid the first few inner mashers when they start to fall. Watch for the outer mashers to begin to rise—as soon as this happens, move into the outer ring's safe areas.

After this wave of mashers, Zeta spawns more holographic copies for you to fight. Again, blast them as quickly as possible, and watch out for the mashers. Note also that the holograms occasionally drop useful weapons, ammo, and grenade power-ups, so be sure to grab items you

need. When you clear the holograms, Zeta again opens his core in order to recharge. Repeat your tactics—hammer away at the core in order to advance to stage three.

STAGE 3

The masher attack for stage three is extremely challenging. Rather than following a particular pattern, Zeta *targets* you with the mashers. Wherever you go, the floor lights up and a masher quickly falls. Converting to vehicle form is a good strategy. Zeta's mashers can't keep up with you if you boost around the room.

The holograms in this last wave are also more challenging. Rather than creating them one at a time, Zeta spawns all of them at once, making it much harder to avoid getting mobbed. Keep moving—staying in vehicle form isn't a bad idea. You can use your vehicle weapons against the holograms, and boost away at speed when you feel claustrophobic. Zeta is much more aggressive with his mashers while you fight these holograms, so continue watching the floor for glowing areas.

When you clear the holograms in stage three, Zeta's core opens again as he recharges. This is your chance to finish him—blast away at the core. Don't go for the Energon along the walls unless you absolutely need it. If you inflict enough damage to the core now, the fight will end. The floor starts to glow and the mashers partially drop, but you're not in any real danger. The final cutscene plays when the battle is won.

CONCLUSION

Zeta Prime's force field falls, and his machinery collapses around him. Megatron drags him from the wreckage and yanks the Omega Key from his grasp. Thinking that he now has access to Cybertron's Core, Megatron gloats...but Zeta Prime laughs. The device that Megatron holds isn't the Omega Key—it merely summons the Omega Key. And so, the Omega Key is now on its way to Megatron; it sounds ominous. We see Omega Supreme activating, becoming his rocket form, and taking to the air.

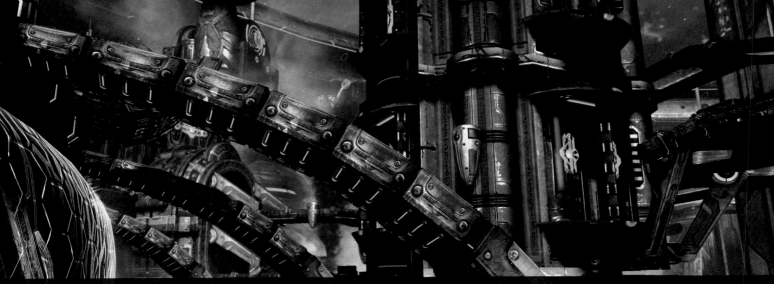

04 DEATH OF HOPE

Zeta Prime has been captured and Iacon inches closer to falling, but the device Megatron believed to be the Omega Key simply activated the key, Omega Supreme. Megatron quickly discovers he can use the device to track Omega Supreme, and races above the skies of Iacon in pursuit of his quarry.

AVAILABLE CHARACTERS

MEGATRON

The heavy hitter of the group. Both his Fusion Cannon and his tank cannon inflict tremendous damage and have a decent blast radius, making them especially powerful against enemy clusters.

SOUNDWAVE

In robot form, Soundwave works great in a support role—he can use his Energon Repair Ray to heal the others. In truck form, Soundwave can move fast and has the added ability to ram enemies.

BREAKDOWN

The Dash ability, combined with the ability to change form into a speedy little car, makes Breakdown extremely quick and maneuverable.

CO-OP TIPS

Big guns proliferate this level. It's a good idea to let one player use the heavy artillery extensively, while others focus on healing (e.g. Soundwave).

The driving portions can be very challenging due to the number of hazards and the fact that all three playable characters move at different speeds in vehicle form. Try to stay together so that anyone who goes down can be revived quickly.

INTRODUCTION

Using the homing device that they obtained from Zeta Prime, Megatron and the Decepticons pilot toward the Omega Key. Suddenly, a giant ship attacks Megatron's fleet—Omega Supreme. As Omega Supreme changes to robot form and grabs Megatron's ship, Megatron realizes that Omega Supreme is the Omega Key. Omega Supreme hurls the ship down into a chasm.

SECTION 1 — THE OMEGA KEY IS ANGRY

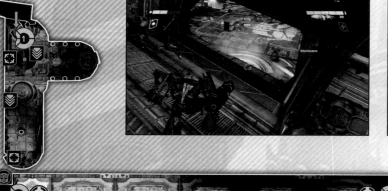

OBJECTIVE:

RENDEZVOUS WITH THE DROP SHIP

STAGE 1

Pick yourself up, dust yourself off, and exit the wreck ①. Your ship has crash-landed on a ledge inside a massive chasm deep below the surface of Iacon. Explore the area for weapons and supplies. Also, be on the lookout for health crates, as you've suffered a small amount of damage as a result of the violent crash. The plan is to move forward and drop down to the bridge. Then rendezvous with the dropship, which has landed in the middle of the bridge ②. Starscream and a troop of Decepticon soldiers wait patiently for your orders.

OBJECTIVE: DESTROY THE BRIDGE SUPPORTS

STAGE 2

Omega Supreme appears out of nowhere the moment you reach the dropship on the bridge ②. He drops out of the sky, crushing your dropship and taking out your support troops in one fell swoop—Starscream transforms into jet mode and flees for higher ground. As Omega starts to shoot rockets at you, notice the large, thruster-like bridge supports that are glowing red on both his left and right sides. Destroy these bridge supports to collapse the bridge underneath Omega and send him tumbling into the chasm.

OBJECTIVE: **FALL BACK TO THE INTERIOR**

STAGE 3

Before you can formulate another plan, Omega Supreme shoots back up from under the bridge in his imposing rocket form. Wasting no time, Omega's wings transform into a giant laser cannon. This laser is immensely powerful; Omega uses it to destroy the bridge bit by bit. Your only hope for survival is to retreat and duck inside the chasm interior ③. Megatron must use Dark Energon to blow open the door.

SECTION ② **ENEMIES WITHIN**

OBJECTIVE: **ASCEND THE CHASM WALL**

STAGE 1

Take a moment to explore the room for ammo and weapons as Omega Supreme tries to break down the door behind you. Specifically, note the Magma Frag Launcher by the monitor in the center of the room. You'll need that momentarily. After a brief moment of calm, a door ④ on the room's right side opens, ushering in a Brute and a Protector.

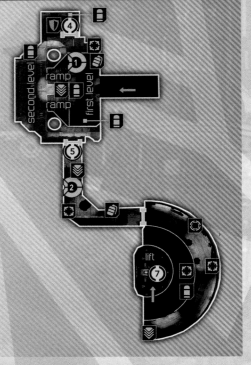

Use the center platform and the columns on the room's sides to try to flank the Brute. Try to get the Brute to chase you up the ramps in the center of the room. It takes the Brute some time to navigate the stairs, which gives your co-op buddy (if you have one) a great opportunity to flank him and shoot him in the back.

STAGE 2

When you defeat one of these two enemies, a door ⑤ on the room's opposite side opens and an Autobot Titan enters, wielding a huge Ion Displacer. He tends to hang out by the door, so use the column by the door and the platform in the center of the room for cover. The aforementioned Magma Frag Launcher definitely comes in handy against this enemy. Peek around the corners and lob salvos at the Titan. Duck back behind cover before you detonate the frag rounds remotely.

STAGE 3

With the Titan dispatched, move through the doorway ⑤ that the Titan was guarding. Starscream's voice comes in over your party's comm channel, informing all Decepticon forces that Megatron has perished and that he is taking command henceforth. This motivates Megatron and company to get back to the surface to regain radio contact with Starscream and the remaining Decepticon forces.

As the door opens, you see Omega Supreme just outside the curved hallway's window ⑥, blasting away at the room you just exited. After completely demolishing the room, Omega wheels around toward you. In no time, he knocks down the force field in the window and opens fire with his sentry guns. Move as quickly as you can to the lift at the end of the hallway. Use the switch to activate the lift ⑦.

ENERGON SHARD CONTAINER

The Energon Shard Container is in the curved hallway ⑥, partially hidden behind a stack of crates on the hallway's left side.

SECTION ③ **CARGO LIFT**

STAGE 1

As the lift shaft closes ⑦, three small locking mechanisms deploy from the floor, effectively keeping the lift grounded. Destroy these three lift locks to start the elevator's ascent toward Iacon's surface.

OBJECTIVE: **ESCAPE THE ELEVATOR**

As the lift rises, Omega Supreme arrives back on the scene in rocket mode, determined to bring Megatron down this time. He opens up his huge cannon and blasts at the lift, destroying whole sections of the lift shaft above you and stopping the lift in its tracks. Omega fires his cannon again, sending the lift into a freefall. This causes the lift's emergency locks to engage, bringing the lift to a sudden halt. Shoot the emergency locks before Omega can target you with his giant beam again. Once you damage both of them, the elevator resumes its plunge until the lift locks reengage. Shoot the locks again to destroy them once and for all, sending the lift downward until it stops at a service exit partway up the shaft.

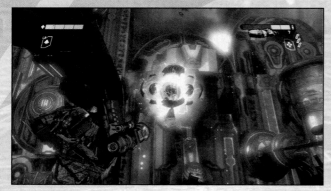

STAGE 2

Exit the elevator shaft to find yourself on a series of scaffolds perilously hanging out over the chasm. Omega Supreme quickly gives chase as you step out onto the scaffold. You have some cover on the left side, but Omega's powerful weaponry can easily destroy those signs, leaving you vulnerable. Carefully navigate the gaps in the scaffolding. Ultimately, you drop down to a safe landing spot further down the chasm (8).

ENERGON SHARD CONTAINER

Drop down through the first break in the scaffolding you encounter after you exit the lift. Once you drop down, perform a 180-degree turn and move back toward the lift shaft. An Energon Shard Container is on the lower scaffolding, up against the elevator shaft.

STAGE 3

When you reach the lower balcony, look around for weapons, ammo, and health if you're running low. With Omega Supreme still chasing you, your natural instinct might be to rush inside the rounded door (9) as soon as it opens. However, this is ill advised, as two Car Soldiers and a Protector wait for you on the other side.

Use the crates on the left side of the doorway for cover, and take down this small squad of Autobots before you proceed through the tube (10).

STAGE 4

A little ways through this tube (10), you trigger a cutscene: A small squad of Decepticons at the tube's opposite end runs toward you,

eager to rendezvous with Megatron. Suddenly, a giant fist punches through the door at the end of the tube, sending the Decepticon troops flying. Omega Supreme slowly spins up his claw tractor beam, sucking in and scraping the remaining Decepticon with ease. He peaks into the tube and identifies his targets. Charging up his claw one more time, Omega releases a powerful blast of energy, which downs Megatron, Soundwave, and Breakdown.

OBJECTIVE: **SHOOT OMEGA'S HAND**

Omega has just used his giant claw hand to knock you down and immobilize you. Slowly spinning up his claw, he begins to suck you in. Shoot at his hand to damage it before he sucks you in and destroys you. Move forward, to the right of the tube's new dead end, enter the tunnel, and drop down the abandoned elevator shaft (11) to escape from Omega.

DECEPTICON COLLECTIBLE #17

After you escape Omega's claw grab, make your way down the tube and turn right to face an elevator shaft (12) with a broken-down elevator hanging from above. Before you drop down, step up to the edge and look up, behind the elevator. You can see the next Decepticon collectible. Shoot it and then drop down into the shaft.

OBJECTIVE: **GO TO THE BRIDGE TERMINAL**

STAGE 1

As you make your way down the next hallway (12), you reach a large, dome-like room with a cadre of Autobots inside. Soundwave scans the nearby radio traffic and determines that this group is coordinating with Omega Supreme, tracking your location through the chasm. Destroying these Autobots would make it easier to avoid Omega Supreme. Proceed to the end of the hallway, where you see a door (13) with a couple of locks.

Destroy the locks to gain access to the Control Dome (14). Before you enter, take a look around for weapons and ammo. In particular, notice the X12 Scrapmaker in front of the Control Dome's window. Also, a grenade crate, which should come in handy, is near the entrance.

ENERGON SHARD CONTAINER

As you make your way down the hallway (12) toward the Control Dome, you should see a small side passage on your left. An Energon Shard Container is located near a stack of crates in this nook.

STAGE 2

When the door blasts open, you immediately see a Titan up on the room's raised central platform (14). He's the biggest threat in the first part of this encounter. Use the sides of the doorway for cover, hang back, and unload on him with the X12 Scrapmaker. Alternatively, you can take the brave route by transforming into vehicle mode and bursting into the room. If you do, be aware that the Titan isn't alone—a couple of Autobot footsoldiers flank him.

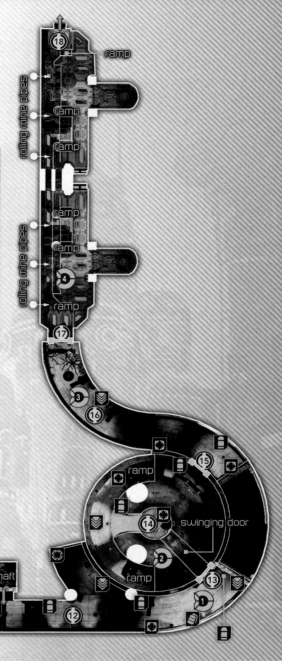

You can also try taking a sharp left inside the doorway, going up the ramp, and using the large support columns for cover. After you eliminate these initial enemies, a group of Autobot Jet Soldiers flies in through the ceiling. A rocket launcher is on the Control Dome's upper level, and a cache of Thermo Mines is toward the rear of the lower level. Both of these power-ups help you take out the remaining Jet Soldiers.

When you defeat all the enemies, use the terminal on the room's central platform ⑭ to swing the giant door back to its original position, revealing your exit ⑮. When you do, you find two Autobot Brutes and two Protectors waiting for you. Use the explosive Energon tanks outside the door to take out the little guys. The Titan's big gun is highly effective against the Brutes.

STAGE 3

Make your way down the curved corridor ⑯, and you quickly reach a locked door. Megatron attempts to blow out the door with the power of Dark Energon, but his efforts are thwarted. An Autobot security measure prevents the door from opening. A group of repair sentries soon pops up and fires on the door, keeping it in place despite the Dark Energon corruption. Destroy the sentries to let Dark Energon fully corrupt the door ⑰, allowing you to continue.

STAGE 4

As you step outside the building, Omega zips by overhead, dropping mines on the road in front of you. Rolling mines spawn from the illuminated red tubes on the left-hand wall along the road. Furthermore, Omega makes a sweep of the entire area, using his mounted weaponry to dog you. Drive as quickly as you can through this area, avoiding the rolling mines and Omega's sentry fire. Enter the building ⑱ at the far end of the road, but watch out for the two Car Soldiers there.

OVERSHIELD

When you drive through the ledge with the rolling mines, stick to the far right. A little ways through the area, you go off a ramp and jump a small gap. An Overshield sits out in the road on the other side of this jump.

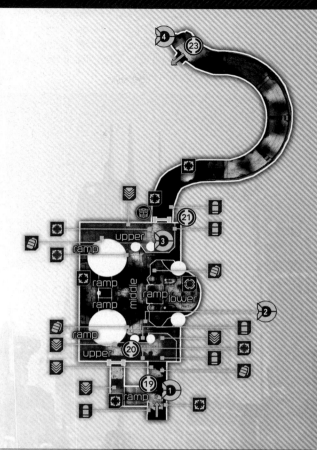

STAGE 1

Inside the building, climb the stairs ⑲ on the left and continue
out the open door to the right, which triggers a cutscene. Omega
swoops into the observation deck and deploys several Autobot
troops, including a giant Tank robot. Megatron and company take
cover as the newly deployed infantry opens up on them. Megatron
radios Starscream for air support. Starscream reluctantly
complies, blasting
Omega Supreme with
a long-range missile.
This draws Omega's
attention; he flies off to
chase Starscream.

STAGE 2

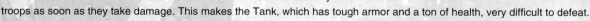

Starscream has successfully distracted Omega Supreme for the moment, so it's up to
you to handle the troops that Omega just deployed. When the fight begins, you take fire
from many different targets, so move around and use the nearby structures as cover. The
balcony on which you start ⑳ is generally a good spot to post up at, but be advised that a
Shotgunner tries to flank you from the left if you hang out here too long.

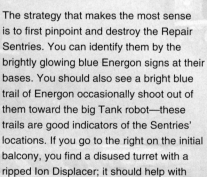

Needless to say, the Tank robot is the biggest threat in the room. You want to take it out
as quickly as you can, but there's a catch. Three Autobot repair sentries are in strategic
locations near the middle of the room. These Sentries start to heal any of the Autobot
troops as soon as they take damage. This makes the Tank, which has tough armor and a ton of health, very difficult to defeat.

The strategy that makes the most sense
is to first pinpoint and destroy the Repair
Sentries. You can identify them by the
brightly glowing blue Energon signs at their
bases. You should also see a bright blue
trail of Energon occasionally shoot out of
them toward the big Tank robot—these
trails are good indicators of the Sentries'
locations. If you go to the right on the initial
balcony, you find a disused turret with a
ripped Ion Displacer; it should help with
taking out the Tank.

STAGE 3

Once you destroy the giant Tank robot (or all of its support troops), a door ㉑ at the arena's far end opens, and a Rocket Soldier and three Snipers file into the observation deck. The three Snipers stay posted up at the far balcony, creating chaos for anyone stranded in the arena's open center area. When the Snipers come out, get to cover as quickly as you can.

You have two options here: One option is to use some of the ranged weaponry that you can find in the observation deck to take on the Snipers at their own game. The other option is to transform into vehicle mode, boost up the ramps on the arena's left side, and try to flank the Snipers. In either case, be advised that a repair sentry is on the balcony where the Snipers are stationed, so you might want to destroy that first.

ENERGON SHARD CONTAINER

A balcony hangs out over the chasm on the observation deck's lowest level, in the arena's center. The Energon Shard Container is in the middle of this platform. Because this area is so wide open, it offers very little protection from the Snipers or the Tank, so be careful when you approach it.

When you clear the observation deck of the Snipers and other reinforcements, you can approach the exit door ㉑ located on the first floor. A pair of Protectors guards that passageway, so use the nearby crates and columns for cover, and dispatch them before you proceed down the curved hallway.

DECEPTICON COLLECTIBLE #18

On the second floor where the snipers were, the eighteenth collectible is near doorway ㉑ on this room's left-hand wall—destroy it.

OBJECTIVE: FIND ANOTHER WAY TO THE BRIDGE

STAGE 5

As you make your way around the domed structure inside the curved hallway ㉒, you see Omega Supreme in drop ship form fly ahead of you and around the corner. When you turn the corner, you see that Omega has transformed back into robot mode and is perched high on a wall. Without warning, he rips a massive chunk out of the wall and hurls it at you with reckless abandon! The structural damage that Omega causes blocks the remainder of the road in front of you. This prevents you from taking the most direct route to the bridge terminal. Fortunately, you can duck into a side passage ㉓ ahead on your left. Get off the road quickly, before Omega peppers the area with missiles.

STAGE 1

After you escape the pursuing Omega Supreme, you emerge in a behind-the-scenes area (23) filled with several maintenance tunnels. Enter the area by destroying the maintenance hatch (24). As you make your way down the narrow hallway, a Car Soldier jumps out in front of you. By this point, you should see a few openings on the left-hand side that lead into the larger maintenance tunnel room (25). If you step out into this opening,

you can see a bridge (26) at the far side of this room. Two Snipers, a Protector, and a repair sentry are stationed on this bridge.

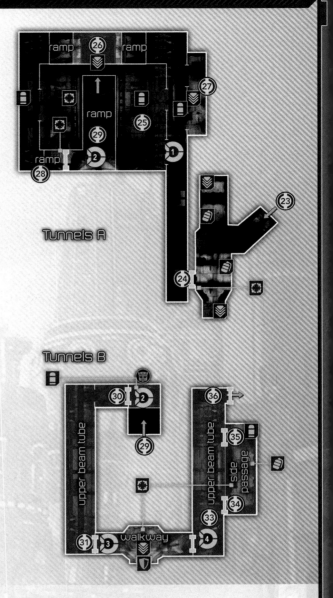

Tunnels A

Tunnels B

If you choose to, you can move into the middle of this open room and fire at the enemies on the bridge. However, take a closer look at the bridge before you do so. You should see a few extra laser tracers focused on the bridge. They originate from another pair of Autobot Snipers positioned at raised locations in the area. These additional Snipers make staying in the narrow hallway advisable. Follow it to the end to get a flanking position on the bridge Snipers.

Also, watch for a hidden nook (27) on this narrow hallway's right side. A Magma Frag Launcher is hidden back there. Use it to pepper the bridge with explosives and take out those Snipers. Be aware that the Snipers here like to shoot at the explosive Energon containers as you approach them. If you move close to one and see it spark, that's your cue to get out of the way. Neutralize the bridge enemies and the Snipers on the raised balconies high above ground level.

STAGE 2

Make your way around the back of the maintenance area, and ascend the ramp (28). You must destroy another door here to access the first maintenance tunnel (29), which leads to the room's upper areas.

As you move into this first tube, a rocket sentry fires at you from the ceiling. You find another hatch (30) to destroy at the end of this

tube. When you open the tube's exit, you get a sign of the danger you face in these maintenance tunnels; a group of Autobots shoots at you from inside the adjacent tube. The power conduit activates, sending massive quantities of highly concentrated Energon through the tube, instantly scrapping the Autobots!

When the tube completes its cool-down cycle and shuts off, make your way quickly and carefully through the tube, and destroy the left-side exit hatch ③ at the other end. Don't straggle behind—the tube reactivates regularly from this point on. Needless to say, it would be bad to get caught in the middle of the tube when it activates.

STAGE 3

As you exit the tube, you step out onto a large balcony ③, and a group of Autobot fliers immediately greets you. A Thermo Rocket Launcher is on this balcony, which should help you permanently ground the Jet Soldiers. Use the large columns and the crates on the balcony as cover.

DECEPTICON COLLECTIBLE #19

From this balcony ③ look directly across to the initial tube you navigated. The nineteenth Autobot symbol for you to destroy is above this tube on the far wall.

OVERSHIELD

If you feel brave, jump down onto the outside of the room's center tube, the one you traversed on the inside to reach the maintenance area's upper levels. After you drop down, turn 180 degrees to see the Overshield sitting on this tube's outside surface. Drop down to the ground level, and travel the tubes again to reach the upper balcony.

STAGE 4

Destroy the hatch to access another power conduit ③. This one is already activated before you arrive. To get a feel for the timing, watch the tube's cycle of powering up and down before you attempt to go through it. It'll be really tough to get all the way to the end of the tube, as its activation cycle seems much quicker than the first power conduit. Fortunately, there's another

way. Look to the tube's right side—you should see another hatch ③ that you can knock down. Quickly duck into this side passage before the beam reactivates. Pull the switch to open the door ③ at the side passage's far end. Then time your movements, making your way through to the end of the tube ③.

SECTION 7 — TERMINAL AMBUSH

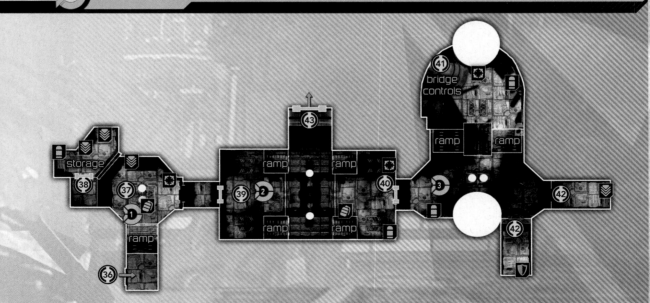

ENERGON REPAIR RAY

Make your way down the ramp into the bridge station. Turn left and look for another destructible hatch ③. Knock down the door to find a small weapons cache with an Energon Repair Ray hidden behind some crates.

OBJECTIVE: ACTIVATE THE BRIDGE

STAGE 1

You've finally made it to the bridge terminal ③. Now you just need to activate the bridge so you can cross it and get on with taking down that pesky Omega Supreme. Descend the ramp, but before you enter the room to your right, take a moment to stock up on goodies. Take special note of the EMP Grenades here.

STAGE 2

As you step into the bridge station ③⑧, you see some falling debris as a few Autobots drop in from the ceiling and then cloak themselves. These Autobot Cloakers can surround you before you know it! Use the EMP grenades you acquired in the previous room liberally. Not only do they stun the Cloakers, they also make them visible. Note all the explosive Energon Crates in the room; try to shoot these when you see Cloakers close to them. The explosion is powerful enough to wax one or two nearby enemies.

STAGE 3

When you clear the bridge station of Cloakers, the switch at the room's far end becomes active. Interact with it to open the door to the bridge control room ④⓪. But don't be too hasty to enter—a Shotgunner waits for you on the other side. As soon as you open the door, he peeks out from cover and tosses an EMP grenade toward the doorway. Stay back from the door to avoid getting stunned and blinded.

Dispatch this first Shotgunner, and be very cautious about how you move through the room. On the elevated position to the left, a Titan, a Protector, and two light sentry guns guard the bridge controls ④①. Use the nearby crates for cover, and try to catch the Titan in an explosion by shooting some of the nearby Energon containers. You should target the sentries and the Titan first, as they're your greatest threat. With the control room cleared of opposition, use the terminal by the window and watch the bridge transform into place. Exit the bridge control room back the way you came, and enter the newly transformed tunnel ④③.

OVERSHIELD

Inspect the two small alcoves ④② at the back of the control room, where the Protector and second Shotgunner came out. The Overshield is in one of the alcoves.

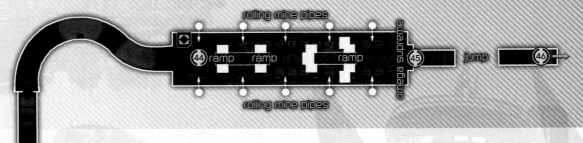

OBJECTIVE: CROSS THE CHASM BRIDGE

STAGE 1

Now that you've made it out to the chasm bridge, change form and get ready to roll. Just as you make it out of the bridge control room, Omega Supreme flies past the bridge tube **(43)** from the right. As you head downhill,

you see Omega drop a cache of rolling mines on the road in front of you. Avoid these mines, and make your way around the curved road toward the other side of the chasm.

As you approach the chasm bridge (44), Omega appears again, flying overhead from your left. He transforms into his imposing robot mode and perches on a structure all the way at the end of the bridge. Dodge the roller mines that spawn from the glowing red tubes on the bridge's sides. Evade Omega's missile barrage as you speed toward the other side…and Omega himself!

You have to drive straight underneath Omega (45) to reach your destination. As you approach Omega, he stops shooting missiles and attempts to slam you with a massive area-of-effect melee attack. This knocks out the tube road in front of you and scatters any hapless Decepticons within Omega's range. Keep driving as fast as you can, jump over the gap in the destroyed tube road, and book it into the bridge station (46) on the other side of the chasm.

OBJECTIVE: ASCEND TO THE TURRET PLATFORM

STAGE 1

Take a moment to explore this bridge station (46) before you proceed toward the elevator. You find plenty of goodies here, so take your time and make sure you're well stocked before you leave. Be sure to grab the EMP Grenades in this area, as well as the X12 Scrapmaker.

OVERSHIELD

Turn left when you enter the bridge station. An Overshield is behind a large stack of crates, just up the ramp on the bridge station's left side.

DECEPTICON COLLECTIBLE #20

On the bridge station's left side, look back at the wall in the direction from which you came. The next Autobot symbol is behind a force field. There's a gap between the force field and the ceiling. Pick up a nearby Flak Grenade and toss it over the force field. If your aim is true, you'll sneak the grenade into that pocket and destroy the last Autobot symbol for the level.

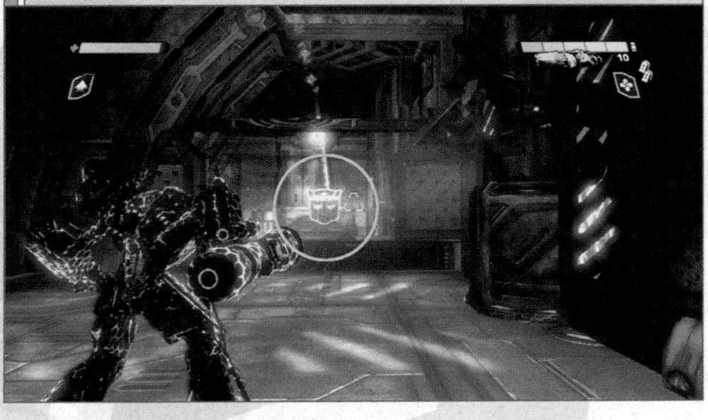

STAGE 2

As the door ㊼ to the lift area opens, you hear an unsettling clicking sound…more Autobot Cloakers! Use the EMP Grenades to spot these guys, and exploit the volatile Energon containers on the platform adjacent to the lift. Once you clear the room of Cloakers, the raised lift descends with an Autobot Brute riding it.

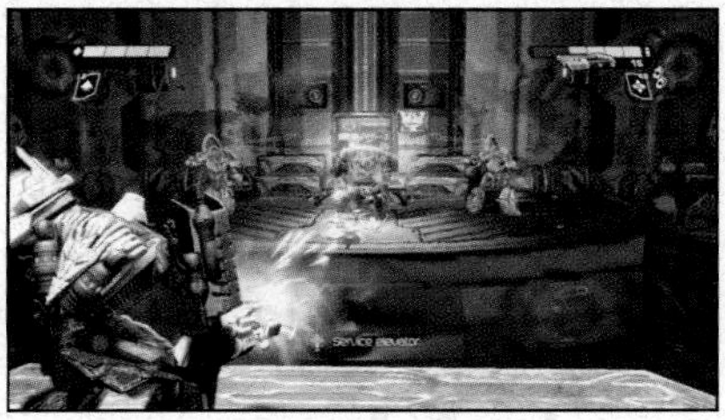

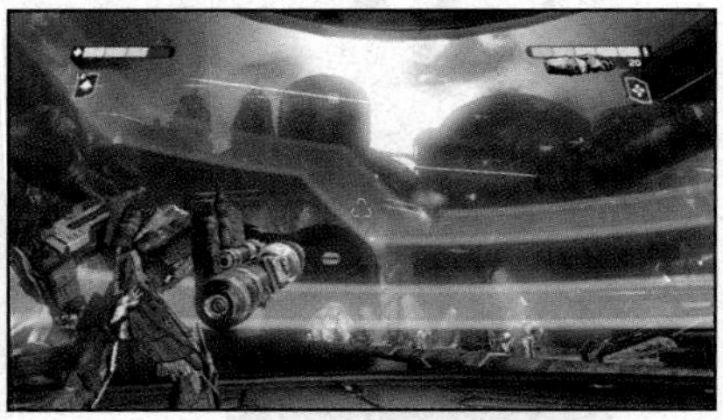

Flank the Brute, and shoot him in the back with the X12 Scrapmaker. Defeat the Brute, and use the switch on the lift ㊽ to activate it. As you ride the lift, use the camera to survey the landscape. The battle for Iacon is raging full force despite Megatron's absence from the frontlines.

OBJECTIVE: CLEAR THE TURRET PLATFORM

STAGE 1

You've finally reached the turret platform ㊾. However, before you can use the Ion Displacers' power to take out Omega Supreme once and for all, you have a small problem to handle. The platform is overrun with Autobots, and they're using the Ion Displacers to destroy the Decepticons' nearby aerial support. You must clear the entire platform of Autobots if you hope to use these turrets to destroy Omega Supreme. This is going to be a big battle.

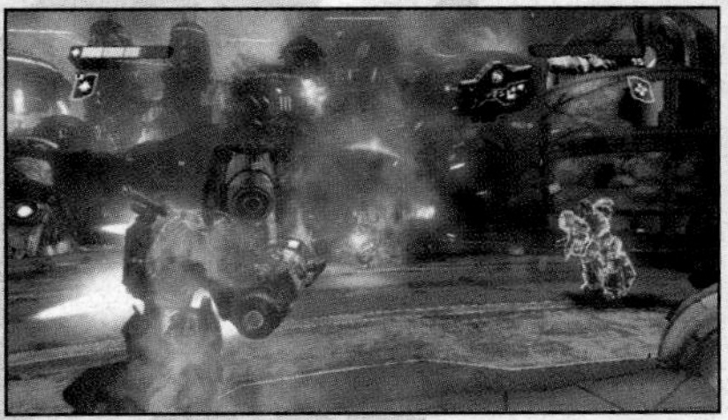

OVERSHIELD

When you step out of the elevator shaft, don't immediately turn left or right. Sneak behind the piece of cover placed straight in front of you to find an Overshield by the destroyed platform.

STAGE 2

When the door opens to the turret platform, you look out into the chasm. A couple of Autobot Shotgunners stand guard. Use the doorway for cover, and take down the two Shotgunners. After this, it doesn't particularly matter whether you choose to turn left or a right. In either case, you ascend a short ramp ㊿ that leads out to the big, open turret platform (51).

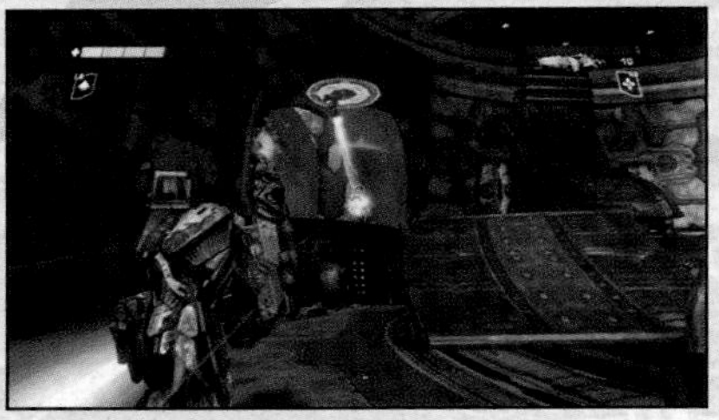

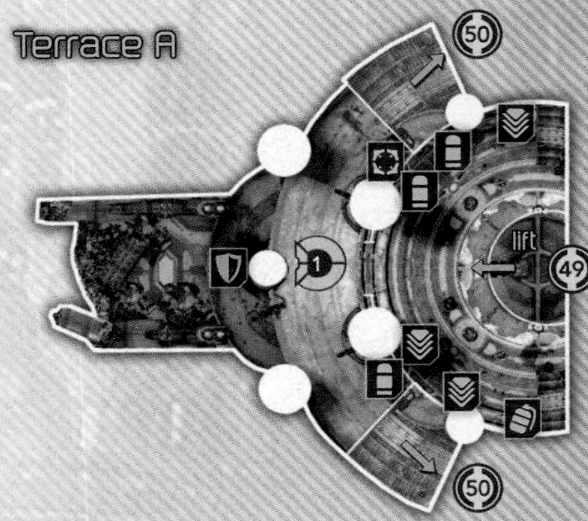

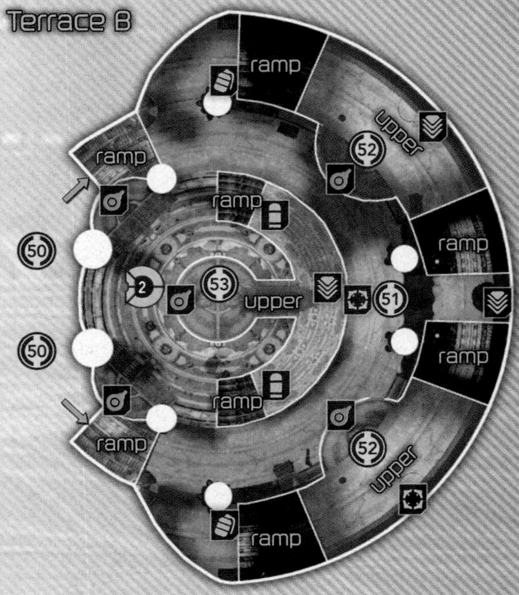

All you've been waiting for is at the top of the ramps. A big Tank is on a raised platform in the arena's center. A Protector mans a Nucleon Shock Cannon directly ahead, in a raised alcove at the back of the arena.

Directly above the Protector, a repair sentry gives jolts of healing energy to the Tank and the support troops as needed.

If you turn hard left or right at the top of the ramp, you can find a passage that leads up into the alcoves, where the Protector is planted in the turret. These side passages (52) would seem like a good option, as they give you cover from the storm of enemy fire in the open center area. Plus, they allow you to flank the turrets safely. However, Titans lurk in these back passages. Furthermore, additional reinforcements (Soldiers, Shotgunners, etc.) drop into the arena as you clear out the initial enemies. This encounter is tough no matter how you choose to tackle it.

First, realize that hanging out in the arena's center is deadly. If you want to play out in the open, keep moving to avoid turret fire and the heavy assault coming from the Tank robot in the center (53). Your best bet is to follow either the left or right side passage. Dealing with the Titan at the top of the ramp is a little hairy, but once you take down one of them, you should have a much easier time of it. He drops an Ion Displacer, which you can put to good use. Move up the passage and blast the repair sentry above the Protector, and then focus some fire on the Protector in the turret.

Once you gain access to an Ion Displacer, use it to take out the other Protector on the turret. If you control these two turrets at the back of the arena, you'll have a much easier time dealing with remaining Titan and, more importantly, the big Tank robot in the center. Stick and move, take the turrets, use the turrets against the remaining enemies, and watch for useful power-ups, such as the Energon Grenade caches in those back passageways. Take these steps, and you should be able to survive the turret platform.

SECTION 10 — BATTLE ON THE TERRACE

OBJECTIVE: USE TURRETS TO DEFEAT OMEGA SUPREME

STAGE 1

With the turret platform cleared, quickly try to stock up on weapons and ammo. Look out for the Thermo Rocket Launcher on the circular platform leading to the center turret. Within moments of clearing the turret platform, Omega Supreme, in his rocket form, finally tracks you down again. The turrets are the only weapons with enough firepower to breach Omega Supreme's thick hull, so strap into the nearest turret and get ready.

The two turrets in the alcoves at the back of the arena are Nucleon Shock Cannons. The two at the front, as well as the center turret, are Ion Displacers. Both turret types are effective weapons against Omega, so pick your poison.

When Omega appears, aim your turret gun at him and let her rip! For his first attack, he unleashes his humongous cannon, so be prepared to hop out of your turret at a moment's notice. Needless to say, you don't want to be stuck inside a turret when a giant laser beam comes for you. Rip the turret gun off its base to stay mobile and still damage Omega. One downside of this strategy is that you can't return to that particular turret until it regenerates its weapon barrel.

After Omega uses his giant cannon to sweep large swaths of the arena, he deploys a giant force field in front of him, which mostly shields his front side from your turret fire. While he does this, he launches a barrage of homing missiles from pods just above his wing thrusters. Keep moving and dodge the missiles, or take aim and blast them out of the sky. Omega alternates these attacks, along with firing his onboard turrets at you. Once you inflict enough damage to Omega Supreme with the turrets, Omega deploys a fleet of Autobot Jet Soldiers. Use the turrets to dispatch them, or use the previously mentioned Thermo Rocket Launcher.

BASICS
CHARACTERS
WEAPONS
WALKTHROUGH
o4
DEATH OF HOPE
MULTIPLAYER
ACHIEVEMENTS

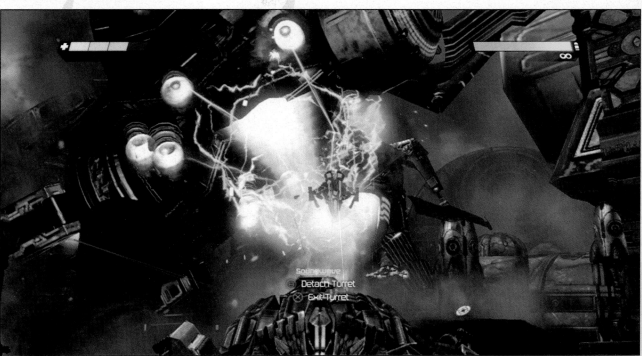

STAGE 2

After you clear the wave of Autobot Jet Soldiers, Omega flies back onto the scene. His movements and attacks are faster during this stage. When you deliver enough damage, Omega deploys another round of Jet Soldiers before he ducks away.

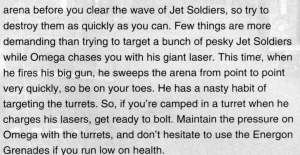

STAGE 3

This time, Omega returns to the arena before you clear the wave of Jet Soldiers, so try to destroy them as quickly as you can. Few things are more demanding than trying to target a bunch of pesky Jet Soldiers while Omega chases you with his giant laser. This time, when he fires his big gun, he sweeps the arena from point to point very quickly, so be on your toes. He has a nasty habit of targeting the turrets. So, if you're camped in a turret when he charges his lasers, get ready to bolt. Maintain the pressure on Omega with the turrets, and don't hesitate to use the Energon Grenades if you run low on health.

CONCLUSION

Omega Supreme, severely damaged from the skirmish, flies out of control, crashes through a building, and falls. Soundwave's analysis reveals that Omega is not yet defeated, so the Decepticons set off in pursuit of Omega Supreme to finish the job.

THE FINAL GUARDIAN

The great Omega Supreme is vulnerable. Megatron and his Decepticons must press their attack if they hope to overcome the guardian of Iacon and force him to unlock the gateway to Cybertron's core.

AVAILABLE CHARACTERS

MEGATRON

When you use his tank form, focus the main cannon into the center of Omega's chest. The splash damage simultaneously hurts multiple sentries. During sequences in which you can damage Omega directly, don't forget to use Megatron's hover ability to increase his weapon damage.

SOUNDWAVE

His barrier ability comes in handy against many of Omega Supreme's attacks. The barrier does not block the Attractor Beam or the Thermo Scatter Bombs, but it temporarily stops everything else. Use Soundwave's repair ray to keep the others alive during the fight.

BREAKDOWN

Breakdown is the quickest of the team. When Omega Supreme calls the batteries to regenerate his sentry turrets, have Breakdown move quickly to the battery, via either his dash ability or his car form, to apply the corruption.

CO-OP TIPS

During most of the fight against Omega Supreme, try to stay somewhat separated. Most of Omega's attacks inflict splash damage, hitting multiple targets simultaneously if they're close to each other. However, don't stay too far apart, or you won't have enough time to reach a player if he or she needs to be revived.

During the fight's second stage, have one player attract Omega Supreme's targeting attention by staying relatively close to him and damaging him with whichever weapon he or she chooses, other than the Ion Displacer turrets. This gives the other player time to target Omega's chest with an Ion Displacer turret.

BASICS

CHARACTERS

WEAPONS

WALKTHROUGH

01

02

03

04

o5
THE FINAL GUARDIAN

06

07

08

09

10

MULTIPLAYER

ACHIEVEMENTS

INTRODUCTION

After temporarily suffering defeat at the hands of Megatron and his allies, Omega Supreme crash-lands in ship form through a nearby building's roof. Megatron and his Decepticons realize that the battle isn't over yet, as they chase him to finish the job and retrieve the key to Iacon's core. Meanwhile, Omega Supreme reaches out to grab a glowing container of liquid Energon. It regenerates him, which allows him to convert into a new form.

SECTION ① MEGATRON VS. THE OMEGA KEY

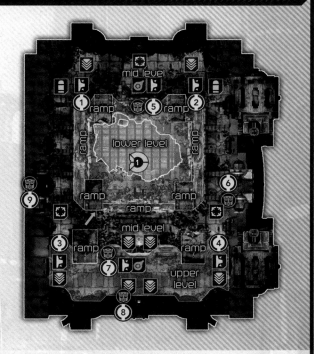

OBJECTIVE: **DESTROY OMEGA SUPREME'S TURRETS**

The battle begins as Omega Supreme completes his transformation into robot mode. During this first stage, Omega uses a few big attacks against you…

MASS-MANIPULATION ATTRACTOR BEAM

Omega Supreme's right hand can lock onto characters and destructible cover in the environment. When the Attractor Beam is about to lock onto you, red discs start to glow around you. You can evade this attack by ducking behind cover until the target lock is broken and Omega grabs a piece of wall or pillar. Omega Supreme throws the piece at the nearest targeted player. This improvised projectile explodes on contact, delivering some splash damage.

If the Attractor Beam grabs you, it lifts you up to Omega's hand, where you are crushed and thrown into the wall. In single-player, this move annihilates you. In co-op, you are downed automatically, and a teammate must revive you. Omega Supreme uses this attack only during the fight's first stage.

BALLISTIC 18 REPULSOR MISSILES

Omega Supreme's left hand locks onto a targeted player and fires a barrage of missiles. The safest way to avoid damage from this attack is to hide behind cover. However, you can also dodge the missiles by using Breakdown's dash ability or by executing a perfectly timed double jump. This attack continues throughout both of the fight's stages. You can also outrun these slow-moving projectiles by transforming into vehicle mode and driving.

VECTOR X CONCUSSION BLAST

If you get too close to Omega Supreme's feet, he charges an area-of-effect attack that severely damages and knocks you backward into the air.

CORE GRID DEFENSE TURRETS

Eight sentry turrets fold out of Omega's chest, shoulders, and back. These sentries can target multiple characters at once, and currently they are Omega Supreme's only vulnerability. To progress, you must destroy these sentries attached to Omega Supreme. Once you destroy four of them, Omega Supreme randomly summons an Energon battery from one of the four locations in the arena's corners ①, ②, ③, and ④. Omega

attempts to use these batteries to recharge his damaged sentry systems. This is your chance to expose Omega's vulnerability during this stage.

OBJECTIVE: CORRUPT BATTERIES TO DEFEAT OMEGA

You must get to that Energon battery and corrupt it before Omega Supreme uses his tractor beam to grab it. If you fail to corrupt the battery, Omega Supreme regenerates, his sentry turrets reactivate, and they resume attacking your squad.

To corrupt the battery, you must step up close enough to interact with one side. Once you successfully corrupt the battery, its color changes from aqua green to purple, and corruption spikes cover its surface. When Omega draws a corrupted battery toward him to drain its power, the corruption spreads to his systems for a short duration.

With Omega Supreme temporarily corrupted by Dark Energon, his armor changes to purple, showing that he is vulnerable. Quickly blast away at him—Omega's vulnerability doesn't last long. After a short time, Omega Supreme purges the Dark Energon corruption, regenerates his sentries, and resumes attacking. You must repeat this process until Omega Supreme falls to his knees, unable to regenerate his sentry turret defense system.

After the first time you corrupt an Energon battery, Omega Supreme calls for Autobot Air Support to attack the Decepticons. Two Autobot Jet Soldiers fly over the outer wall near the summoned battery. These Autobots try to distract you long enough that you miss the window of opportunity to corrupt the battery with Dark Energon.

DON'T DILLYDALLY

Although there's no specific timer to compel you to hurry during the fight's first stage, it is important to avoid taking too long here. All of the cover in this arena is destructible, and Omega's attacks quickly rip away at it. If all the cover is destroyed during the fight's first stage, you'll have nowhere to hide from Omega Supreme's Attractor Beam.

OVERSHIELD

When you first begin, an Overshield power-up is directly in front of you, in the pit next to Omega Supreme.

DECEPTICON COLLECTIBLE #21

You can see the twenty-first Autobot symbol ⑤ where you begin the fight. It's on a wall, in the pit with Omega Supreme.

DECEPTICON COLLECTIBLE #22

The next Autobot symbol ⑥ is hidden from plain sight. Ten arches connect to pillars in this arena. The arch closest to the Magma Grenade Launcher power-up protects the collectible. The symbol is hanging where the arch connects to the wall; you can see it only when Omega Supreme destroys the arch.

DECEPTICON COLLECTIBLE #23

You can find the twenty-third Autobot symbol ⑦ on the arched ceiling, directly above the Photon Burst Rifle weapon power-up. Just walk over to the Burst Rifle and look straight up.

OBJECTIVE:

DESTROY THE ARMOR PROTECTING OMEGA SUPREME'S CHEST

The battle's second stage begins with Omega Supreme standing up again after you believe he's defeated. As Omega Supreme rises, Soundwave points out that the internal shielding protecting his core is now vulnerable. The armored plating covering his chest has now opened, allowing you to damage his source of power directly.

Your goal is to blast away at Omega's core, enough to take the fight out of him and win the battle. This is no small task; Omega is in a weakened state, but his attacks are much more vicious during this stage.

THERMO-SCATTER BOMBS

Omega Supreme begins the second stage with a barrage of homing bombs that fire from a launcher mounted between his shoulders. The best way to evade this attack is to keep moving to the left or right. If you're playing as Breakdown, the dash ability comes in handy here. Any of the characters can change form and drive to avoid suffering damage from this attack.

A-INFINITY ACCELERATOR

Omega Supreme's main second-phase attack comes from his right hand. His Mass-Manipulation Attractor Beam changes to a very powerful energy cannon. Omega Supreme locks onto you and unleashes an awesome wave of explosive energy blasts. The most effective ways to evade this attack are to change form into a vehicle and drive to the left or right, or to dash. Taking cover offers only limited protection, because this attack instantly destroys any cover objects, leaving you exposed to further attacks.

ION DISPLACER TURRET

During this stage, two Ion Displacer turrets become available. Each has an interact switch next to it; press it to make the floor panels open. Rip these turrets from their bases as quickly as possible, as it's very dangerous to remain stationary during this phase of the battle.

DECEPTICON COLLECTIBLE #24

The twenty-fourth Autobot symbol (8) is embedded in the destructible wall near the Photon Burst Rifle power-up. To destroy this symbol, wait until Omega Supreme destroys this wall.

DECEPTICON COLLECTIBLE #25

You can see the final Autobot symbol (9) from only one place in the arena. To spot this symbol, walk over to the ledge where the Energon battery spawns (near the Magma Frag Launcher power-up). Peer across the arena to the other side, and look for the arch above the outer wall. The symbol is just behind the outer wall below this arch. It is easier to hit this symbol with an Energon Battle Pistol, Photon Burst Rifle, or the Null Ray.

"DEVASTATOR!" ACHIEVEMENT/TROPHY

It's easiest to earn this Achievement/Trophy during the fight's second stage, Omega Supreme's Last Stand. During the fight, notice that many walls, pillars, and arches offer temporary cover against Omega Supreme's attacks. Thirteen walls, 10 pillars with attached arches, and 9 additional pillars without arches add up to 32 destructible cover pieces. As they accumulate damage, these cover pieces progress through multiple stages of destruction, but to unlock the Achievement/Trophy they must be destroyed completely. Although you cannot directly damage or destroy them, you can lure Omega Supreme into destroying them by using them for cover as Omega attacks.

CONCLUSION

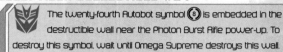

Omega Supreme has fallen, corrupted by the influence of Dark Energon. Triumphant, Megatron forces the guardian to open the Omega Gate and lead the Decepticons to the core of Cybertron itself.

06 # DEFEND IACON

Iacon, the capital city of the Autobots, is crumbling under the onslaught of Megatron and his Decepticons. Rumors have spread of the defeat of Omega Supreme and Autobot leader Zeta Prime. If the Autobots have any hope to band together and repel the enemy, a new hero must emerge.

AVAILABLE CHARACTERS

OPTIMUS

With the Autobots' leader Zeta Prime defeated, Optimus has reluctantly stepped up to organize the remaining forces in Iacon and repel the Decepticon invasion. Wielding his Energon battle axe and short-range Ion Blaster, Optimus prefers an honorable close-range fight. He can also rally friendly troops with his Warcry to temporarily provide a boost to their damage output and reinforce their armor.

RATCHET

Taking a defensive role, Ratchet has several tools at his disposal to provide support for the group. On the battlefield, Ratchet can repair damage with his Energon Repair Ray and create energy shields behind which the team can take cover. He can also deploy a sentry that engages his enemies and draws fire from the group as they advance or flank their opponents.

BUMBLEBEE

Small and agile, Bumblebee is always ready to charge headfirst into a fight. He can flank his enemies quickly via his vehicle's boost mode, or dodge their attacks with his robot form's dash ability. Bumblebee is an extremely effective fighter at any range, and should not be underestimated.

CO-OP TIPS

Ratchet can use his Energon Repair Ray to revive downed players.

Make sure you get everyone close together when you activate Optimus's Warcry so that the entire team benefits from the boost.

Bumblebee starts with an Energon Battle Pistol as his default weapon; using its scope, he can identify long-range threats for the group.

BASICS
CHARACTERS
WEAPONS
WALKTHROUGH
01
02
03
04
05
06
DEFEND IACON
07
08
09
10
MULTIPLAYER
ACHIEVEMENTS

INTRODUCTION

Having just met up with Bumblebee and Ratchet, Optimus heads to one of Iacon's command centers. With Zeta Prime gone, the Autobots lack a leader to coordinate Iacon's defenses against the Decepticons. Optimus assumes a temporary leadership position, rallying the Autobots to fight back against the Decepticons.

SECTION 1 — IACON UNDER SIEGE

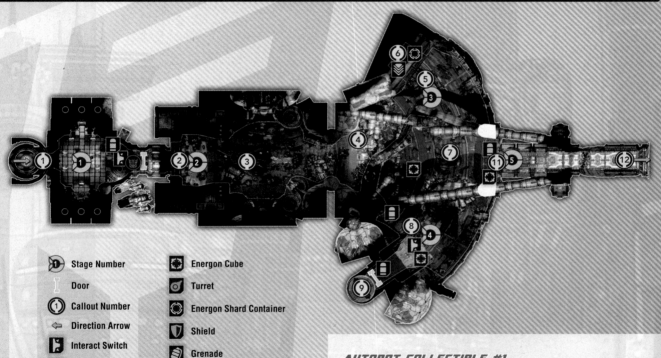

Stage Number	Energon Cube
Door	Turret
Callout Number	Energon Shard Container
Direction Arrow	Shield
Interact Switch	Grenade
Weapon Pick-Up	Autobot Symbol
Ammo Pick-Up	Decepticon Symbol

AUTOBOT COLLECTIBLE #1

This collectible is located in front of a monitor on the elevated catwalk. You can see it behind the hologram image in the beginning of the level.

OBJECTIVE: ACTIVATE PLANETARY GUNS

STAGE 1

Upon exiting the elevator into the command center ①, Jetfire appears on the hologram communicator. Optimus informs Jetfire that their leader, Zeta Prime, is dead. We learn that the Decepticons have control of the air space above Iacon, and that the planetary guns are currently offline. Optimus informs Jetfire that he will fight

to the control tower and reactivate the defense systems. Grab some extra ammo and head out of the command center.

STAGE 2

When you step out of the command center, you see a small group of Autobot soldiers. Two of them are using mounted Ion Displacers, firing at a Decepticon warship. Take cover as the

warship is shot down and crashes nearby. When the smoke and debris clears, jump over the crate stack ② and head out toward the plaza. Behind the wrecked warship ③, you encounter a couple of Decepticon survivors from the wreck. Quickly dispatch them and collect the Energon shards to fuel your abilities.

"PAGING RATCHET" ACHIEVEMENT/TROPHY (1/5)

You encounter the first wounded Autobot ④ after you navigate around the destroyed statue at the plaza's entrance. A bombing run from a squad of Decepticon Jet Soldiers takes down a group of Autobots. Revive the wounded Autobot before you proceed down the stairs.

STAGE 3

As you move down the stairs into the plaza ⑤, try to avoid to the energy fires; they inflict damage if you touch them. Near the bottom of the stairs, two Autobot Car Soldiers drive out of a nearby tunnel, launch off a ramp, and drive toward the plaza.

ENERGON SHARD CONTAINER

If you turn left into the tunnel at the bottom of the stairs, you can find a weapon crate and an Energon Shard Container ⑥

When you enter the plaza, you trigger a cutscene in which two Decepticon Car Soldiers drive over some nearby wreckage and attack your group. Another Decepticon

soldier takes up a position at the top of the stairs, behind some debris ⑦. Double-jump over the larger wreckage to flank your enemy. Use the smaller debris as cover as you advance on the enemy.

STAGE 4

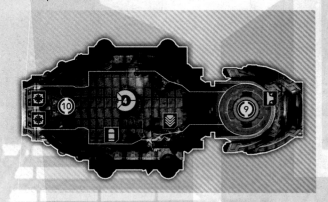

Another group of Decepticon soldiers engages you when you get closer to the planetary gun control room ⑧. Several of them fall back behind cover, attempting to block access to the door. After you defeat this first group, the door opens and Decepticon reinforcements ride the lift down into the plaza. Try to massacre the enemies as the lift door opens and they are in a tight cluster. The enemies are more difficult to engage after they spread out into the open.

Enter the lift ⑨ and ride it up to the planetary gun control room. You encounter two Decepticons guarding the terminal. Destroy them and use the terminal ⑩ to activate the planetary guns. Shortly after you activate the guns, a warship is shot down and

crashes into the planetary gun control tower, deactivating the energy shield. Jump out of the tower and back down into the plaza.

STAGE 5

Eliminate the wounded Decepticons from the wrecked ship. Change form into a vehicle and drive over the debris, making your way toward the terminal bridge ⑪. As the bridge opens, look out for Decepticon Jet Soldiers. Knock out the Jet Soldiers from a distance, and try to avoid getting stuck on the bridge when they perform a bombing run attack.

SECTION 2 — THE BROKEN LIFT

OBJECTIVE: REACH IACON SPEEDWAY

STAGE 1

Refill your health with the two Energon crates before you enter the damaged terminal building ⑫. Shortly after you walk through the doorway, you trigger a cutscene that introduces the Decepticon Brute. Don't panic—the best strategy against the Brute is patience. The Brute has a vulnerable spot on its back, so you must time your shots accordingly. Wait for him to miss a melee attack or to switch targets, and try to circle behind him. If you shoot him elsewhere on his body, he may stumble and expose his back for a short duration.

Remember to jump when the Brute performs his area-of-effect smash attack. This protects you from having your HUD and reticule scrambled and your foot speed reduced. If you get low on ammo during the fight, look to the sides of the room—two ammo power-ups are nearby. After you defeat the Brute, an automated repair system reactivates and heals some of your damage. It then shifts focus to repair the malfunctioning door at the back of the room, thus opening your exit ⑬.

STAGE 2

As you exit the lift onto the skywalk ⑭, you see a nearby building explode and collapse. As it falls over, it takes out a section of the skywalk ⑮. Change into a vehicle and boost over the gap. Remember to use your vehicle jump to gain extra height and distance when you launch off ramps.

STAGE 3

As you step into the next building  ⑯ from the skywalk, you see a vignette with a Decepticon War Machine. You see it charge up and emit a pulse of Dark Energon. After the pulse, the nearby door ⑰ opens, and several Dark Energon spikes grow out of the ceiling and floor. Most of these spikes are destructible, but they cause light damage when they explode.

Proceed down the next hallway and engage the Decepticon soldiers. As you get toward this hallway's end, Jetfire contacts to inform you that a large squad of Decepticon Seekers is inbound.

STAGE 4

As you step out of the hallway and onto the balcony ⑱, a group of Decepticon Car Soldiers and several Decepticon Jet Soldiers confront you. Neutralize the ground units before you deal with the Jet Soldiers. Try to stay under the balcony, as it provides more protection against the Jet Soldiers.

"PAGING RATCHET" ACHIEVEMENT/TROPHY (2/5)

If you head off to the right a short distance along the outside of the balcony section, you see an Autobot soldier ⑲ fighting a Decepticon Jet Soldier. The Autobot suffers heavy damage and goes down. Take out the Decepticon Jet Soldier and then revive the Autobot. If you follow him after he is revived, he opens a nearby secret room, giving you access to some valuable loot.

AUTOBOT COLLECTIBLE #2

As you proceed along the balcony toward your destination, you can see several Decepticon Rocket Soldiers attacking from a nearby bridge to your right. You can see the Autobot collectible on the bridge's second tier—shoot it.

STAGE 5

Climb the stairs ⑳ to the left until you reach the turrets ㉑. A mix of Decepticon Jet Soldiers in the air and Decepticon Rocket Soldiers on the bridge assaults you. Shift your focus between the two different units. You can use the fine aim functionality while you're in the turret; it zooms the camera in slightly and helps you spot the enemies easier.

After you mop up several waves of these enemies, a larger Decepticon warship emerges to fire a barrage of rockets onto the platform. These rockets are large and slow, and they are easy to shoot and destroy. Focus your fire onto the warship's four weapon target areas to take it out. In case of an emergency, you can also rip the turret from its mounted position and go mobile with it. You incur a slight movement penalty, and the weapon's ammo supply is limited when you remove the gun from its mount. After you destroy the warship, Jetfire appears, opening the door ㉒ to the Iacon Speedway for you.

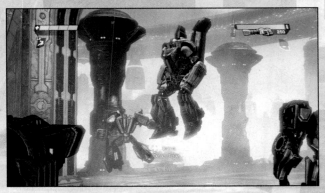

BASICS
CHARACTERS
WEAPONS
WALKTHROUGH

o6
DEFEND IACON

MULTIPLAYER
ACHIEVEMENTS

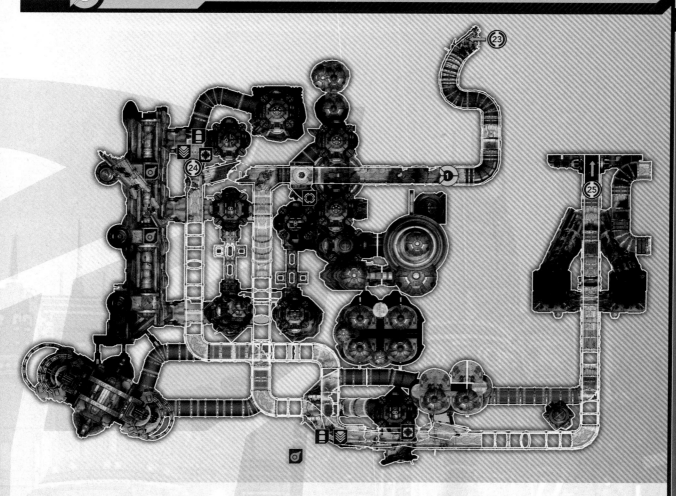

OBJECTIVE: GET TO THE DECAGON

STAGE 1

Enter vehicle mode and travel through the speedway (23). You can take either path through this section. At several points throughout this section, follow the tunnel as it transforms outward in front of you. The Decepticons have created several roadblocks that feature heavy mounted turrets. You can either speed through the section in your vehicle, or change into robot form and try to snipe them.

Grab an Energon Battle Pistol (24) and try to quash the Decepticons, using the wreckage from the damaged speedway as cover. As you get deeper into the tubes, you

hear Soundwave give the order to detonate the thermal charges in the Iacon speedway (25). A cutscene triggers, showing the speedway explode and your group of Autobots falling down into a lower section of the city.

STAGE 2

Pick yourself up out of the wreckage, and enter the doorway to the right (26). As you near the next doorway, a Sniper appears and takes out a nearby guard. This Autobot drops his Energon Battle Pistol. Pick it up and use it to engage the enemy Snipers. Use the doorway or nearby wreckage as cover.

ENERGON SHARD CONTAINER

When you first enter the side passage after the crash, look to your right to find two Energon Shard Containers.

"PAGING RATCHET" ACHIEVEMENT/TROPHY (3/5)

When the first Sniper appears, he takes out an Autobot solider (28) and critically injures another. You must rush out into the open and revive this Autobot. Try to eliminate the Sniper before you move to revive your comrade; otherwise, you'll be under fire the whole time.

If the Sniper loses his target, he will switch to a scanning pattern. Run from one side of the half-pipe to the other, defeating the Snipers as you find them. The Snipers target the explosive barrels in the area. Avoid these, or shoot them before you get too close. You can also use the explosive barrels to your advantage, as several are near some of the Snipers' positions. Jump up the broken bridge (27) to reach this area's upper section.

STAGE 3

On the second level, be careful of the gap in the bridge (29) to the next level. Use your vehicle form to speed across the gap. Several more Snipers spawn as you reach the half pipe's upper levels. Stick to the side alcoves for cover, ammo, and power-ups as you progress through this section. Enter the terminal building (30) on the upper level.

SECTION (4) FALSE PROPAGANDA

STAGE 1

As you enter the damaged terminal building (30), a Megatron hologram appears. You can find a grenade crate just behind the hologram. Smash it and claim the Flak Grenades. As you get closer to the door, you trigger a cutscene. Soundwave spots the Autobots and instructs his Decepticon soldiers to engage them.

REPAIR RAY

If you go to the damaged terminal's upper-right section, you can find a Repair Ray just around the corner.

STAGE 2

You have a few seconds before the Decepticons take out the door (31) to the terminal building. Use your Flak Grenades when the enemies are clustered together. Several explosive Energon barrels are in this hallway. You can use them to inflict additional damage to the Decepticons. Reinforcements jump down from the wrecked ceiling at the back of the damaged hallway.

After you clear several waves, a large Decepticon Titan jumps down from the ruined ceiling. Engage him from cover, and exploit any explosive Energon barrels…if they're still around. Fall back into the terminal building, and use the wreckage and elevated platforms to try to flank the Titan. Enter the path to the right (32) at the end of the platform. Fall to the lower level and continue forward.

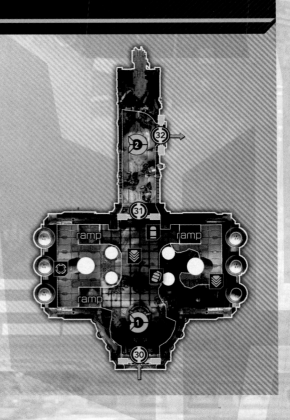

SECTION 5 — CORRUPTED HALLS

OBJECTIVE: DEFEAT THE DECEPTICON CORRUPTOR

STAGE 1

Several Dark Energon spikes manifest as you move through this section ㉜. You have to destroy some of them to clear your path and continue forward. To avoid damage, evade or fire at the Dark Energon spikes that arise. Turn left, then right into the large corridor. Enter the room with the Decepticon War Machine ㉝.

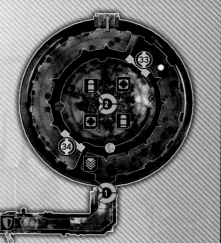

STAGE 2

After the cutscene, start to destroy the armor on each of the War Machine's legs. During this stage, the War Machine alternates between two attacks: a ground thump and a homing rocket barrage. Stay away from the War Machine during the ground thump, and take cover behind the pillars when the War Machine launches missiles. Between ground thump attacks, grab health and ammo from the center of the room.

After you take out the armor on the legs, the War Machine ceases his ground thump attack and produces a large Dark Energon corruption beam. The War Machine sweeps the room with the beam in either a clockwise or a counterclockwise direction. In doing so, the energy beam destroys all of the pillars and cover in

the room, making it more difficult to dodge the missile attacks. Use your vehicle form to boost away from the energy beam and dodge homing missiles. When you're not avoiding these assaults, attack the War Machine's vulnerable core unit. A side door opens ㉞ after you defeat the War Machine; destroy the Dark Energon spikes around the doorway and follow this passage to the next speedway.

SECTION 6 — IACON SPEEDWAY

OBJECTIVE: CONTINUE TO THE DECAGON

STAGE 1

Follow the path ㉟, destroying or avoiding the Dark Energon spikes. Turn left at the end and continue down the tunnel until you reach a blockage. Destroy the Dark Energon spikes and head out onto the speedway.

Detach Turret

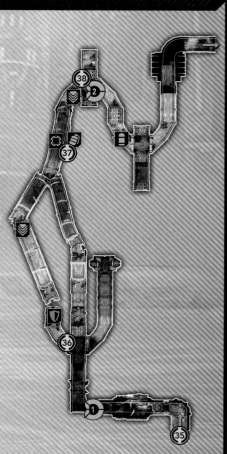

OVERSHIELD

The first part of speedway is split into two paths. If you clear the corruption spikes on the left, you reveal an alternate path ㊱ and an Overshield power-up.

ENERGON SHARD CONTAINER

After the paths merge, turn around at the bottom of this section and backtrack. You can find a grenade crate and an Energon Shard Container ㊲ at the end of this tunnel.

STAGE 2

Grab the Scatter Blaster at the bottom of the wrecked speedway before you proceed down into the tunnels ㊳. This is a tighter, close-quarter combat section, and the semi-auto shotgun comes in handy. Destroy the corruption spikes blocking your path, and advance into the speedway. Several squads of Decepticon Protectors and Soldiers guard these tunnels. Try to quash them before they fall back to positions that are more defensible. Watch out for reinforcements firing at you from behind the Dark Energon roadblocks.

STAGE 3

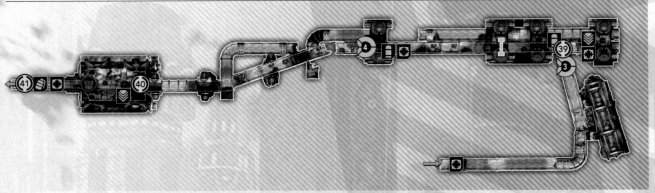

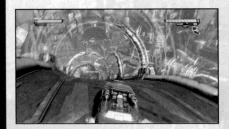

You reach a section of speedway where you must drop down onto a lower level ㊴. Shortly after you make this transition, a squad of Decepticon Jet Soldiers swoops down onto your position. If you fall back to the right, you can engage the Jet Soldiers from a small alcove with a weapon crate and health.

STAGE 4

After you decimate the first group of Jet Soldiers, several Decepticon Car Soldiers drive into your position, opening up the rest of the speedway. Eliminate the Car Soldiers and proceed carefully across the wrecked speedway. Another group of Jet Soldiers attacks you—use the Thermo Rocket Launcher to teach them a lesson. Activate the boosters and launch out of the wrecked speedway ㊵.

AUTOBOT COLLECTIBLE #3

As you jump out of the tunnel, the Autobot collectible is directly across from you. It's on the other side of the damaged speedway, above the next tunnel entrance ㊶.

STAGE 5

Move down the tunnel ㊶ and grab some health and grenades before you continue forward. As you step out into the streets, you see two Autobot Titans advancing on several Decepticons. The Decepticons defeat the Titan on the right, and he drops his Ion Displacer. You can pick up this weapon and use it to make a huge dent in the Decepticon enemies here.

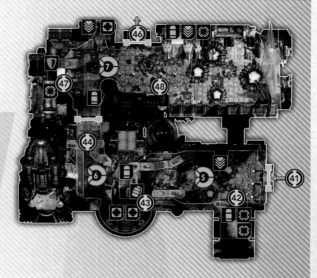

Take out the elevated Decepticon Rocket Soldier, and then focus on the ground forces. Stick to the sides of the streets to avoid getting caught in a crossfire in the middle. Advance using cover, or climb the wrecked bridge for an elevation advantage. A small building halfway down the street contains some health and an alternate path to flank some of the enemies further down the street.

ENERGON SHARD CONTAINER

A tunnel ㊷ on this area's left side, behind the Titan, contains some ammo and Energon Shard Containers.

STAGE 6

Watch for the Snipers in the next area, and use the explosive canisters to take out the remaining ground forces. You can also fall back into this area's side room ㊸ on the left, or head underneath the bridge to engage the Snipers. Once you clear out the enemies, double-jump up the debris onto the bridge. Use the switch ㊹ to open the large blast door ㊺.

STAGE 7

As you continue into the next section, you see that this part of the streets is under siege from another Decepticon War Machine. The War Machine's core unit is already exposed, so focus all of your fire here. Check all of the nearby alcoves for additional health, ammo, and weapons. Use the spikes and alcoves as cover when you engage the War Machine. Once you defeat it, the Dark Energon spikes blocking the exit are destroyed. Enter the door ㊻ to the left, and ride the elevator ㊾ up into the Energon production facility.

OVERSHIELD

The alcoves ㊼ to the left of where you entered contain Overshields and Energon Shard Containers.

"PAGING RATCHET" ACHIEVEMENT/TROPHY (4/5)

To the right of the second War Machine, on an elevated part of the streets, an Autobot soldier ㊽ takes heavy damage and enters a wounded state. Race over and revive him before he is defeated during the fight.

BASICS
CHARACTERS
WEAPONS
WALKTHROUGH
06
DEFEND IACON
MULTIPLAYER
ACHIEVEMENTS

SECTION 7 CENTRAL VENTILATION SYSTEM

OBJECTIVE: USE THE VENTILATION SYSTEM FANS TO REACH DECAGON SPEEDWAY

STAGE 1

As you exit out into the Energon production facility, a Decepticon Seeker bombing run takes out a group of Autobots. Use the nearby Thermo Rocket Launcher ⑤⓪ to lock onto the Jet Soldiers, and then fire some homing rockets. Watch out for bombing run attacks, and try to stay behind pillars and underneath the overhangs for cover from the Jet Soldiers.

AUTOBOT COLLECTIBLE #4

The fourth Autobot collectible is stashed underneath the bridge in a bundle of blue wires and cables—shoot it.

STAGE 2

If you ascend the ramp, several Decepticon soldiers rush out to ambush you. Instead of heading up the ramp, you can flank them by jumping up the transport train ⑤① on the left. As you get closer to the wind turbines ⑤②, two more Decepticon Jet Soldiers fly into the area. Destroy them before you jump onto the fan blades.

STAGE 3

In order to reach the Decagon Speedway, you must jump onto the fan blades ⑤③ and ride them through ⑤④ the rest of the Energon production facility. Time your jumps and be careful not to fall. Two Decepticon Jet Soldiers attack you in the area containing multiple wind blade columns ⑤⑤. Halfway through the second section, you can jump onto a hovering platform ⑤⑥ and engage the Jet Soldiers from there. After you jump from the last set of fans, continue down the walkway and enter the last speedway ⑤⑧.

"PAGING RATCHET" ACHIEVEMENT/TROPHY (5/5)

Before you jump down from the third turbine, you see an Autobot soldier fighting the Rocket Soldier on a nearby balcony below. Wait until your fan is close to this balcony, and combo your double-jump with a midair dash. After you revive this Autobot, the secret room behind him opens ⑤⑦, giving you access to a Null Ray and Thermo Mines.

You encounter no resistance driving along the last speedway ⑤⑧. The Decagon building is undergoing a transformation off in the distance. Boost over the speedway's damaged section and enter the armory ⑤⑨.

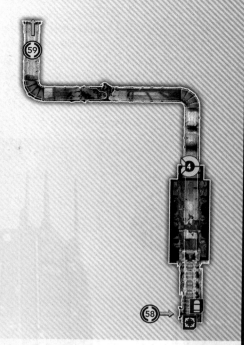

SECTION ⑧ THE DECAGON PLAZA

OBJECTIVE:

RETAKE THE DECAGON PLAZA FROM THE DECEPTICONS

STAGE 1

Upon entering the armory ⑤⑨, Ironhide rides a lift down through the space, informing you that he will attempt to flank the enemy from behind while you make the frontal assault. Grab some extra ammo, grenades, and weapons before you leave ⑥⓪ the armory.

OVERSHIELD

Use the switch on the left side of the armory to open a secret compartment with an Overshield.

STAGE 2

The Decepticons have locked down the entrance to the Decagon, and they brought heavy resistance here to protect it. Advance between cover points as you move toward the entrance ⑥①. Try to use the environment to flank your enemy. Look out for explosive Energon containers throughout this space, and use them to your advantage when enemies are nearby. Your vehicle form allows you to race very quickly to the left and right sides as you engage your enemies. If you get into trouble during a fight, retreat and search for health, or jump behind cover and regenerate.

The first encounter has you squaring off against a Titan and several Decepticon soldiers. Focus on the Titan first, and then take out the Decepticon fodder. You can stay back and pick them off from a distance with the scoped Energon Battle Pistol. Or you can charge headfirst with grenades and an assault rifle. Remember that, when the Titan is defeated, he drops a heavy Ion Displacer that you can power-up.

As you reach the first set of stairs, watch out for two Decepticon Rocket Soldiers on elevated positions. You can double-jump onto the nearby debris and get onto the same platforms. Some ammo is halfway through courtyard, and you can find some health beyond

the second set of stairs leading up to the entrance. When you clear the enemies, head to the destroyed statue that blocks the door 62 into Decagon.

ENERGON SHARD CONTAINER

After you climb the second set of stairs, you can find an Energon Shard Container on the left side of the plaza behind some debris.

STAGE 3

Once you clear the Decagon plaza and reach the top of the stairs, a cutscene shows Ironhide ambushing a couple of Brutes. After gameplay resumes, Ironhide runs over and lifts up a damaged statute that blocks the path into the Decagon. Drive underneath it to enter the Decagon foyer 63.

STAGE 4

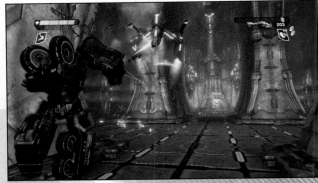

Inside the Decagon 63, grab the Thermo Rocket Launcher and proceed with caution. Several Jet Soldiers and Decepticon ground units soon emerge. Neutralize the Jet Soldiers first, and then weave between the arches to advance toward and flank the ground units.

OVERSHIELD

Before you run up the wrecked elevator shaft 64, you can find an Overshield crate elevated on the right side of the debris.

STAGE 5

Jump down out of the wrecked elevator shaft 65 and confront the Decepticon Brute. Alternatively, you can grab the nearby Plasma Cannon and fire fully charged projectiles near the Brute's feet. Splash damage from the Plasma Cannon's projectiles can harm the Brute's vulnerable back attachment. After the repair sentries repair the malfunctioning door, enter the data grid room 66.

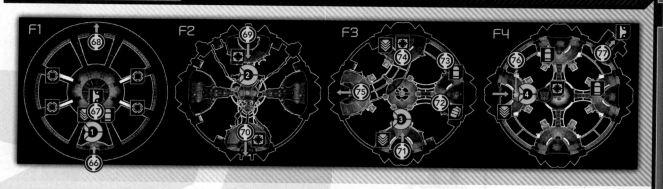

OBJECTIVE: RESTORE THE COMMUNICATION GRID

STAGE 1

When you enter the Decagon room's (66) interior, you notice that the data grid communication streams are misaligned. By shooting the rotator component, you can charge the machine and get the unit to rotate back to position. When the beams are correctly aligned with the receptacles on the floor, use the interact terminal (67) to jumpstart the machine. If you do this correctly, the unit powers on and the data grid comes back online. Because the elevator to the broadcast control room is wrecked, you must ride the data cubes (68) to the higher levels.

OBJECTIVE: GET TO THE BROADCAST ROOM

STAGE 2

When you reach the second floor (69), you come to a data cube assembly line. Time your movements through the area to avoid taking damage from the energy beams. Move around the lightning directly in front of you. Jump onto the cube when it moves up to hop over the first beam. Move forward when the next energy beam turns off. Next, watch the spinning prongs that fire electricity. Time your movement to avoid them. At the back wall, hop onto the next data cube (70) and ride it upward.

As you get to the upper bridge section, watch out for two Decepticon Protectors and two Decepticon Snipers. On this next level (74), you can find an Energon Battle Pistol in a nearby weapon crate, and some health inside the nearby cube storage shed. Cap the Snipers from a distance, move forward to the cover on the bridge's center, and engage the Protectors. When you defeat these enemies, jump onto the next data cube (75) and ride it upward.

STAGE 4

As you reach the top level (76), you enter the midst of a dogfight between Autobot and Decepticon Jet Soldiers. Use the cover that the storage sheds provide, and move into

this area's center if you need health. Some ammo crates are scattered along the outside of this space. Once you permanently dispatch the enemy Jet Soldiers, Decepticon soldiers emerge from the maintenance lift and open the exit door (77). Enter the door, get onto the lift, and activate it.

STAGE 3

As you step off the data cube onto the third level (71), two Decepticon Car Soldiers jump down onto your level. A Decepticon Protector also takes up an elevated position. Use the beam receptors as cover and move forward. Follow the right path from the center (72). Before you ascend the ramp (73) on the right, grab the grenades from behind the data cube storage shed.

AUTOBOT COLLECTIBLE #5

As you ride the last data cube (beyond the Snipers), you can find the Autobot collectible two-thirds of the way up the central pillar's side.

SECTION 10 — COMMUNICATION ROOM

OBJECTIVE: DEFEAT STARSCREAM

STAGE 1

Grab some health, ammo, and weapons before you enter the main communication room (78) to confront Starscream.

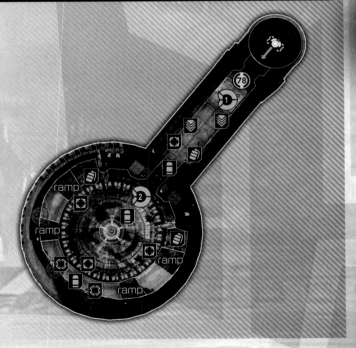

As you enter the room, a cutscene shows Starscream flying into the area. For this first stage, be ready to dodge Starscream's rockets as he hovers around the space. Periodically, you hear him taunt and then fly out of the arena. When this happens, prepare for his bombing run attack. Starscream flies a figure-eight pattern through the ceiling's wrecked holes, launching a barrage of homing missiles at you. Use your dash ability or get behind the pillars to dodge the missile attacks. Look around the room for additional ammo and health power-ups. If you run up onto the elevated control deck, you'll find two Energon Shard Containers.

BASICS
CHARACTERS
WEAPONS
WALKTHROUGH
01
02
03
04
05
06
DEFEND IACON
07
08
09
10
MULTIPLAYER
ACHIEVEMENTS

STAGE 2

When you deplete half of Starscream's health, he assumes his robot form. This provides him with a few new attacks. Starscream attempts to slow you down and blind you by throwing EMP Grenades. Back away from the blasts and try to look away to avoid their detrimental effects.

Starscream also jumps into the air and hovers as he deploys a 360-degree missile barrage attack. On the ground, he can quickly dodge and evade your attacks. While he's in robot form, stick to assault rifles and grenades to inflict quick bursts of damage. Once you defeat Starscream, the end level cinematic plays.

CONCLUSION

The Autobots learn that Zeta Prime is not dead. They resolve to carry out a daring mission: go to Kaon and save him.

KAON PRISON BREAK

In an effort to save Zeta Prime. Optimus enacts a bold plan to allow the Decepticons to capture him and a few others. The plan works all too well. and soon the Autobots find themselves in route to Kaon. the capital city of the Decepticons.

AVAILABLE CHARACTERS

OPTIMUS

In truck form, Optimus delivers devastating damage with his forward rockets. He can clean up stragglers with his powerful Ram attack. His Warcry ability provides an immediate boost to the entire team's defense and offense.

SIDESWIPE

Sideswipe can outmaneuver anyone on the road, shred through targets with his mounted machine guns, and then convert to robot form and plow through enemies with his hard-hitting Whirlwind ability.

BUMBLEBEE

Bumblebee's combination of Dash and Shockwave can make him a deadly hit-and-run fighter. He can pounce on a group of enemies, unleash instantaneous destruction, and then escape unscathed, only to continue punishing foes from range.

CO-OP TIPS

When it's activated, Optimus's Warcry provides its help to all allies in range. The more allies it affects, the stronger the overall effect. So, make sure that the player controlling Optimus uses Warcry only when all three team members are within range.

Once you find the Energon Repair Ray, it's a good idea for one team member to use it for the rest of the level, keeping the team at optimum health, even when Energon Cubes are in short supply.

Watch for the flashing Revive indicator when one of your teammates goes down. You have only a short window of time to revive the teammate, so move fast. Don't forget that if you're the one who's down, you can continue to help the team by shooting enemies from the prone position.

EMP Grenades, which paralyze enemies, can be an extremely effective part of a coordinated attack. Make sure you call out to teammates before you deploy one, so that they can take full advantage of the enemy's weakness.

BASICS
CHARACTERS
WEAPONS
WALKTHROUGH
01
02
03
04
05
06
07
KAON PRISON BREAK
08
09
10
MULTIPLAYER
ACHIEVEMENTS

INTRODUCTION

Knowing that a frontal assault would be futile, Optimus and his team have become willing prisoners of Megatron's fortress-like prison at the center of Kaon. Once inside, they have a plan to break out, locate Zeta Prime, and escape with him back to Autobot-held territory. Everything hinges on careful coordination with Air Raid, who has gathered intelligence about the prison complex and is waiting on its outskirts for just the right moment.

SECTION 1 PRISON ENTRANCE

OBJECTIVE: INFILTRATE THE KAON PRISON

STAGE 1

The opening cinematic ends with the Autobots being escorted into the prison. They are stripped of their weapons and bound by Energon shackles that prevent them from changing form or using their abilities. During this sequence, move the camera around to take in the sights and witness Megatron's harsh treatment of Autobot prisoners. After Air Raid flies in ① and releases the team, drop into the air ducts

through the hole in the room's forward-right corner. Before you go too far, you see Air Raid getting captured. Now two Autobots need rescue.

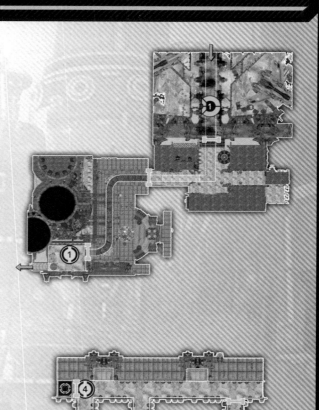

STAGE 2

Inside the vents ②, remember that you have no ranged weapons, so use your melee attack to break through either of the grates blocking your way. Past the grates, a small group of Spiderbots attacks. Vanquish them with your melee weapon before they gang up on you. There are three exits from this area ③, but each one leads to the

same guardroom ⑤. Choose your optimal ambush point, and then bash through the grates to attack the guards below.

ENERGON SHARD CONTAINER

After you drop ② into the vents from above, melee the grate to the right. Then turn left and go straight to the end of the hallway. Another grate ④ conceals an Enegron Shard Container.

STAGE 3

Once you drop into the guardroom ③ from the vents, the two soldiers in this room turn and attack. Quickly use your Dash ability to close

the gap, and melee them before their guns damage you too much. Before you move to the next area ⑤, restore any health you lost with the Energon Crates.

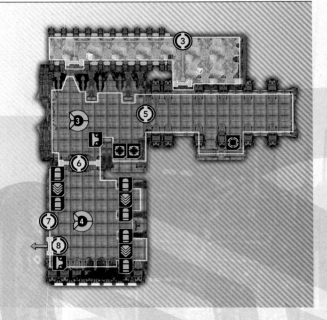

ENERGON SHARD CONTAINER

Go down the hallway ⑤ and look into the alcove on your right. An Energon Shard Container is there.

STAGE 4

Activate the switch ⑥ and be prepared for another close-range fight. Dash in and take out the two guards with melee, or use an ability to dispatch them quickly. After you clear the room, pick up a Photon Burst Rifle and stock up on ammunition. The switch in the corner opens the nearby door ⑧, giving you access to the courtyard ⑨.

AUTOBOT COLLECTIBLE #6

Look out the barred window ⑦. The Decepticon symbol floats in the air directly to the right of the building that's across from you.

"BEAK BREAKER" ACHIEVEMENT/TROPHY (1/3)

Looking out the barred window ⑧, note that two large spikes jut out from the sides of the building across from you. Laserbeak is perched atop the spike on the right side. Shoot him with the Photon Burst Rifle, and he flies away. This is part one of the "Beak Breaker" Achievement/Trophy.

SECTION 2 COURTYARD

STAGE 1

Activating the switch in this room opens the door ⑧ and alerts the courtyard Protectors ⑨ to your presence. They maintain their distance, but more will come if you don't advance. Use the doorway or the crates on the bridge as cover. Once you step out of the room, watch for sniper fire coming from the right side. Change into vehicle form for a lower profile, or double-jump to the walkway just to the right of the bridge. Destroy the remaining Protectors.

OVERSHIELD

Double-jump up to the circular catwalk ⑩ just to the left of the first bridge. Circle around it to the right side. You can find an Overshield there.

STAGE 2

At this point, you can circle around the tower to the right or enter the room from which the Protectors attacked. Both vantage points

provide ample cover and good sightlines to the first few Snipers on the high platform. Either way, you eventually want to gear up with some Flak Grenades, which are stacked near the window of the room across the first bridge. Also, look for health and ammo power-ups sprinkled around this area.

STAGE 3

The path snakes left and then opens out to the right, where a wall of prisoner holding cells blocks the way. Stay behind cover and use your Photon Burst Rifle's scope as you eliminate the last few Snipers.

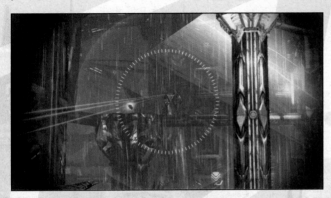

STAGE 4

Climb the ramps and proceed around to the left to reach the switch ⑪ that slides the prisoner cells out of the way. Once the path is clear, a wave of soldiers wheels in and attacks. For the best results, use your Flak Grenades and press the attack forward. Otherwise, expect enemy reinforcements.

STAGE 5

Enter either doorway ⑫ to access the next area. A giant Wallcrawler ⑬ ascends from below and attacks with mounted Rocket Sentries. Destroy the Rocket Sentries as quickly as you can to avoid excessive damage. With its outer defenses demolished, the Wallcrawler sinks back down and opens its shutters, revealing three Rocket Soldiers inside. One or two well-thrown Flak Grenades through the windows can make short work of these enemies. After the door opens, activate the switch inside to ride down to the next section ⑭.

SECTION ③ MEGATRON'S AMBUSH

STAGE 1

The Wallcrawler opens out into a hallway ⑭ lined with a few new weapon choices. This area precedes a major string of encounters, so make sure to gear up. The plasma cannon can be especially useful here. After the cinematic, waves of enemy Car Soldiers drive into the arena from the three

ramps at the area's edges. Because there is little cover, it's wise to move fast and make full use of the arena. Each of the arena's four corners hosts either an Energon Cube or an ammo power-up, all of which respawn after a short period. Quickly use your vehicle form to access the power-ups you need.

STAGE 2

The action pauses when Megatron resumes speaking. Take this opportunity to collect Energon Shards and refill your health and ammo. The next attack wave comes from corruption crystals that grow out from the four circular pads on the ground. When they detonate, Spiderbots burrow out from the ground and attack in swarms. The Spiderbots will make short work of you if you stand still, so keep moving. Use your resource ability liberally to survive this wave.

STAGE 3

When Megatron resumes his speech, clean up any remaining Spiderbots and refill your health and ammo before the final wave. In this round, more enemy Car Soldiers launch off the ramps, this time supported by Jet Soldiers. Avoid their bombing runs and keep moving. When the Jet Soldiers activate their hover attack, target their exposed leg thrusters for quick kills.

STAGE 4

Once you clear all the enemies, Megatron's faces retract, and a hidden mechanism teleports the squad to a dungeon cell ⑮. When they come to, they find themselves behind bars, once again stripped of their weapons. Notice that Air Raid is being escorted through the hallway in front of you, followed by Soundwave and Rumble, who approach the cell to confirm that the Autobots are secure. When they leave, Optimus suggests that he has a way out. If you're playing as Optimus, look for the interact prompt to appear on the wall— activate it. Otherwise, wait for Optimus to approach the wall and use his axe to carve an opening.

OBJECTIVE:

ESCAPE YOUR JAIL CELL
STAGE 4

Exit the cell and collect some weapons ⑯. You need them in the upcoming encounters. Be sure to explore each hallway, and notice all the imprisoned Autobots. Don't worry; you get a chance to free them later. You can acquire some EMP Grenades here for the first time as well. After you get the next Autobot Collectible, activate the switch at the exit door ⑱.

AUTOBOT COLLECTIBLE #7

After you exit your cell, turn right and go all the way to the end ⑰ of the hallway. A Decepticon symbol floats in the last jail cell on the right side—shoot it through the bars.

SECTION ④ **TO THE DUNGEONS**

OBJECTIVE: **LOCATE AIR RAID**

STAGE 1

When you're ready to move to the next area, activate the switch at the exit door ⑱. Two Decepticon soldiers stand guard at the end of the hallway beyond the door, but they are unaware of you. Take them out from here, as more enemies wait in the main chamber. When you turn the corner, you enter an L-shaped room ⑲. Four Sentries are mounted on the pillars, and two Rocket Soldiers are on the room's far side. Those enemy rockets can be punishing, so use the cylindrical structures in the middle of the room as cover, or use your Dash ability to dodge them.

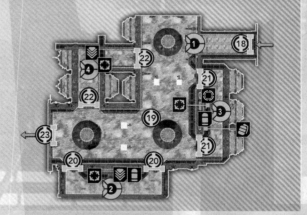

STAGE 2

When you defeat all the enemies, a call for reinforcements goes out over the PA system. Notice that three sets of two doors (⑳, ㉑, and ㉒) are on each side of the room. The reinforcements arrive in three waves, one from each set of doors. The first wave is composed of four soldiers. You may notice additional soldiers watching the action from above, but they can't jump down through the force fields.

There is plenty of cover here, but don't forget your EMP Grenades. You can use them to paralyze groups of enemies. After the first set of doors opens, go inside the hallway ⑳ to find some health ammo and a new weapon.

STAGE 3

The second wave ㉑ brings in three more soldiers and one Brute. The Brute is easier to deal with in isolation, so try to take out the soldiers first. The new hallway that opens contains more health, ammo, and EMP Grenades, so don't be shy about using your grenades, which can be very effective against the Brute. Just remember to focus all your fire on his vulnerable backpack. Also in this hallway, see if you can spot Arcee admiring her manicure in one of the jail cells.

ENERGON SHARD CONTAINER

An Energon Shard Container is also in this new hallway ㉑.

STAGE 4

When the last set of doors opens ㉒, a Brute and a Titan move in to attack. This can be a tricky battle. If you take lots of hits, use all the side hallways to hide from the Titan's fire and to flank the Brute. If you take out the Titan first, grab his Ion Displacer and use it to shred the Brute. You move a lot slower with this heavy weapon, but you can compensate with your Dash ability. In the hallway ㉒ from which these enemies enter, you can find find a health crate and a Plasma Cannon. Also, see if you can spot Jazz getting a workout in one of the jail cells.

STAGE 5

After this final wave, Optimus locates another wall ㉓ that he can blast through with his special axe ability. Break open the next grate to create an opening that leads into a sewer area. At a flowing river, recycled Autobot parts are ground into metallic flakes.

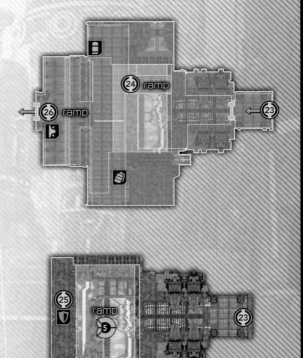

The way to the next section is up the ramp ㉔. If you want to brave the river, some nice power-ups are on the other side. Just be careful, because the river's current can pull you into the spinning grinders on the left side. If you get too close, they'll grind you up. In the water, press away from the grinders as you go, and use your jump and Dash abilities to make it safely across.

If you're still carrying the Ion Displacer from the Titan battle, you can no longer double jump. It might be wise to drop it before you cross the river, and then reclaim it on your way out. The hallway at the top of the ramp also contains grenades and ammo.

OVERSHIELD

An Overshield is in the center of the platform ㉕ on the other side of the river.

ENERGON REPAIR RAY

An Energon Repair Ray is on the other side of the river ㉕, hidden behind a grate on the left side.

SECTION 5 AIR RAID'S RESCUE

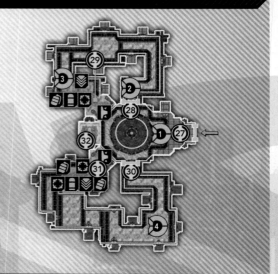

OBJECTIVE: FREE AIR RAID

STAGE 1

After you navigate the sewers and activate the switch at the exit door (26), you enter a solitary confinement area (27). Air Raid is held in a high security containment field. Cloakers guard this entire area. Three Cloakers attack at close range as soon as the cinematic ends. To locate them, look for the telltale signs of their Plasma Cannons charging. Once you damage them, try to finish them off before they regain their footing and disappear again. When you neutralize all three Cloakers, Air Raid explains that you must activate two switches to free him—you can see the switches through the windows. The first switch (29) is on the right side. Enter the door (28) when its access lights turn green.

STAGE 2

These winding tunnels are perfect hunting grounds for Cloakers, so be on your toes. They use the small holes on the tunnels' sides to ambush you and perform hit-and-run tactics. Only the Cloakers can use these access holes, so don't bother trying to follow them. On your first trip through these tunnels, a few Cloakers dodge out in front of you, but you can ignore them, as they don't attack. Instead, worry about the Spiderbots that come rushing out of the holes. Make your way to the end, where you can see back into the main room where Air Raid is. Some grenades, health, ammo, and a Plasma Cannon are here. Activate the console (29) to unlock the first layer of Air Raid's containment cell.

STAGE 3

Now you have to make your way back through the tunnels, but the Cloakers attack you for real this time. Four Cloakers ambush you on the way back. Once again, look for their glowing weapon charges, and try to kill them before they dodge back into their access holes. If they escape, you never know where they'll attack from next. The Plasma Cannon is especially effective here, as its splash damage de-cloaks the Cloakers even without a direct hit. EMP Grenades also instantly de-cloak and paralyze them.

STAGE 4

The next console (31) is through another series of tunnels (30), so cross the main room and enter the other door, which is now unlocked. This time, the Cloakers attack in greater numbers, and Spiderbots accompany them. In all, six Cloakers attack, as well as two groups of Spiderbots: a wave of three followed by a wave of five toward the end. The final area contains health, ammo, EMP Grenades, Flak Grenades, and a Neutron Assault Rifle. Interact with the second console (31) to deactivate the shield around Air Raid and set him free. When this happens, notice through the window that a wave of Spiderbots pours into the main room and attacks Air Raid. Speed back to the main room (27) and help him. You don't have to worry about any more Cloakers at this point.

OBJECTIVE: RESCUE OTHER PRISONERS

STAGE 5

Air Raid explains that he can lead the way to a central command room, where the team should be able to access the jail cell controls for the entire prison and release all the Autobot prisoners. Air Raid flies up to the upper level and activates a lift (32).

Hop onto the lift and hit the switch to carry you upward. Circle around either side of the upper level until you see a switch at the exit door (33). Some ammo and a weapon crate are here in case you're running low after the Cloaker encounters.

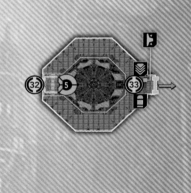

STAGE 6

The command room (34) is through this door. The Decepticons put up stiff resistance, so be ready for a fight. A hallway lined with monitors stretches to the left, with a group of Protectors at the end. Exploit the monitors for cover, and use grenades liberally to clear out the Protectors. If you linger in the back, they bring in reinforcements, so try to keep moving forward. Once you break free into the main room, a Brute rounds the corner from the right side. Use the room's two pillars to keep the Brute at bay, and wait until he slips up to attack his backpack. It's a small room, so keep your distance when his backpack detonates to avoid taking damage. While the Brute is distracted with your squad mates, try standing on the monitors to shoot down at his vulnerable backside.

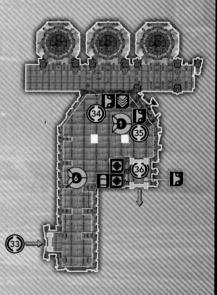

SECTION 6 PRISON COMMAND ROOM

STAGE 1

Air Raid activates a screen on the room's right side. It displays information on Zeta Prime's location and releases the shield covering the main security console against the window (34). With the shield released, activate the console (35). This unlocks all the jail cells in the prison, instigating a prison-wide jailbreak. The Autobots, visible through the window, begin to pour out in large numbers. Activating this switch also opens this room's exit behind you. Turn around and flip the switch (36) at the exit door to access the next area.

OBJECTIVE: **ESCORT THE PRISONERS TO SAFETY**

STAGE 2

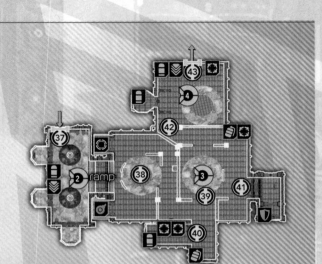

A cinematic begins when the door opens (37). It shows a friendly Autobot Brute breaking out from his jail cell and then rushing into battle. At the end of the cinematic, you're in an upper level of the dungeons. Follow the Brute out to the left, and help him clear out the enemies. Two Rocket

Soldiers are in this larger room (38), and when you clear them out, more regular soldiers rush in from the right side.

Enemy reinforcements keep coming until you move up, so maintain your forward momentum. Explosive containers are at the far end of this room, so use them judiciously when enemies group together. Through the force field below you, note that hordes of escaped Autobot prisoners are running free. As you enter this room (39), turn around and look to the right and left; two alcoves (40) contain nice power-ups.

ENERGON SHARD CONTAINER

An Energon Shard Container is in the alcove (40) in the back-left.

NUCLEON SHOCK CANNON

A Nucleon Shock Cannon is in the alcove (40) in the back-right.

STAGE 3

As you turn the corner, take care of any stragglers shooting you from the room to the right. This room also contains some health and ammo. More enemies pour in from the back corner and from the hallway directly across the main chamber. Explosive containers in each direction allow you to unleash widespread devastation. This area's exit is in the left corner (42), in the direction of the arrows, but explore all the side hallways to find helpful items.

OVERSHIELD

When you enter this area, head straight to the hallway (41) across the room. Turn right to find an Overshield in front of a locked door.

STAGE 4

Coming around this last corner, you see more enemies entering the area from the hallway immediately to your left ④. Press forward, take them out, and grab some ammo from that alcove if you need it. Look down through the force field floor to see if you can spot Arcee, now freed from her jail cell and directing prisoners to safety.

When you approach the exit door ㊸, the door opens and a Brute charges in. Use the ample space here to avoid his melee attacks, and remember to avoid his ground pound attack by jumping. A weapon crate that yields a long-range gun is to the left of the exit door—this might come in handy during the next encounter.

STAGE 1

In the hangar ㊹, the Autobot prisoners pile into dropships below to make their escape. Two squadrons of Jet Soldiers fly in to

attack. The first is a group of three. Try to pick them off before they enter the upper landing on which you stand—their bombing runs and hover attacks can be deadly at close range. The second wave is a group of four Jet Soldiers, and they are a bit more aggressive. This upper landing area offers health, some ammo, and a Photon Burst Rifle. When you defeat all of the Jet Soldiers, Air Raid flies to the other side of the right exit door ㊺ and opens it for you.

OBJECTIVE: **LOCATE ZETA PRIME**

STAGE 2

Optimus directs Air Raid to help the fleeing Autobots escape the prison safely, so he flies down to the hangar's ground floor and begins to direct traffic. Look out the windows to the left and try to spot Jazz, now freed from his jail cell and helping with the escape. Follow the walkway and activate the switch to open the exit door ㊼. A Thermo Rocket Launcher is at the bottom of the ramp, and another Wallcrawler is around the corner to the right; it takes you to the lower levels ㊽.

AUTOBOT COLLECTIBLE #8

 Look out the window ㊻ on the landing area's far left side. A Decepticon symbol floats above the entrance to the dropship that the Autobots are boarding—shoot it.

"BEAK BREAKER" ACHIEVEMENT/TROPHY (2/3)

After you first enter this room, turn around and look above the entrance door. Laserbeak is perched on the left side of the overhang. Shoot him to make him fly away. This is part two of the "Beak Breaker" Achievement/Trophy.

SECTION 8 · DESCENT INTO MADNESS

STAGE 1

Enter the Wallcrawler 49 and start the ride by activating the switch in the center. As is moves down, mount one of the Ion Displacer turrets. Depending on which turret you occupy, you'll have to deal with a different threat. Two windows face out over enemy Wallcrawlers that shoot mortars at you. These are extremely tough, but if you focus Ion Displacer fire on them, they eventually explode. You can also focus fire directly on the side-mounted mortar cannons to take them out individually, but it's more efficient to concentrate on the main body. One window faces out over some curved walkways, where crowds of Decepticons mobilize and Rocket Soldiers fire rockets up at you. Finally, the fourth window looks out over some arched turret emplacements. You can shoot these enemies directly, or you can shoot the angled supports on which they stand. Deliver enough damage to the support, and the whole structure collapses, defeating the enemy on top of it in the process.

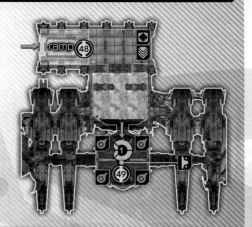

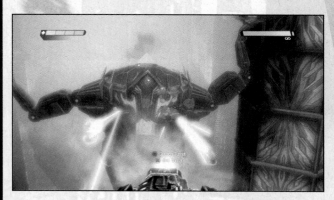

SECTION 9 · THE FINAL APPROACH

STAGE 1

Exit the Wallcrawler and follow the tunnel 50 around to the right. A cinematic plays, introducing the Rocketeer enemy type. This next section is a long expanse of open terrain, where you are under constant mortar fire. Use your vehicle form to traverse most of it. The ground around you gets destroyed in sections, so be careful of going too fast. As you exit the first tunnel, a swath of ground to the right is destroyed, so steer to the left, and then go up the ramp in front of you 51. The Rocketeer is vulnerable from behind, so flank him to take him out, or just ignore him and keep driving.

OVERSHIELD:

An Overshield is to the right, below the Rocketeer's platform. Jump across the destroyed floor to grab it.

STAGE 2

On the other side of the first ramp, a piece of ground is destroyed on the left side. Steer to the right and then navigate through the archway. On the other side, steer close to the inside of the left pillar (52), as the floor in the middle is blown apart. Two more Rocketeers launch rockets at you from platforms on another ramp's (53) left and right sides. Drive past them if you wish, but defeat them and grab some power-ups from their platforms if you're low on health or ammo.

AUTOBOT COLLECTIBLE #9

 At the top of the ramp (53) exiting this area, look to the right and shoot the floating Decepticon symbol floating above the platform.

STAGE 3

Beyond the ramp (53), the ground on either side is destroyed, so gun it up the middle. A Rocket Soldier attacks from a large structure (54) ahead, and some Car Soldiers steer in from behind it. A deactivated Wallcrawler with two weapon crates is to the left of the structure. Another Wallcrawler (55) guarded by two soldiers is across from that; it contains health and ammo. Clear out these enemies, or just drive around the obstacles and follow the arrows to the right.

STAGE 4

As you drive up the ramp (56) to the right, a Wallcrawler (57) slides down and crashes through the floor. Three soldiers jump out of it and attack. Take them out, or ignore them and drive underneath the Wallcrawler's arms. The route bears to the left once you're past the Wallcrawler.

"BEAK BREAKER" ACHIEVEMENT/TROPHY (3/3)

Laserbeak is perched on top of the large pillar (58). Shoot him to make him fly away. This is the final part of the "Beak Breaker" Achievement/Trophy.

STAGE 5

Follow the path to the left, where the ground splits (59) into an upper and a lower path. Choosing the lower path protects you from the Rocketeer on the other side. Once you make it across, you reach another Rocketeer platform (60) and two Car Soldiers. Deal with them and follow the path to the right.

OVERSHIELD

Go around the Rocketeer platform to the left to see an Overshield on the ground behind it.

STAGE 6

Two sections of ground are destroyed in front of you here (61), so be careful. To avoid falling, make a sharp right and then a sharp left. Two more Car Soldiers wait for you on the other side, and then the path leads up another ramp (62) to the left.

STAGE 7

The path curves around to the left and branches off into two routes. This is the final stretch (63). Three Snipers and two waves of Car Soldiers guard it. The Snipers can target you while you're driving, so it's best to eliminate them. There is ample cover here, but avoid getting so focused on the Snipers that you let the Car Soldiers blindside you. Race up the final series of ramps to reach the entrance to Zeta Prime's containment cell (64).

 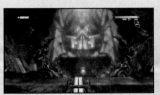

AUTOBOT COLLECTIBLE #10

You reach a transparent catwalk lined with claw-like structures before the last ramp (64). The tenth Decepticon symbol is beneath this catwalk. Shoot it from is the left or right side below the ramp that leads to this catwalk.

OBJECTIVE: **DEFEAT SOUNDWAVE**

STAGE 1

Before you enter Zeta Prime's chamber (65), load up on weaponry, grenades, and Energon Shards. Activate the switch (66) to open the door and enter the room (67). At the far end, Zeta Prime is chained up in a machine that is torturing him and draining his life force. Approach Zeta Prime to trigger a cinematic.

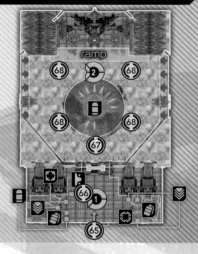

During the cinematic, Soundwave, who is hidden at the base of the platform blasts the team with an audio scrambler attack and then changes form into robot form. He throws up a powerful force field around him, and then begins his attack.

STAGE 2: PHASE 1

The first phase of this boss battle begins as Soundwave continues firing his audio blast attack. If you get hit by it your movement speed is slowed and your screen gets scrambled, so avoid it at all costs. Soundwave's shield is impenetrable; so don't waste ammo trying to hurt him yet. There are four Sentry mounts (68) in this room, two in front and one on either side. Soundwave begins activating these Sentries, but only two at a time during this phase and they appear in random locations. Destroy the sentries as soon as they pop up. Once destroyed, the Sentries drop ammo, health, or Energon Shards, so make sure to keep recharging yourself with these resources.

PHASE 2

Before long, the Sentries retract and Soundwave summons his first minion—Frenzy. A brief cinematic plays, showing Frenzy jumping out of Soundwave's chest cavity. Frenzy attacks with a mini-shotgun, but his main attack is a hover blast that does significant damage. When you see him jump in the air, use your Dash ability to avoid the projectile or get behind the pillars or the mound in the center of the room.

Focus all your fire on Frenzy. When he reaches zero health, he falls down and then Soundwave exits his protective forcefield to revive him. This is your chance to attack Soundwave directly. You'll need to deal significant damage to him while he is exposed, so try to get Frenzy down towards the back of the room. This gives you more time to attack Soundwave. If you do enough damage to Soundwave, then he will recall Frenzy, who runs back to the platform with him. If not, then Soundwave returns alone and Frenzy will continue attacking. Bring him down again to cause Soundwave to exit the forcefield again. Once both Soundwave and Frenzy are on the platform, the battle goes into the next phase.

PHASE 3

In this phase, Soundwave continues his Audio Blast attack and reactivates the Sentries. This time, he activates three Sentries at a time in random locations. Destroy as many as possible in order to refuel your health and ammo bars.

PHASE 4

After the second round of Sentries, Soundwave summons Rumble. Rumble attacks at range with a pistol and also has two special attacks. The first special attack is a close-range ground pound that causes damage and knocks you back when in range. Keep your distance from this attack, because it can deplete your health very quickly.

His second special attack is a bull-rush style stampede attack. He charges forward and slams into you, causing heavy damage. Dodge this attack at all costs by strafing around it or using your Dash ability. Just like with Frenzy, you need to focus fire on Rumble until he goes down. Once he goes down, Soundwave will come out of his shield to revive him. Do as much damage as you  can to Soundwave before he returns. Once both Soundwave and Rumble are back up on the platform, the next phase begins.

PHASE 5

In this phase, Soundwave continues his Audio Blast attack and reactivates the Sentries. This time, he activates all four Sentries at once. Destroy as many as possible in order to refuel your health and ammo bars.

PHASE 6

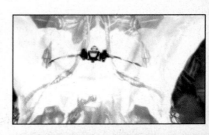

When all the Sentries have deactivated, Soundwave summons the third and final minion—Laserbeak. Laserbeak pummels you from the air with rapid-fire machine guns. Try to avoid this damage by using the cover in the room. His most damaging attack is the Laser Bombing Run. He flies across the room, strafing the ground with a deadly laser beam.

Don't get caught in the path of this beam, because it will drain your health severely. Just as with the previous minions, you'll need to damage Laserbeak until he goes down in order to lure Soundwave out of his shield. This time, while Soundwave is exposed, bring him down to zero health to defeat him. Once he is defeated, a closing cinematic will play.

Soundwave regenerates his life force by draining it from Zeta Prime, but Optimus interrupts him and Soundwave counterattacks. In the resulting commotion, Soundwave and his minions escape. Unfortunately, the Autobots are too late; the Decepticon machinery is the only thing keeping Zeta Prime alive.

CONCLUSION

Optimus, Sideswipe, and Bumblebee bring Zeta Prime's lifeless body to the Council. Optimus is made the new Prime, and the Council informs him that Megatron has corrupted the core of Cybertron. Optimus's first mission as Prime is to travel to the core and purify the stain of Dark Energon.

TO THE CORE

Having embraced his destiny as leader of the Autobots, Optimus Prime leads a small band of Autobots to save the core of Cybertron itself from the clutches of Megatron. But to do so, they must first rescue the mightiest Autobot guardian ever created: Omega Supreme.

AVAILABLE CHARACTERS

OPTIMUS

Always a strong choice, Optimus Prime starts with his own custom Ion Blaster, which is quite a powerful weapon. His Dash ability helps keep you clear of danger. His vehicle form has potent rockets that you can use to blast your enemies to smithereens.

WARPATH

The only tank in this level, Warpath means business. He has strong defensive abilities, which aid his survival through those tough encounters with Megatron's troops. Barrier and Shockwave keep enemies at bay while he blasts them with his powerful tank shell.

IRONHIDE

Ironhide begins the level with the Scatter Blaster, an automatic shotgun that packs a serious punch. His abilities, Dash and Whirlwind, are a nice mix of defense and offense, giving him welcome versatility.

CO-OP TIPS

Optimus Prime should always be in your co-op group to exploit his powerful Warcry ability. The damage and armor buff it provides can help turn the tide of battle in your favor.

Try using Warpath's Barrier ability to force enemies to come to you. Then have Ironhide unleash a Whirlwind to shred them when they get inside the Barrier.

INTRODUCTION

Megatron has succeeded. Dark Energon has corrupted the core of Cybertron. As the new Prime, Optimus must lead a small group of Autobots deep into the world's core to cleanse it. But before Optimus Prime and his Autobot friends can descend into the core of Cybertron, they must rescue the mighty Omega Supreme from capture.

SECTION ❯ 1 ❯ OMEGA'S HOLDING CELL

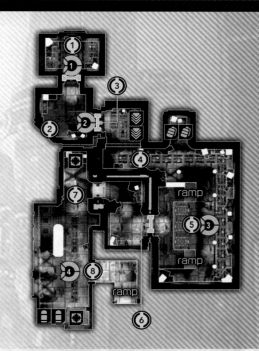

OBJECTIVE: DISRUPT POWER TO THE FACILITY

STAGE 1

After the introductory cutscene, you find yourself in a room ① with only one exit. The door is locked, held shut by two destructible locks. When Optimus finishes his speech, shoot both locks to exit

the room. When you step through the open door, you get your first look at Omega Supreme being tortured ②.

STAGE 2

You face another door held shut by two destructible locks. When Optimus finishes speaking with Ratchet about Omega Supreme, shoot the locks to open the door ③ and advance. As you step through the door, you see a Neutron Assault Rifle and a Semi-Auto EMP Shotgun. Grab one of these for your secondary weapon, and follow the buddies to your right ④.

STAGE 3

Your next goal is to disrupt power to the facility, just as Ratchet and Optimus discussed. Destroy the three power generators ⑤. Afterward, Ratchet enables a holo-map, giving you new instructions on how to proceed to free Omega Supreme.

When the holo-map disappears, the door ⑥ behind you opens and three enemies enter the room: two Car Soldiers and one Rocket Soldier. The Rocket Solider usually hangs back and fires at you from long range, so take advantage of the cover in the room. Dispatch them and move forward. If they give you too much trouble, move back toward your entrance to this room to find some Flak Grenades. Pick up more ammunition from the next room.

OBJECTIVE:

RESTORE FULL SECURITY ACCESS
STAGE 4

When you enter the next large chamber ⑦, you immediately face combat. Two Decepticon Protectors are on the floor and a Rocket Solider is up on a balcony. Use the storage crates for cover, and put down the Rocket Soldier first, as he is exposed. With the Rocket Soldier out of the equation, slink out from cover to destroy the two Protectors. If you get into trouble, a health crate is behind you, back toward the entrance. If you need ammunition, cross enemy lines to find ammo crates behind them. This room's exit is the hallway ⑧ along the left wall.

STAGE 5

A lone Rocket Soldier blocks your path as you move to the hallway ⑧. Deal with him and move up the steep ramps. When you get to the top ⑨, stay cool. You see four Overshield power-ups, but don't get too close. When you approach, they vanish and turn into EMP Grenades that blur your view when they detonate. If you play it right, you can set off the trap and suffer only slight distortion. Next, take an immediate right and grab your own EMP Grenades. You need them against the Cloakers that are here.

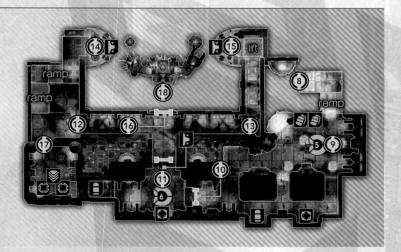

OBJECTIVE: **RELEASE OMEGA SUPREME'S RESTRAINTS**
STAGE 6

Engage the two Decepticon Protectors guarding the security console ⑪. Once they're destroyed, interact with the console to open the door behind it. Inside, you can proceed to the left ⑫ or to the right ⑬. Both directions lead to one of two interactive switches (⑭ and ⑮) that help free Omega Supreme from his bonds. They're located on ledges near Omega Supreme's shoulders—you must activate both of them. You encounter enemies in either direction, so prepare for a fight.

To track them, watch for their plasma cannons' glowing orb or their heat distortion. Lob an EMP Grenade near them—they de-cloak and become stunned—easy pickings. Slay them and follow the objective marker to the back of the room. Disable the destructible locks on the exit door ⑩.

You find Cloakers as you move from one switch to the other. Once you interact with both switches, return to the center to find Omega Supreme's chamber door ⑯ open. Two Protectors are ready to engage you.

AUTOBOT COLLECTIBLE #11

Look for a destructible portion of wall ⑰ at the back of the room. on the left. The hidden Decepticon symbol is in a secret room behind this piece of wall.

ENERGON SHARD CONTAINERS & ENERGON REPAIR RAY

Two Energon Shard Containers and an Energon Repair Ray are in the same secret room ⑰ behind the destructible wall.

SECTION ② PROTECT RATCHET

OBJECTIVE:

DEFEAT THE DECEPTICONS AROUND OMEGA SUPREME

STAGE 1

With Omega Supreme ⑱ finally free of his bonds, it's time to move inside and repay his captors. A squadron of Rocket Soldiers surrounds Omega. Move into the chamber, and use the cover to Omega's left and right to take down the soldiers on the bridge ⑲. Drop down into the chamber to clean up the remaining guards.

With his captors eliminated, Omega informs the group that he is too damaged to open the Omega Gate. Ratchet reports that he is on his way and that the team should hold out for him to arrive. Omega advises the group to set up a defensive perimeter. The

impending fight is the longest and hardest encounter that Optimus and his crew have faced. Throughout the fight, Omega unlocks more defenses that the team can use to fend off the incoming Decepticons. Use this time to unlock the first series of defenses, two Energon repair sentries (⑳ and ㉑). Hold off the next brief wave of Decepticons to clear the way for Ratchet.

OBJECTIVE: PROTECT RATCHET

STAGE 2

With Ratchet on the scene, healing Omega, the Decepticons step up their attack. The first wave is an army of Car Soldiers. Your primary goal is to keep the enemy fire off Ratchet. If Ratchet goes down, you must clear a path to him and revive him immediately. If Ratchet goes offline, it's game over. Use the ammo and Flak Grenade power-ups on the side to stay equipped throughout the battle.

OBJECTIVE: ACTIVATE THE DEFENSES

STAGE 3

With the first wave destroyed, it's time to unlock the next series of defenses. You must unlock three interact stations: a grenade closet (22), a weapon closet (23), and a secured repair station (24). This next attack wave is much more deadly than the preceding waves. The team must fight Snipers, Rocket Soldiers, and the deadly Titan. The Energon Battle Pistol and the Energon Grenades are very useful in

this conflict. If Ratchet goes down, you can revive him by tossing an Energon Grenade at his feet. This lets you stay in the fight and simultaneously revive Ratchet. Before the wave starts, it's a good idea to retreat to the secured repair station and exploit one of the three Overshield power-ups.

OBJECTIVE: PROTECT RATCHET

When the Titan arrives, your best bet is to destroy him immediately. His slow walking speed gives you plenty of time to pummel him before he reaches Ratchet. If the Titan does get to Ratchet, he can down Ratchet in seconds. Fight from behind cover, and use Flak Grenades to pound the Titan. Once you neutralize him, his Ion Displacer is yours for the taking. Pick it up to make quick work of any remaining Rocket Soldiers.

STAGE 4

Two waves down, one to go. Take a moment between waves to unlock the final set of defenses. On the lower level, the team can release two Nucleon Shock Cannons ((25) and (26)). On the upper bridge (19), the team can unlock a set of rocket sentries (28). If you haven't already discovered it, a mounted Ion Displacer (27) is also on the upper bridge; it can be very useful during this final wave. If any Overshield power-ups are left, it's a good idea to grab one before the next assault begins. The final wave is the most deadly yet. Jet Soldiers, Snipers, Car Soldiers, and Titans all try to destroy Ratchet and prevent the group from saving the core of Cybertron.

Use the Ion Displacer (27) to tear the first group of Jet Soldiers from the sky. Watch for more Snipers to drop into the battle; they can spell a quick death if you don't take care of them immediately. The battle climaxes with a long assault of Titans and Car Soldiers. This is a great time to break out the big guns. Grab one of the Nucleon Shock Cannons ((25) and (26)) to wipe out large groups of Car Soldiers.

When the final Decepticon falls, Omega finally gets enough energy to open the Omega Gate. Stay sharp; one final challenge stands between you and Cybertron's corrupted underground.

OBJECTIVE: **DEFEAT THE DECEPTICON TANK**

STAGE 1

The Omega Gate opens to reveal a giant Tank Soldier. The Tank rolls into the arena, destroying anything that stands in its way. Ratchet informs the group that he needs just a little more time to fully heal Omega. It's up to Optimus and the crew to keep this Tank off Ratchet if Omega Supreme has any chance of surviving. The Tank Soldier's front and sides are heavily shielded. His only weak spot consists of a small, destructible back panel. Grab one of the remaining Nucleon Shock Cannons or Ion Displacers, and begin to flank the Tank. Watch out for his powerful cannon blast. When you get behind the Tank, focus fire on his vulnerable spot long enough, and he transforms into his towering robot form. Avoid his Magma Frag Grenades and powerful spread attack as you focus all fire on his chest plate.

When you deal enough damage to the Tank, Ratchet informs the group that he has done it—Omega's full power is restored. Optimus and the team watch in awe as Omega pulls the Decepticon Tank into the air, ripping it to pieces. With the path (29) to the core finally open, it's time for Optimus to leave Ratchet and Omega and venture deeper into Cybertron's corrupted interior.

OBJECTIVE: **FIND A WAY TO THE CORE**

STAGE 1

Ratchet stays behind to repair Omega, while you head into Cybertron's core. Change into your vehicle mode, and burn down the hallway (30) ahead of you. There are no enemies or power-ups to find. A door opens (31) at the end of the hallway. Move through to find a small room with a hole in the floor (32); it leads down into the depths of Cybertron. You can find some health here if you need it, along with two weapons: an Energon Battle Pistol and a Scattershot Gun. When you're ready, make the long leap down.

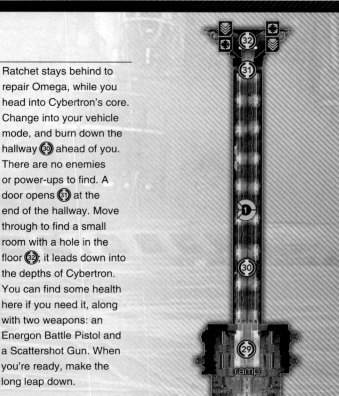

STAGE 1

Once you reach the bottom (33), bear witness to the core's corruption. Jump down and meet the Space Slug for the first time. You'll be seeing him again soon… When the Space Slug exits, a special switch (34) appears (if you're playing as Optimus Prime); interact with it to force open the clogged, corrupted hallway. If you aren't playing as Optimus Prime, stand back and watch the show as he clears the corruption in your path. Move down the hallway (35), and avoid the falling objects as you progress toward the next encounter.

AUTOBOT COLLECTIBLE #12

If a member of the team controls Optimus, he or she has a chance to use his Charged Axe interact to open a hidden path (37) to the left. A sneaky Decepticon symbol hides at this path's end, before you drop into the Decepticon trap.

STAGE 2

You find yourself in a large room (36) surrounded by corruption that's too thick to blast out of your way. With nowhere to go, you must fight the Car Soldiers coming your way. Multiple waves of Car Soldiers and Rocket Soldiers attack here, so get ready. The Car

Soldiers always leap down from the overhead balconies to engage you up close. Meanwhile, the Rocket Soldiers remain on high ground, pelting you from a distance. Take them down.

When you eliminate all of them, the action breaks for a moment to introduce the master of close-range combat, the Shotgunner. He is graced with an Overshield, so it takes some extra heat to bring him down. A few of these foes confront you here, so brace yourself. When you finish dealing with them, a Space Slug breaks through the wall of corruption and consumes the remaining enemy, leaving a path for you.

Once again, if you are playing as Optimus Prime, you see a special interact at the end of the hallway. Proceed in that direction. If you aren't playing as Optimus Prime, follow him to the end of the hallway and watch him do his handy work. When the corruption is clear (38), move forward and make another long drop (39) deeper into the core.

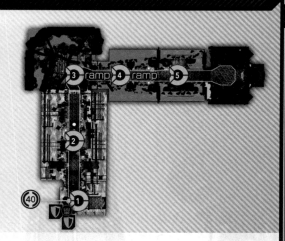

OBJECTIVE: ESCORT THE SLUGS

STAGE 1

When you land in the core (40), you wind up in a room with no exits and two walls of corruption. The Space Slugs come out when you approach the wall on your right. But this time, they have turrets mounted on their backs. Watch as you hop on, mount up, and get ready for the ride of your life.

OVERSHIELD

After you drop into this area, turn around to locate a destructible wall panel. You can find two Overshield power-ups inside the secret room behind the panel.

AUTOBOT COLLECTIBLE #13

When you drop into this area (40), turn around to see a destructible wall panel. A hidden Decepticon symbol is inside the newly revealed secret room.

STAGE 2

You are riding a Space Slug with a turret mounted on its back. You have unlimited ammunition. The Space Slugs dictate which way you go, so you can focus on blasting any enemies you see.

Use your zoom to tighten the weapon's spread, and then release the zoom to scan for new targets. They are plentiful, practically everywhere you look.

STAGE 3

After they break through a large wall of corruption, the Space Slugs stop in a large room. Enter the Corrupted Worm. It moves from right to left, leaving large holes in the walls across from where you sit. Jet Soldiers emerge from these holes. Blast them out of the air with your mounted turret. After a short time, the Corrupted Worm returns, breaking through the wall. It lobs balls of corruption toward you and the team. Blast them before they hit you. More Jet Soldiers also fly in from the holes, further complicating things. Once you destroy them all, the Corrupted Worm shrieks in defiance and jumps away, and the Space Slugs resume their progress.

STAGE 4

With the Space Slugs moving on, you soon face a Decepticon Destroyer. You can't destroy him with direct fire, so take Optimus's advice and blast the supports for the bridge on which he stands. Watch out for the Rocketeers along the back wall. They hide behind their shields, waiting for the perfect time to strike. When they pop out, blast them.

STAGE 5

The Space Slugs break through another wall of corruption and move forward. Continue shredding any enemies that appear. After a short time, the Corrupted Worm returns, flying in front of you. It launches more balls of corruption at you. Shoot them out of the air as before. Eventually, the Space Slugs move forward and the Corrupted Worm moves out of your way. The Space Slugs break through a final wall of corruption. The Corrupted Worm then smashes through the wall and breaks the floor behind you—tumbling down you go.

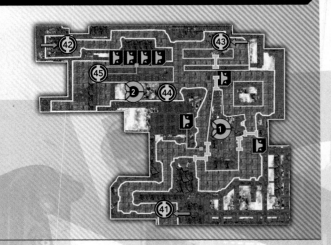

OBJECTIVE: REGROUP WITH YOUR SQUAD

STAGE 1

The squadmates wake to find that they are separated from each other. Optimus Prime starts on the lower south pathway (41). Warpath begins at (42), and Ironhide begins at (43). Your first goal is to regroup with the rest of the squad. Depending on which member of the squad you're playing, you have to open locked Energon floodgates, avoid deadly mashers, and fight groups of Spiderbots. Continue forward, and the squad members eventually locate each other. Though the group finds him, Warpath is still separated from the team. Continue moving forward to find a way to unite the squad.

STAGE 2

Optimus and Ironhide soon come to the shore of an Energon River (44). Warpath must raise a series of bridge supports (45) to allow his squad mates to cross safely. Optimus or Ironhide must destroy the Energon spouts to stop the flow of Corrupted Energon raining down on the platforms.

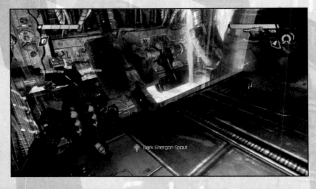

Dark Energon Spout

SECTION 8 — DIVIDE AND CONQUER

STAGE 1

You can find some health crates and a Scatter Blaster, should you need them. The Corrupted Worm makes a flyby, ripping through the landscape in front of you 46 as you move forward. Spiderbots spew forth from the rift it creates. They can't withstand much damage, so defeat them any way you wish, either with a weapon or a swift stomp of your foot. Eventually, Car Soldiers and Jet Soldiers arrive to complicate things. You can find ammunition and EMP Grenades in the area—use them liberally.

One member of your party, Warpath, remains separated, but that teammate can mount a Nucleon Shock Cannon turret 47 to support the squad. Once you slay all the enemies, Optimus or Ironhide must unlock the final Energon floodgate 48. Enter the rift the Corrupted Worm created to find the way to reach it. With the final gate open, the team reunites.

STAGE 2

Around the next bend 49, the squad finally catches its first glimpse of Cybertron's core. An army of Space Slugs mounts a final defense against the attacking Decepticons. Ride the lift in the next room 50 down to the core exterior.

"SLUGFEST" ACHIEVEMENT/TROPHY

> After the Divide and Conquer fight, shoot the corrupted pillar so that it smashes the Tank Soldier before he can execute the Slug. If you save the Slug, you receive the Slugfest Achievement/Trophy.

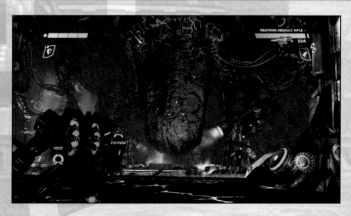

SECTION 9 — SEA OF CORRUPTION

OBJECTIVE: LOCATE THE ENTRANCE TO THE CORE

STAGE 1

From the lift 51, convert into your vehicle form and drive down the ramp leading to the sea of corruption 52. You can find various ammunition and health crates around the sea. You can identify the entrance 53 to Cybertron's core via an objective marker. However, a large and dangerous sea lies between you and it. In order to cross it and reach your objective, you must blast large chunks of corrupted metal that cling 52 to the ceiling. They splash down, providing you a way to cross.

There are many paths to the core entrance. After you drop the first chunk of corrupted metal and jump to the subsequent platform, quickly turn left and jump across to the rock. Drop another chunk of corrupted metal into the sea to make your way across. You can find a hidden cache of Energon shard containers and an Ion Displacer (54). Remember that you cannot double-jump when you carry a large weapon like the Ion Displacer, so you must dash to cross the rest of the corrupted sea. Turn around and make your way to the core of Cybertron's entrance (53). Prepare yourself—the end is near.

ENERGON REPAIR RAY

Near the back of the room, shoot down two pieces of corrupted metal. This creates a path to a platform (54) holding an Energon Repair Ray.

ION DISPLACER & NUCLEON SHOCK CANNON

To the left of the first destructible pillar, shoot down a piece of corrupted metal (55). This creates a path to both an Ion Displacer and a Nucleon Shock Cannon. Attempt to retrieve one of these weapons only if your character is equipped with the Dash ability; you need it to work your way to the core entrance.

AUTOBOT COLLECTIBLE #14

Find the hidden path to the right (56) at the bottom of the first long ramp. A Decepticon symbol is at the end of a series of pillars.

AUTOBOT COLLECTIBLE #15

Shoot down the piece of corrupted metal on the far side of the room. This creates a path to a platform with Energon Grenade power-ups (57). A Decepticon symbol is near the back of this platform.

SECTION 10 **THE HEART OF CYBERTRON**

OBJECTIVE: **DEFEAT THE MENACE ON THE CORE**

STAGE 1

You have found the core of Cybertron (58). It's covered with corruption, and a corrupted creature has taken up residence there. The Corrupted Worm has made the core its home, and it intends to fight you for it. There is only one way

to damage the Corrupted Worm. You must shoot it directly in the mouth, which it protects with its huge metal mandibles. The Worm is vulnerable only when it pauses to siphon Dark Energon from the core. The Worm ceases its attack, and it sucks in streams of Dark Energon from the core. Shoot the mouth at that moment. Remember that shots to other parts of its body may rip away chunks of armor, but they inflict no actual damage. If you blast the mandibles, you can expose the mouth.

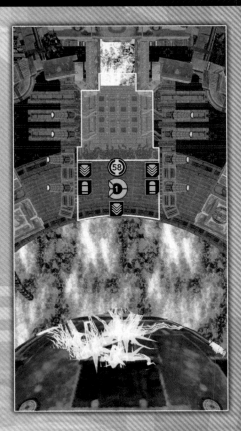

This boss has many attacks, and each is as deadly as the last. First, it slams its two front legs into the ground to your left and right. It then rakes its legs back toward itself. This leaves two massive streaks of corruption spikes in its wake. You must destroy these as quickly as possible. If you don't, the Corrupted Worm uses them in conjunction with its next attack, which is a debilitating ground slam. The Worm rears back, signaling an incoming slam. Jump high into the air just as the impact arrives, or suffer a knockdown and visual distortion. If corruption spikes remain on the ground during his slam, they explode, inflicting damage to anyone around them.

The Corrupted Worm possesses two glowing bits that look like they could be eyes. Beware, as they actually shoot Energon projectiles. The Worm sidesteps to the arena's left, middle, or right and then blasts along a straight line. Providing you avoid the Worm's direct path, you don't have to worry about these attacks.

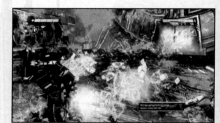

When you deal enough damage to the Corrupted Worm, it retreats up the side of the core, finding time to recuperate from your attacks. During this retreat, it launches white sacs full of Spiderbots to the ground. You cannot destroy the sacs in midair, but try to defeat the Spiderbots as soon as possible, because they drop ammunition and even weapons. The Corrupted Worm retreats only

twice. The first time, it waits patiently for you to defeat all of the Spiderbots scurrying at your feet. However, the second time, the Worm is not so polite, so exterminate the Spiderbots as quickly as you can.

At certain points during the fight, the Corrupted Worm transforms its mouth and mandibles into a deadly laser. It emits a thick, destructive beam toward you, sweeping back and forth across the arena. Dodge the beam to avoid damage. The beam also sweeps low and high, so remain alert. The Corrupted Worm always stops its beam attack in the middle of the battle area, as the laser spins down and stops. Continue to assault the Corrupted Worm's soft center when it's exposed. With enough blasting, it falls from the core into the Energon below.

CONCLUSION

Cybertron's core is free from the corruption that engulfed it, but it has suffered too much damage to survive. The core speaks of an answer. It must shut itself down, but it takes millions of years to repair itself. The planet will grow cold and barren, but there is hope: the Matrix of Leadership entrusted in Optimus Prime, leader of the free Autobots. As long as his spark glows, the core of Cybertron lives on.

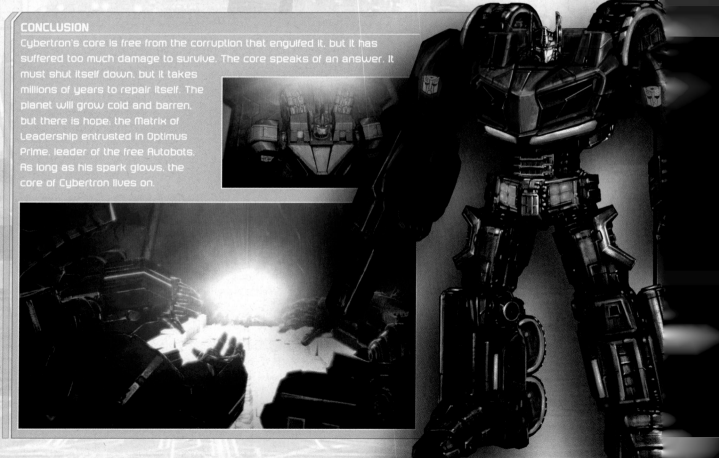

09 AERIAL ASSAULT

The core is too damaged by Dark Energon to sustain life on Cybertron. In order to repair itself, the core must shut down for millions of years. Sadly, Optimus Prime, carrying the Matrix of Leadership's power inside him, must order the evacuation of the entire planet if his race is to survive.

AVAILABLE CHARACTERS

AIR RAID

The runner and gunner of the group in personality as well as power, Air Raid's ability to go invisible allows him to sneak in and inflict massive close-range damage. That's where his devastating Whirlwind attack comes in. If he bites off more than he can chew, he can also use invisibility to give himself room to recover.

JETFIRE

As an Autobot scientist who once worked on the relay station that Megatron repurposed for his villainous plans, Jetfire knows the best way to destroy the station from within. Jetfire is better at engaging enemies from mid to long range, where he can also observe the team's health and use his Energon Repair Ray when necessary (even to repair his spawned sentry gun).

SILVERBOLT

Designated leader of Mission Aerial Assault by Optimus Prime, Silverbolt takes his duties seriously. His Barrier ability can protect his team from enemy fire, and his Shockwave ability proves its worth in the thick of battle. Silverbolt is a versatile all-around fighter.

CO-OP TIPS

The player using Jetfire should focus on making sure everyone is healed between battles. During larger fights, Jetfire is well advised to heal the team in the midst of combat rather than waiting until the battle ends. Have other players save excess ammo power-ups for Jetfire's Energon Repair Ray.

If Air Raid's Whirlwind ability is charged, allow him to sneak invisibly into a group of enemies before he unleashes it. Jetfire can even focus on healing Air Raid during his Whirlwind, enabling him to dish out a lot of damage without taking any in return.

Silverbolt's Barrier ability can save everyone from suffering a lot of damage during big encounters. If things get hectic, don't hesitate to activate the Barrier and get everyone behind it.

INTRODUCTION

As the Autobots flee Cybertron in their transport ships, Megatron unleashes a lethal surprise. Unknown to the Autobots, Megatron harvested the pieces of the ancient space station in Cybertron's orbit. He used the pieces to create a mammoth gun that runs on Dark Energon. It can destroy the entire Autobot fleet. Facing the complete annihilation of the Autobots, Optimus devises a desperate plan. He sends Silverbolt, Jetfire, and Air Raid up the Energon Bridge beam that powers the gun to find some way to shut it down. The Autobots' escape from a doomed Cybertron and the very future of their race depends on their success.

SECTION 1 — ATTACK ON THE RELAY STATION

OBJECTIVE: FOLLOW THE BEAM

STAGE 1

Boost your way along the Energon Bridge beam ①, dodging the wreckage of the Autobot fleet. If you follow the beam, you should eventually reach the Decepticons' energy relay station. Hopefully, you can find a way to stop the beam that powers the gun. Don't fly into the beam or outside the containment field surrounding it, or your circuits will surely fry.

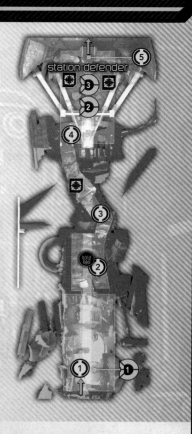

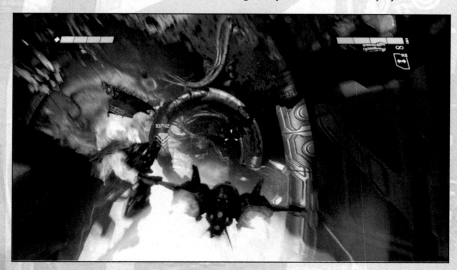

OBJECTIVE: ENTER THE RELAY STATION

AUTOBOT COLLECTIBLE #16

 As soon as you fly through the first glowing orange hole, look down. A glowing Decepticon symbol is on the floor ②. Shoot it to collect it.

If you're damaged, a health power-up is just past the cave's halfway point. When you resume flying up instead of down, fly past two crossbeams, and then watch the cave floor to find the health.

Soon, you fly through a section of cave where the Energon Bridge beam bore straight through a large piece of space debris. Mind the floating space mines ③ that the Decepticons set to guard the relay station's perimeter. A rocket or a concentrated machinegun burst destroys them. On Hard difficulty, they require an extra rocket and a lot more damage— you're better off just flying around them.

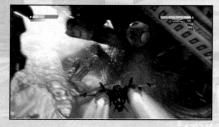

STAGE 2

Emerging from the cave ④, you come face-to-face with the Decepticons' relay station ⑤. As you fly closer, five Decepticon Jet Soldiers fly out to intercept you. Your jet rockets with lock-on may be your best bet for taking out enemy Jet Soldiers, particularly at longer range. Watch for their bombing runs, which can cause significant damage and get the Jet Soldiers behind you. Boost or barrel roll out

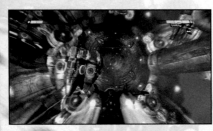

of the way if this happens. On easier difficulties, you may find that your jet's machineguns are the fastest way to take out the enemy flyers.

When you destroy the initial Jet Soldiers, the Decepticon Station Defender breaks out the front of the relay station.

STAGE 3

If you get low on health, fly down to one of the two Energon platforms to pick up an Energon Cube. They regenerate every 30 seconds. Strafe left and right as you shoot at the Station Defender. Boost to avoid the side gun projectiles, and barrel roll to avoid the rockets.

Keep moving or you'll get pounded with damage. You can also shoot the incoming rockets out of the air with your jet machineguns.

In the Station Defender fight's first phase, your jet rocket and machinegun fire work well to destroy the two side guns. However, you might try using rockets with the lock-on to blow apart the two uppermost gun cover pieces. Then use machinegun fire to reduce the gun's main health.

After you destroy the Station Defender's two side guns, Decepticon reinforcements join the fray. Also, the Station Defender unleashes horizontal and vertical beam attacks. Shoot the Station Defender's red center as it powers up. Jet machinegun fire does the most damage, although you can use the lock-on with rockets. Barrel roll away from the Station Defender's larger rocket barrages. Watch for the red tracer lasers that precede the horizontal and vertical beam attacks. They preview the ensuing beam's path so you can get out of the way.

With the Station Defender out of commission, fly into it and activate the switch. The core is exposed. Shoot and destroy the core to find the way forward.

SECTION ② COOLANT CHAMBER

OBJECTIVE: INFILTRATE COOLANT ROOM

STAGE 1

In the illuminated green area ⑥, walk forward, drop down a small ledge, and turn the next corner. A medium sized coolant pump ⑦ is in the middle of an alcove. Destroy it along with the one ⑧ on the central coolant pool's opposite side. Decepticons then arrive in an elevator ⑨ that rises from the room's center. Take them out, and then visit the supply room to the left of the elevator.

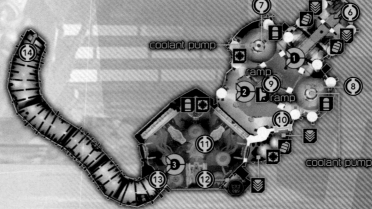

coolant pump

ramp

ramp

coolant pump

ENERGON SHARD CONTAINER

Once you destroy the two coolant pumps, and the supply room ⑩ along the left wall is open, enter and look along the back wall's right side for the Energon shard container.

OBJECTIVE: DESTROY THE COOLANT PUMP

STAGE 2

Restock with weapons, health, and ammo. Then use the interact switch that's in the elevator. The vent that covers the far wall opens, and enemy Jet Soldiers storm the room. When you defeat them, fly into the next room ⑪. Watch for enemy Rocket Sentries down near the coolant.

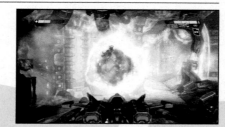

AUTOBOT COLLECTIBLE #17

Two destructible doors are in the room with the Rocket Sentries. A glowing Decepticon symbol is behind the left door. Blast through the door ⑫ and then shoot the collectible to claim it.

STAGE 3

After you get the collectible, shoot through the forward transparent door ⑬ in the room that houses the rocket turrets. Fly through

the door and down a narrow tunnel. Dodge the icicles hanging from the ceiling, and take care to avoid touching the coolant on the tunnel floor ⑭.

SECTION ③ INTO THE BELLY OF THE MACHINE

STAGE 1

You eventually emerge from the tunnel into a large room ⑮, where Decepticons shoot at you from an upper ledge. If you remain in jet form here, watch for enemy fire coming from farther back in the room—the two Rocket Sentries in the room's center are good examples. You may want to change to robot form and, from the ground, shoot at the Decepticons on the ledge. Use the crates to jump up the ledge. Then carefully move forward, deeper into the room, using the corners for cover. If you can, destroy the two central Rocket Sentries before you engage the rest of the Decepticons.

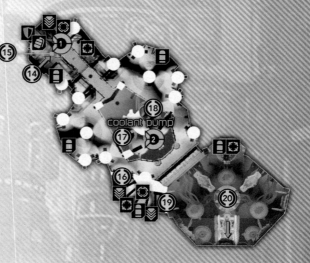

If you're feeling brave, you can fly to the room's back right. If you boost hard, you can get there without suffering too much damage. You can take refuge in and then fight your way out of a small supply hallway ⑯.

ENERGON SHARD CONTAINER

Leaving the tunnel ⑮ fly straight ahead until you reach a wall. Drop to the ground. The Energon shard container is just to your left.

ENERGON SHARD CONTAINER

An Energon shard container is in the supply hallway ⑯. In the room's back right.

OVERSHIELD

An Overshield is to the left of the exit of the tunnel ⑮. Look on the ground to the left for cables that run into the wall. The Overshield is to the left of the cables in the back corner.

STAGE 2

Once you clear the room of enemies, inspect the enormous coolant pump in the room's center. Destroy the two small engines (⑰ and ⑱) on either side of the pump. The pump explodes and the large side vent wall opens ⑲.

OBJECTIVE: LOWER THE RELAY STATION COOLANT

Fly into the next room. Another coolant elevator with Decepticons in it rises. Clear out the Decepticons and fly into the elevator (20). Use the switch to activate the elevator. You descend under the coolant to a sub-level of the relay station. What *are* those creatures swimming out in the coolant?

SECTION 4 — COOLANT CONTROL ROOM

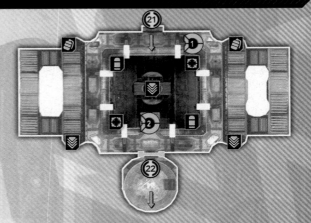

STAGE 1

When you're below the coolant, proceed forward through the next set of doors and enter the next room (21). You find a switch that reveals the X12 Scrapmaker.

Quickly get the X12 Scrapmaker. Also, you can find EMP Grenades on the upper walkway, to the left and right of the entry door. Grab them and get ready to fight Cloakers. Throw the EMP Grenades near the Cloakers to reveal them briefly. Finish them off with the X12 Scrapmaker.

STAGE 2

When you defeat the Cloakers, an elevator door opens on the room's far side. Ride the elevator (22) down, and follow the hallway around to a large room (23). It contains coolant tanks that slowly fill and empty.

ENERGON SHARD CONTAINER

Floor-to-ceiling force field windows that contain coolant occupy this room's left and right sides. An Energon shard container is on the floor in front of each of these windows.

STAGE 5

Follow the objective marker to the front of the room, toward a switch (24). Along the way, note the health power-up locations in the room. A hologram of Megatron appears, force fields block the exit hallways, and Decepticons swarm the room. Megatron sends three waves of Decepticons at you. The first two waves should be straightforward. Before the second wave starts, drop proximity mines near the force fields where the Decepticons emerge.

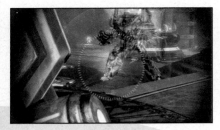

The last Decepticon wave consists of a Brute and two Titans. Take out the Brute quickly, and then coordinate the attack on one Titan at a time. Use Silverbolt's Barrier ability in the middle of the room to provide cover from the Titans' machineguns. If the destructible red tanks are still around, try to lure a Titan close to one and then detonate it. It's risky, but if a Titan already has a lot of damage, Air Raid's Whirlwind attack can inflict a large dose of damage to seal its fate. Make sure you find the room's two Energon Cubes.

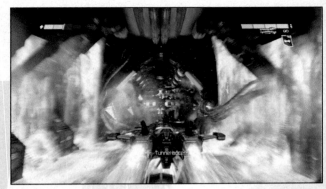

Once you dismantle the Decepticons, use the switch (24) to lower the coolant. With lowered coolant levels, it's only a matter of time until the relay station overheats and shuts down. Fly through the door that opens into the coolant tunnels.

SECTION (5) COOLANT TUNNELS

OBJECTIVE: OVERLOAD THE PULSE REGULATOR

STAGE 1

This is a fast-moving flying section (25), hurtling through the winding coolant tunnels at high speed. At the end of the tunnel's first section, fly down through the broken floor, make a hard right turn, dodge some Energon waterfalls, and then fly up and out of a broken hallway floor (26). After you fly through the tunnels, you should end up in a hallway (27) with windows that overlook a large room and an enormous Decepticon.

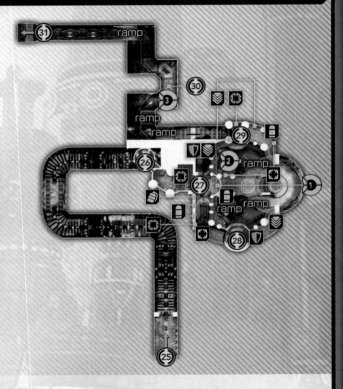

"POWERGLIDE PERFORMER" ACHIEVEMENT/TROPHY

Starting where the doors open, if you can fly all the way from the tunnel's beginning to its end within 23 seconds, you'll earn the "Powerglide Performer" Achievement/Trophy.

OVERSHIELD

From the hallway entrance (27), turn left and walk to the dead-end to find an Overshield.

ENERGON SHARD CONTAINER

On your way back along the hallway, after you get the Achievement/Trophy and the Overshield, drop back down into the broken tunnel from which you just flew (26). The Energon shard container is down on the catwalk to the right.

ENERGON SHARD CONTAINER

Once you jump or fly out of the shattered floor into the upper hallway, turn right (27) and walk along the hallway. The windows down into the main room are to your left. Another Energon shard container is just ahead on the right.

STAGE 2

Continue along the hallway to the right until you reach an elevator (28). Activate the switch to ride it downward, and prepare to fight in this large chamber. Watch for Sniper tracer lasers. Locate their origin, transform into jet mode, and take out the Snipers first. Having gained the

higher ground, you should have good cover to clear out the rest of the room. To take out the giant Decepticon Tank in the middle of the room, concentrate on damaging one area, such as the chest, to remove armor. Then, focus on shooting the exposed, glowing weak spot. You may also want to try lobbing grenades down from the upper ledges.

OVERSHIELD

As you leave the elevator (28) and enter the room, turn around to look up and to the elevator's left. You can find an Overshield on the highest ledge, just to the left above the elevator.

ENERGON SHARD CONTAINER

Flying directly over the enormous Decepticon's head, you can see two ledges along the far wall (29). Look for the Energon shard containers on these ledges' far left sides.

STAGE 3

Reinforcements arrive through a door across from the elevator. Cut them down and exit through the door (29).

STAGE 4

The station is now in full meltdown mode, and most of the Decepticons are doing what they can to escape the chaos. Follow the hallway until you reach a room (30) where you can see a

smaller area filling with coolant and Decepticons fleeing along the Dark Energon beam to the right. Two Decepticons attack you here.

STAGE 5

Keep moving through the exploding station. Fly down a long hallway until you reach a room (31) at a dead-end. Take out the defending Decepticons and the reinforcements that come through the side doors.

SECTION 6 — THE NERVE CENTER

STAGE 1

Decepticons defend two switches (33) in the back of the room (32). Rush the room and wax the Decepticons. Decepticons manning the two turrets in the room's center are your first priority.

OVERSHIELD

To find an Overshield, fly above the large beam that runs the length of the room's center. Look near the ceiling, above the beam.

AUTOBOT COLLECTIBLE #18

A glowing Decepticon symbol is also above the large central beam. Shoot it to claim this Autobot Collectible.

ENERGON SHARD CONTAINER

Fly to the back of the room, to the large window that looks out into space. Find the two Energon shard containers: one on the window's right side and one on its left.

STAGE 2

Activate the two switches ㉝ in the back of the room. The large, rotating Pulse Regulator opens to expose its core. Note the two regenerating Energon Cubes near the switches. Also, a number of power-ups are near the back window that looks out into space. Restock

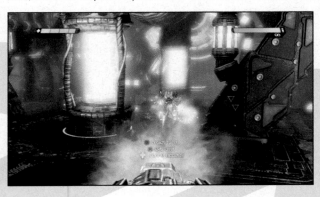

on weapons and ammo. Before you shoot the exposed Pulse Regulator, consider detaching the turrets and equipping them as weapons.

Return to the Pulse Regulator and shoot the three containment bands. The final battle for the relay station

begins as Decepticons rush the room. Watch out for Snipers that occasionally appear on the upper platforms. Also, try to keep the Decepticons from using the turrets in the room's center. Turn the turrets back on them.

The relay station finally overheats, and explosions rock the Nerve Center. The Autobots narrowly escape through the window ㉞.

SECTION ⑦ APPROACHING TRYPTICON

OBJECTIVE: ENTER THE ORBITAL GUN

STAGE 1

Fly forward ㉟, avoiding the projectiles from the spiky space mines. Shooting the mines' red spots destroys them.

STAGE 2

You soon reach an old piece of the scientist station ㊱ that was used to help create Megatron's space gun. A large barrier blocks your path, and numerous enemies camp here. Hang back and take out the Decepticon Jet Soldiers first. Then focus on the three enemies manning the Nucleon Shock Cannons. Above

all, keep moving—the Cannon projectiles are slow and easy to spot, but a few blasts easily knock you out of the sky.

When you clear the initial enemies, an elevator rises, revealing a switch. However, as the elevator door opens, Cloakers stream out and

attack. Destroy the Cloakers with your jet rockets, or land and use detached turrets. Enter the glowing, spherical elevator room and use the switch inside. The elevator transforms, and you rise into the air to see the barrier transform and open.

Restock on weapons. Then fly through the transformed barrier and finally up into the space gun ㊲ that has been attacking the Autobot fleet.

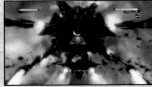

OVERSHIELD

As you enter this area ㊱, fly straight past the first turret and over the bubble-like room on the scientist station's floor. You can see an Overshield on the floor's far edge. It's directly between the spherical room and the back barrier.

ENERGON SHARD CONTAINER

As you enter ㊱, fly past the first turret. Land in front of the glowing, spherical structure in the middle of the floor. The container is to the right, where large cables meet the spherical building.

ENERGON SHARD CONTAINER

You can also find an Energon shard container near the scientist station's back edge, close to the back wall barrier. It's tucked behind a pillar's broken base directly in front of the Overshield.

ENERGON SHARD CONTAINER

An Energon shard container is on the floor under the large ledge on which the turrets rest. Look directly between the two turrets, along the back wall.

AUTOBOT COLLECTIBLE #19

Before you fly through the open barrier, look to its left for a small, lone section of station. The glowing Decepticon symbol is on the lower floor section. Shoot it to claim it.

SECTION 8 — **DECEPTICON DESTROYERS**

OBJECTIVE: DISABLE TRYPTICON

STAGE 1

You encounter stiff resistance from Decepticon defenders inside the space gun ㊳. When you engage the two enormous Decepticon Tanks, fly to the left or right to find

small side rooms ㊴ that provide cover. Take out the Snipers in these upper rooms, and then carefully engage the Decepticons. Focus on the Decepticon Jet Soldiers as you avoid the Tank fire. Be wary of the Titans that march next to each Tank. If you can destroy them and pick up their Ion Displacers, you can use them to great effect against the Tanks.

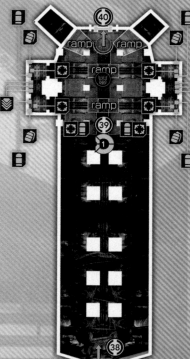

When only the Tanks remain, shoot the red spots on their backs to convert them to robot form. Then concentrate on one area of the chest to penetrate their protective armor and expose a glowing weak spot. When you defeat all the Decepticons, Trypticon laughs off the Autobots, inviting them deeper into the base. Enter the next tunnel ㊵ in the back of the room.

AUTOBOT COLLECTIBLE #20

Fly straight down the middle of the room on your way into this area ㊴. Then fly down into the hallways that run under the Tanks to see a glowing Decepticon symbol. Shoot it.

OVERSHIELD

Two Overshields are directly below the rooms in the fight area's upper left and right. The doors to these areas are on the same vertical level as the Tanks. You have to hop over a small gap to reach them.

ENERGON SHARD CONTAINER

Four Energon shard containers are in the hallways that run under the main floor. Look for the two bridges that cross over the room's center. Fly under a bridge, land, and look on the floor to the left and right. The containers are a short distance away.

STAGE 1

Carefully time your boost to fly forward through the first masher ④① without being crushed. As you turn the next corner, avoid flying too close to the creatures crawling along the floor, or you can be temporarily disabled. It's better to clear the way first with rockets or machinegun fire. Pass two more mashers ④② and then dodge your way up a long, white hallway ④③ that contains moving lasers. Barrel rolling at the last minute can save you from getting sliced by the lasers.

STAGE 2

You've reached Trypticon's Conversion Cog ④④. Turrets and an armored shell protect it. Hang back and barrel roll to dodge the rockets. Use your jet rocket lock-on to take out the turrets ④⑤. As you destroy the turrets, the armor should peel away to expose the Cog. Shooting the exposed, glowing cog starts Trypticon's transformation. To avoid being crushed, boost and fly hard toward the exit ④⑥.

The Autobots fly outside Trypticon as he changes form, and they eventually come face-to-face with his original form.

SECTION 10 A TITAN FALLS

OBJECTIVE: **DESTROY TRYPTICON'S JETPACK**

STAGE 1

Shoot Trypticon's jetpack when his back is toward you. Damaging it causes Trypticon to spin toward you in a rage and unleash attacks. Barrel roll and fly hard to the left and right to avoid vertical laser attacks and rockets. Keep shooting at the jetpack until Trypticon falls out of control to the planet surface.

CONCLUSION

With his jetpack destroyed, Trypticon falls out of control and on fire toward Cybertron. Optimus Prime radios to inform the Autobot flyers that he's monitoring Trypticon's fall and will take it from there.

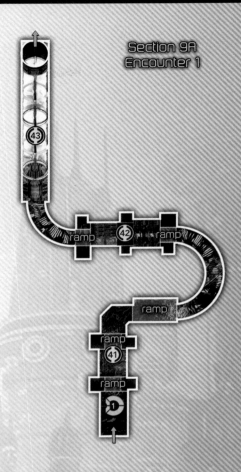

Section 9A
Encounter 1

Section 9B
Encounter 2

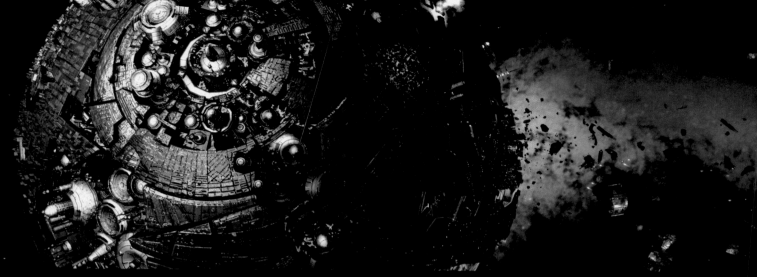

ONE SHALL STAND...

The orbital cannon is offline, but it has revealed its true form to be none other than a savage monster named Trypticon. It races to the planet's surface like a meteor, hungry to enact revenge on the Autobots.

AVAILABLE CHARACTERS

OPTIMUS

Optimus starts with the Warcry Resource Ability, which helps boost the Autobots' damage and armor. This is very useful in the battle's final stage. Optimus can also use the Truck Ram ability in vehicle form. This can help Optimus get from one side of the arena to the other to avoid the large tail attacks.

BUMBLEBEE

Bumblebee's car-mounted machineguns are very effective for destroying the liquid Energon canisters. Bumblebee can also use his car form to Dash or jump-roll to avoid Trypticon's attacks. Bumblebee also has the Shockwave Resource Ability, which is useful against the Spiderbots in the final stage.

IRONHIDE

Ironhide has the Whirlwind Resource Ability, which can destroy multiple Spiderbots simultaneously. Ironhide can also use the Truck Ram ability in vehicle form. This can help Ironhide get from one side of the arena to the other to avoid the large tail attacks.

CO-OP TIPS

Players should try to split up when Trypticon uses his Gravity Smash and Dark Energon Scorpion Strike attacks. Trypticon can target only one player in one part of the arena at a time. This reduces the chances of everyone taking damage from the attack.

When you find the secret cache at the beginning of the level, have one player take the Energon Heal Grenades, while a different character takes the Energon Repair Ray. That way, if a player gets downed during the fight, another teammate will have healing equipment to try to revive that player. If one player has all of the healing equipment and gets downed, he or she can't do any good.

During the battle's final stage, Spiderbots drop the only available Energon shards. Optimus' Warcry ability is incredibly useful to all three Autobots. So, players should try to let Optimus pick up as many of the Energon shards as possible to refill his Resource Ability gauge.

INTRODUCTION

Optimus and the Autobots race through the devastated streets of Iacon. Off in the distance, they see a huge, fiery ball that looks like a meteor crashing into the heart of the city. As Autobot citizens try to avoid the destruction near the crash site, Silverbolt transmits information to assist Optimus with his battle plan against Trypticon.

SECTION 1 DOWN BUT NOT DESTROYED

OBJECTIVE: INSPECT THE CRASH SITE

STAGE 1

You start in the street ①. Signs of destruction are all around you as Autobots move to evacuate the area. It's up to you to check out the area where Trypticon crashed.

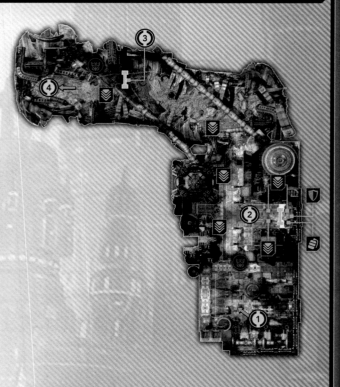

AUTOBOT COLLECTIBLE #21

You can find the first Decepticon symbol in the streets near the beginning of the level. You see the Autobot drop ship just about to take off. Along this path, a street sign hangs from an overhead support post. The symbol is on the back of the sign, so you have to pass the sign and turn around to see it.

STAGE 2

From the drop ship area, look down the street to the right to see Ratchet. If you walk up to him, he approaches an access terminal and opens a nearby door ②. A cache of power-ups including Energon Grenades, an Overshield, and the Energon Repair Ray is behind this door.

OBJECTIVE:

FIND A WAY THROUGH DEBRIS BLOCKING PATH

STAGE 3

Leaving the streets of Iacon, you enter the devastated impact area. You reach what seems to be a dead end ③. A large pile of rubble blocks the way to the crash site. A large Energon battery lies in a pool of liquid Energon. If you shoot this canister, it becomes unstable and destroys the barrier behind it, allowing you to continue to the crash site.

AUTOBOT COLLECTIBLE #22

You can find the next Decepticon symbol in the impact area. Immediately after you destroy the leaking Energon container ③, a Decepticon symbol is on a wall to the right as you pass through the opening in the rubble pile.

ENERGON SHARD CONTAINER

An Energon shard container is located on some destroyed steps near the opening in the rubble pile.

OBJECTIVE:

INSPECT THE CRASH SITE
STAGE 4

Past the pile of rubble, you come to a dead end ④ with some wounded Autobots. Simply walk forward, and Trypticon reveals himself by spiking his tail up through the street, destroying the group of wounded Autobots.

Trypticon's Tail

SECTION ② THE THREAT EMERGES

OBJECTIVE:

DESTROY TRYPTICON'S SHOULDER-MOUNTED CANNONS
STAGE 1

The Autobots fall into an arena-like area ⑤ with the immense and menacing Trypticon looming over them. The battle begins when Trypticon finishes talking to the Autobots. All three playable characters have the ability to dash. Use this ability as often as you can to evade Trypticon's attacks. In this first phase, Trypticon alternates between two big attacks.

REVERSE POLARITY "SPLITTER" CANNONS

Trypticon's two shoulder-mounted cannons fire huge, unstable energy particles at you. Each cannon fires two projectiles that split and lock onto you. Using the dash ability or double-jumping are effective ways to evade this attack. You can also transform into vehicle mode and drive around to avoid taking damage.

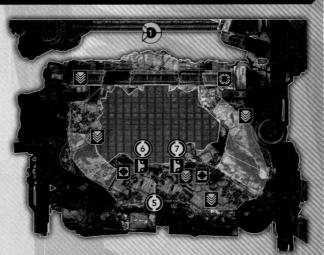

HEAVY FUSION MOUTH MORTAR

Using the same technology as Megatron's Fusion Cannon, Trypticon can spit enormous balls of fusion energy at you. These projectiles don't move very fast, so you can easily dodge them by jumping and dashing.

OBJECTIVE:

SHOOT ENERGON BATTERIES TO OVERLOAD SHOULDER CANNONS

Trypticon is nearly invincible and cannot be damaged directly by any weapon. Instead, you must use the environment to deal with Trypticon's shoulder cannons. After the dialogue between Trypticon and the Autobots finishes, a switch becomes available that controls the left Energon canister relocation conveyor. When the conveyor starts moving, Energon canisters slowly pass by Trypticon's shoulder cannon. Using the Neutron Assault Rifle, Null Ray, or Photon Burst Rifle, you can damage the canisters, causing them to destabilize and explode. It takes four Energon explosions to destroy one of Trypticon's shoulder cannons. Once you demolish the left one, activate the switch that controls the conveyor on the right, and repeat the sequence.

AUTOBOT COLLECTIBLE #23

Find the Decepticon symbol behind a rubble pile, under the catwalk across the front of this arena. It's at ground level and is easy to damage with weapon or melee attacks. You have to turn your back to Trypticon in order to see this symbol.

AUTOBOT COLLECTIBLE #24

You can find the next Decepticon symbol on this same level at the back of the arena. Locate the small alcove with a Plasma Cannon power-up. The symbol hangs on the wall in the alcove to the left behind the rubble.

ENERGON SHARD CONTAINER

An Energon shard container is on the catwalk's right side, up at the front of the arena.

OBJECTIVE: DAMAGE TRYPTICON'S CHEST COILS

After you obliterate both shoulder cannons, the Autobot jets from the previous chapter arrive to help Optimus Prime and the others. Trypticon knocks them out for the rest of the fight, but not before Air Raid drops one Overshield at the front of the arena. After Trypticon deals with the Autobot air support team, he destroys the rest of the catwalk at the front of the arena. The battle continues. In this second phase, Trypticon introduces two new attacks.

HEAVY FUSION MOUTH MORTAR FRENZY

Trypticon now increases his Heavy Fusion Mouth Mortar attack's rate of fire. Each time Trypticon uses this attack, two chest-mounted coils begin to overheat, and Trypticon opens the shields to cool them. These two glowing red chest coils are his only vulnerabilities during this part of the fight. When you destroy one of them, the remaining shield automatically closes to protect the other chest coil. You must wait until the next time the attack occurs to damage the other coil.

GRAVITY SMASH

In addition to Trypticon's Mortar attack, he periodically roars and charges an attack with his tail. This causes small pieces of debris to float around you, and the air changes as if a storm is about to hit. When the attack is fully charged, Trypticon smashes his tail down onto one side of the arena. You can avoid this attack only by being on the arena's opposite side.

Once you destroy both chest coils, Trypticon spins around, swinging his tail down to smash the platform on which you stand. As you fall to a lower level, Trypticon chases you and changes form.

OVERSHIELD

Just after the Autobot air support sequence, look at the floor in front of where you regain control. An Overshield power-up is there.

OBJECTIVE: **DESTROY TRYPTICON'S POWER SOURCE**

STAGE 1

The battle's second stage begins with Trypticon in a crouching, scorpion-like form ⑧. After another exchange of dialogue between him and the Autobots, Trypticon attacks with completely new techniques.

AERIAL DISPERSION GRENADES

Trypticon fires a barrage of homing grenades into the air. They split apart and track multiple targets. The launchers for these grenades are located on Trypticon's back. You can evade the grenades by using the dash ability with any of the three characters, or by changing into vehicle form and driving in any direction. Double-jumping and strafing to the side also reduces the damage you take from these grenades to some degree.

RAPID-FIRE BLASTER

When Trypticon changes into his scorpion form, a cannon transforms out from the top of his nose. This cannon fires a stream of fast-moving projectiles. They do not possess a huge splash damage radius, so you can strafe and jump to the left or right to evade this attack. Transforming and driving in vehicle form or using the dash ability also helps you avoid this attack.

DARK ENERGON SCORPION STRIKE

As he prepares this attack, Trypticon raises his tail behind him in the shape of a scorpion's. Sentry turrets that fire homing missiles line both sides of Trypticon's tail; they attack whenever he raises his tail to charge his scorpion strike. When the attack is fully charged, Trypticon's tail aims at a target to the arena's right, left, or center. Again, small pieces of debris float around you.

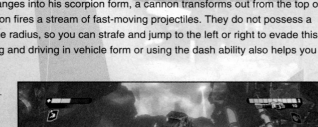

When Trypticon's tail strikes the ground, scattered groups of large corruption spikes grow around the arena. You have a short window of time to destroy the corruption spikes

before they explode and spawn Spiderbots. The Spiderbots attack the nearest Autobot. Trypticon stops to laugh at the Autobots and watch as the Spiderbots chase them around the arena. When a Spiderbot is killed, it drops Energon shards, which fills the character's Resource Ability gauge. This can be very useful.

In the midst of Trypticon's attacks, the Autobots find they're having trouble damaging him. Ironhide scans Trypticon's exterior, and he identifies external power cores mounted on Trypticon's back. Once Ironhide finds this weakness, the dorsal power cores begin to glow red one by one as they are destroyed.

After you destroy all three power cores, Trypticon's defense systems begin to fail. He falls backward and catches himself with one hand. After a short line of dialogue, he falls off the platform's edge, into the abyss below.

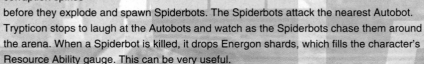

AUTOBOT COLLECTIBLE #25

You can find the final Decepticon symbol in a small crack in the wall behind a burning debris pile. This is located on the arena's lowest level, over to the left from where you start the fight's second stage. An ammo power-up and an X-12 Scrapmaker weapon lie near the symbol.

"FIRST WE CRACK THE SHELL..." ACHIEVEMENT/TROPHY

After you defeat Trypticon, he tries one last time to kill the Autobots by slashing with his claw into the arena. If you're under his claw as he does this, you'll be downed automatically. However, you won't die, and Trypticon falls off the platform. To be under the claw, move up to the front of the arena, between the two health power-ups. Do this correctly to receive the special "First We Crack the Shell..." Achievement/Trophy.

CONCLUSION

Trypticon is defeated, but the victory is bittersweet. Optimus Prime and the others watch as their brothers evacuate the planet in the galactic transports.

MULTIPLAYER

Transformers: War for Cybertron features an exciting variety of competitive multiplayer modes for individuals and teams alike. With support for up to ten players in a game, there are many reasons to keep playing.

COOPERATIVE CAMPAIGN

Up to three players can play Campaign mode cooperatively through Xbox LIVE. The game host has the option to enable competitive scoring—this adds a whole new dimension to cooperative play, as two or three players compete for points as they play through the campaign level.

CO-OP CAMPAIGN SCORING

DEFEATING ENEMIES

Each enemy you defeat adds points to your score. Here's a breakdown of what each enemy kill is worth:

ENEMIES	POINTS
Spiderbot	5
Brute	100
Titan	100
Cloaker	75
Car Soldier	25
Jet Soldier	50
Rocketeer	25
Rocket Soldier	25
Sniper	50
Shotgunner	75
Sentry	25
Tank	200

You can also accrue special score bonuses by taking out enemies in rapid succession.

MULTIKILL	POINTS
2 Multikill	50
3 Multikill	100
4 Multikill	200

SCORE MULTIPLIERS

As you take out enemies quicker and in more creative ways, your score multiplier increases to as much as 5x. As long as your score multiplier is active, any points you acquire filter through this multiplier, allowing you to boost your score at an impressive rate. Note that your score multiplier evaporates over time when you cease accruing points, so the longer you stay in combat the longer your multiplier remains active.

ACTION	MULTIPLIER
Headshot Multiplier	1.5x
Melee Kill Multiplier	1.25x
Assist Kill Multiplier	.75x

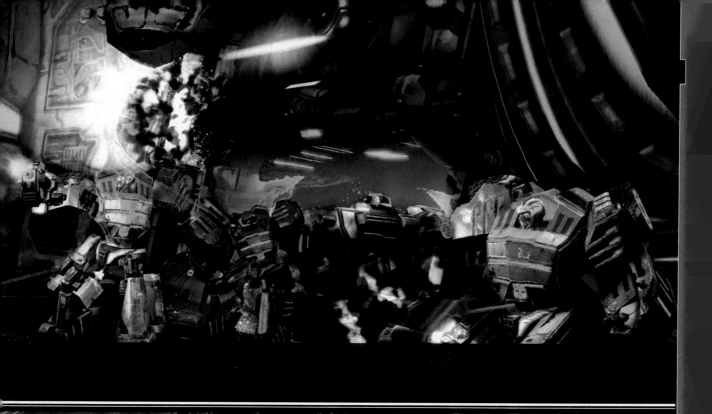

ADDITIONAL SCORING INFO

If you're downed, 100 points are deducted from your total score. If you are completely defeated, you lose 250 points. Reviving a downed teammate earns you 15 points. During most boss fights, all players in co-op earn points as they progress through the fight. However, players that inflict the most damage to the boss's vulnerable spots receive many more points. The moral of the story: contribute to the team and do your part during boss battles.

Players receive additional points for destroying objects in the environment, from tiny loot crates to giant stalactites. When you play co-op with scoring enabled, watch for these objects in order to squeeze a few extra points out of the game. Blasting destructibles is a great way to maintain your score multiplier between firefights.

GAME TYPES

TEAM DEATHMATCH

Autobots vs. Decepticons. Work with your teammates to eliminate the opposing faction's competitors.

DEATHMATCH

A free-for-all gladiatorial battle in which you must eliminate all other combatants until one warrior reaches the Goal Score to win.

CODE OF POWER

In this game mode, each faction must grab the opposing faction's Code of Power and bring it back to its base to score a point. You have a limited amount of time to retrieve the Code and return it to your base. Each team takes turns assaulting and defending, swapping roles each round.

COUNTDOWN TO EXTINCTION

Your team must work together to take the neutral bomb and plant it at the opposing team's base. But be careful; the enemy team can defuse the bomb and retaliate. Shifting offensive and defensive roles makes Countdown to Extinction the most teamwork-intensive of all game modes.

POWER STRUGGLE

In this mode, a Power Node moves randomly to different locations on the map. Your team must work together to hold the Node and gain points, defeating any enemies that try to take the Power Node from you.

CONQUEST

Similar to Power Struggle, the goal in Conquest is to acquire points for your team by holding Power Nodes. However, in Conquest, multiple fixed Power Nodes are scattered across the map.

SCOUT

WEAPONS

- Plasma Cannon
- Energon Battle Pistol
- Null Ray
- Scatter Blaster
- EMP Grenades

ABILITIES

- Cloak
- Mark Target
- Decoy Trap
- Dash

VEHICLE FORM

Car

KILLSTREAKS

3 KILLS	5 KILLS	7 KILLS
Orbital Beacon	Energon Recharger	Orbital Beacon 2.0

The Scout is the stealth warrior. It uses hit-and-run tactics to deliver sudden damage and circumvent enemy defenses.

ENERGON LEVEL:	4
MELEE WEAPON:	Energon Sword

KILLSTREAKS

	NO. OF KILLS	REWARD	DESCRIPTION
	3 KILLS	Orbital Beacon	Displays enemies' location
	5 KILLS	Energon Recharger	Health continually regenerates for a brief time
	7 KILLS	Orbital Beacon 2.0	Causes a level-wide EMP Blast and tags all enemies with Mark Target

ABILITIES

CLOAKING

Cloaking can be very helpful on offense or defense. If you're attacking an entrenched enemy position, use Cloak to get next to enemies before they know you're there. If you're taking hits and need to get away, or just want to ambush pursuing enemies, draw the enemy toward you, and then hide behind cover and Cloak. When the enemies approach, get close to them, and unleash a melee attack or shotgun blast to dispatch them quickly.

DASH

You can use the Dash ability many different ways. Use it to dodge incoming enemy fire, or combine Dash with double-jumping to traverse long distances and access hard-to-reach places.

DECOY TRAP (UNLOCKS AT LEVEL 2)

The Decoy Trap ability is very handy as a defensive measure. Try placing these traps in doorways to stun players who don't watch where they're going. If you're being chased, just set a trap, preferably around a corner or near another power-up. When an enemy hits the trap, he or she is stunned and extremely vulnerable to attack. Simply walk up to your stunned opponent and pull the trigger. However, be warned that your decoy traps can be spotted and destroyed.

MARK TARGET (UNLOCKS AT LEVEL 5)

Mark Target identifies targets for both you and your teammates. While enemies are marked, they also receive increased damage and your teammates can see them through walls—a useful marking device is one placed on an enemy carrier.

SURPRISE ATTACK	Cause extra damage after coming out of Cloak	1
BACKSTAB	Cause extra melee damage from behind	1
VENDETTA	Increase time Mark Target stays on victim	7
SHOCK TREATMENT	Decoy causes damage over time to victims	10
TARGETING CHIP	Do more damage with Mark Target	17
STINGER	Increase time enemy is stunned from Trap	23

DEFENSIVE SKILLS TIER 2	DESCRIPTION	LEVEL
HEALTH MATRIX	For every kill, the Scout gets health back	3
GHOST	Time added to Cloak	3
LEG SERVOS	Faster foot speed	8
DIMENSIONAL STEP	Armor/No Teleport FX tell when in or out of Cloak	13
FUEL EFFICIENCY	Increase distance of Dash	19
EMP BLINDERS	Flash-bang doesn't blind you	24

GENERAL SKILLS TIER 3	DESCRIPTION	LEVEL
WEAPON STABILIZER	Reduce recoil for all weapons	6
EMP INTENSIFIER	Increase Radius of flash-bang	6
BLASTER AMPLIFIER	Two more clips of reserve ammo added	9
FIRST AID	Time decreased for health regeneration	15
EXPLOSIVE CAPACITOR	Carry 1 extra flash-bang	21
RAPID RECHARGE	Time between ability use is decreased	25

SCOUT TIPS

For beginners, the Scout excels in certain game modes. But depending on the game mode, some may find it difficult to use the Scout effectively. With enough practice, you can do very well in any mode. The following tips should help through the rough times:

CODE OF POWER & COUNTDOWN TO EXTINCTION (A.K.A. CTF & BOMBRUN)

The Scout is great for running the flag. The Scout usually has a hard time as a carrier because of its low health compared to the Leader and Soldier. The Scout must rely on quickly navigating the map while the other classes lend support. The Scout is very good for escorting a carrier. He or she can deploy a quick EMP Grenade to blind opponents trailing the carrier. While they're blinded, the Scout can mop up a few of them and cloak into the darkness while your carrier gets away.

SCOUT IN CONQUEST

The Scout does very well as a defensive class for this game type. The Scout relies on cloak to surprise enemies that try to take over your team's captured node. Let the heavier classes try to gain control of a node, while you provide backup from the outside. Continue providing backup until it's under control.

POWER STRUGGLE

This game mode can be difficult for apprehensive or non-aggressive players. For beginners, try using ranged weapons to support your teammates trying to control the struggle zone. Firing from the outside can be dangerous, so be aware of your surroundings.

SCIENTIST

WEAPONS

- Energon Repair Ray
- Photon Burst Rifle
- EMP Shotgun
- Neutron Repeater
- Energon Grenades

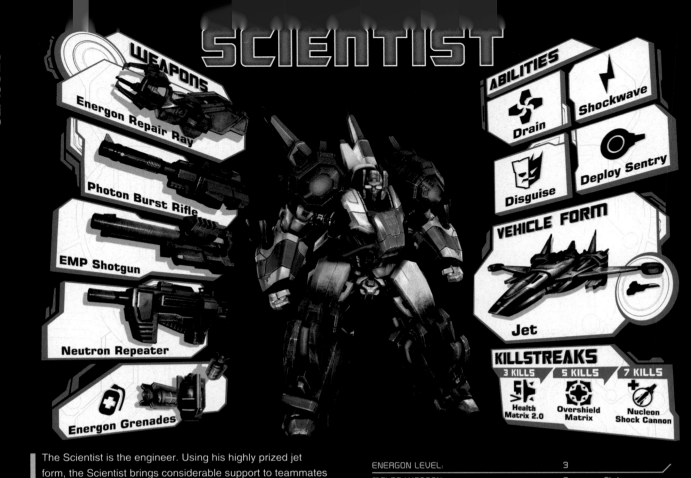

ABILITIES

- Drain
- Shockwave
- Disguise
- Deploy Sentry

VEHICLE FORM

Jet

KILLSTREAKS

3 KILLS	5 KILLS	7 KILLS
Health Matrix 2.0	Overshield Matrix	Nucleon Shock Cannon

The Scientist is the engineer. Using his highly prized jet form, the Scientist brings considerable support to teammates anywhere on the battlefield.

ENERGON LEVEL:	3
MELEE WEAPON:	Energon Club

KILLSTREAKS

NO. OF KILLS	REWARD	DESCRIPTION
3 KILLS	Health Matrix 2.0	Teammates receive health for every kill
5 KILLS	Overshield Matrix	Teammates receive Overshields
7 KILLS	Nucleon Shock Cannon	Spawn a useable detached rocket turret

ABILITIES

SHOCKWAVE

This ability is very useful for pushing enemies away from your teammates. It also deals a small amount of damage to victims of this blast. Furthermore, it can knock enemies off some maps to their deaths.

SPAWN SENTRY

Sentries can be very helpful for offensive and defensive support. Plant sentries up above doorways or in windows to assist in taking down enemies. Your Energon Repair Ray can heal sentries. At later levels, you can upgrade the sentry to provide additional offensive support that includes rockets or even the ability to heal your teammates. Sentries can even see cloaked enemies, so you can also use them as a defensive tactic. A Scout's EMP Grenade can temporarily disable Sentries.

DRAIN (UNLOCKS AT LEVEL 2)

The ability to drain multiple enemies of their health while replenishing your own can prove very handy in sticky situations. This is especially true when you're face-to-face with a heavy class, like a Soldier. Drain and shoot it at the same time to quickly end the aggression.

DISGUISE (UNLOCKS AT LEVEL 5)

Disguising yourself as an enemy Scientist can be very handy for reconnaissance or for sabotaging enemy fortifications. Infiltrate the enemy's base and, for a discourteous surprise, plant a turret while you shoot them. But be careful—your chassis will give you away. You may still represent the opposing faction, but the shape of your own faction's chassis is a dead giveaway to a keen enemy's eye.

RANGE FINDER	Increase range of Energon Repair Ray	1
ENERGON STORM	Increase damage Shockwave deals	1
ROCKET SENTRY	Spawn Rocket Sentry	7
REPAIR SENTRY	Spawn Repair Sentry	10
FRIENDLY FIRE	Damage buff when coming out of Disguise	17
REPULSION AMPLIFIER	Increase radius of Shockwave	23
DEFENSIVE SKILLS TIER 2	**DESCRIPTION**	**LEVEL**
BATTLE MEDIC	Take reduced damage while healing team	3
SENTRY ARMOR	Increase the health of the sentry	3
MASTER OF DISGUISE	Disguise persists even when shot	8
ENERGON OPTIMIZATION	Increase heal rate of Heal Ray	13
LEECH	Increase rate of health regained from Drain	19
SENTRY POWER CORE	Increase power of Sentry	24
GENERAL SKILLS TIER 3	**DESCRIPTION**	**LEVEL**
WEAPON STABILIZER	Reduce recoil for all weapons	6
SANCTUARY	Healing grenade bubble stays out longer	6
BLASTER AMPLIFIER	2 more clips of reserve ammo added	9
FIRST AID	Time decreased for health regen	15
EXPLOSIVE CAPACITOR	Carry 1 Extra healing grenade	21
RAPID RECHARGE	Time between ability use decreased	25

SCIENTIST TIPS

The Scientist is a great defensive class that offers offensive support via Drain and Sentries. This is the only class that heals itself with its heal grenades—it also inherently has the lowest health. Take advantage of your jet form to navigate the map quickly and reach objective points quicker than most classes. You can also use your jet form to exploit a map's verticality by providing air support.

CODE OF POWER & COUNTDOWN TO EXTINCTION (A.K.A. CTF & BOMB RUN)

The Scientist isn't the best carrier, but he's excellent at supporting your team's carrier. Heal your carrier as needed, and drop Heal Grenades to assist your team's escorts. A well-placed Sentry can impede tracking enemies. Switch to jet form to get in front of an enemy carrier. Then use Shockwave to knock him back, away from his goal.

CONQUEST & POWER STRUGGLE

Spawn Sentry can fortify nodes your team already controls. Drain or Shockwave help when enemies try to take your node. Knock them back with Shockwave to clear their capture timer, giving teammates time to arrive. Initiate Disguise, then sneak into an enemy-controlled node to halt the flow of points and contest the node.

DEATHMATCH & TEAM DEATHMATCH

In Team DM, pair with an ally to heal him as needed. With enough XP, the Scientist can be a powerful solo character. Spawn Sentry upgraded to a rocket turret increases its damage, practically forcing enemies to face two opponents when they encounter you. Drain damages multiple enemies and replenishes your own health. You can boost Drain at higher levels, increasing the health you gain. Airborne maneuverability combined with the ability to heal oneself and inflict major damage can make the Scientist a formidable opponent even in normal DM games.

LEADER

WEAPONS

Fusion Cannon

Magma Frag Launcher

Ion Blaster

Energon Battle Pistol

Thermo Mines

ABILITIES

Warcry

Barrier

Moleculon Bomb

Transform Disruptor

VEHICLE FORM

Truck

KILLSTREAKS

3 KILLS	5 KILLS	7 KILLS
Intercooler	Poke v2.0	Thermo Mine Re-Spawner

The Leader is the protector of allied troops. Its role is to move the lines of the battlefield by boosting the teammates' strength and defense.

ENERGON LEVEL:	5
MELEE WEAPON:	Energon Axe

KILLSTREAKS

	NO. OF KILLS	REWARD	DESCRIPTION
	3 KILLS	Intercooler	Greatly decreases the cooldown time for ability use
	5 KILLS	P.o.K.E. 2.0	Deadly melee attack that causes enemies to explode
	7 KILLS	Thermo Mine Respawner	Spawn a trail of thermo mines

ABILITIES

WARCRY

Warcry is an area-of-effect (AOE) buff, which can help your team tremendously when you charge into an enemy base. It grants everyone within the AOE radius increased damage output and increased armor.

BARRIER

A shield that blocks most incoming enemy fire—who doesn't want that? If you're stuck between a rock and hard place and need somewhere to recover, just use this ability to gain a short reprieve before you rejoin the fray. Just be quick, as the enemy can continue to shoot it, decreasing its duration. And be warned that enemies can walk through it.

MOLECULON BOMB (UNLOCKS AT LEVEL 2)

Having the power to slow your enemies and (at higher levels) cause damage to them can prove invaluable. Anyone on your team can push around this bomb to place it in just the right position. Be quick, as it has a timer and self-detonates, damaging anyone within the blast radius.

DISRUPTION (UNLOCKS AT LEVEL 5)

This forces your opponent to assume the robot or vehicle mode opposite the one he or she is using prior to the attack's effect. So, if the attack strikes a vehicle, it forces the target into robot form, and vice versa. Forcing your opponent to change his or her mindset is one of the best ways to disrupt his or her game plan.

	RALLY	Increase radius of Warcry	1
	ROLL OUT	Increase Ram damage	1
	DUCK AND COVER	Add DOT to Moleculon Bomb	7
	NO SURRENDER	Increase the duration of Warcry	10
	CORRODE	DOT added to Disruption	17
	RAGE	Damage and armor increase for Warcry	23

	DEFENSIVE SKILLS TIER 2	DESCRIPTION	LEVEL
	FLAK ARMOR	Reduced damage from explosions	3
	EMPOWERED SHIELD	Increase health of Barrier	3
	MARTYRDOM	Drop a K-Mine of Death	8
	CHAOS MASTER	Increase time of T-Form Disruptor	13
	ION BOOSTER	Speed increase for teammates around Mole Bomb	19
	RESERVE POWER CELLS	Ability to shoot while downed	24

	GENERAL SKILLS TIER 3	DESCRIPTION	LEVEL
	WEAPON STABILIZER	Reduce recoil for all weapons	6
	SEEKER	Increase search radius of K-Mine	6
	BLASTER AMPLIFIER	2 more clips of reserve ammo added	9
	FIRST AID	Time decreased for health regen	15
	EXPLOSIVE CAPACITOR	Carry 1 Extra K-Mine	21
	RAPID RECHARGE	Time between ability use decreased	25

LEADER TIPS

Via its intrinsic abilities, the Leader is great at performing offensive and defensive roles almost simultaneously. Meant to excel at charging at the front lines as well as bringing up the rear, the Leader is a valuable asset to any team regardless of its makeup.

CODE OF POWER & COUNTDOWN TO EXTINCTION (AKA CTF & BOMBRUN)

These game types are perfect for the Leader class, as it can fill both offensive and defensive roles with equal élan. Use your Moleculon Bomb and Disruption to slow your enemies and force them to drop the bomb or flag.

CONQUEST & POWER STRUGGLE

Great for clearing out an occupied zone, the Leader can shine when he or she is properly equipped. Use the Magma Frag Launcher to eliminate multiple foes from a contested area. Set up Thermo Mines to defend a region while you leave to capture another spot. Buff your teammates with Warcry before you enter a skirmish to increase your team's damage output.

SOLDIER

WEAPONS

X12 Scrapmaker

Neutron Repeater

EMP Shotgun

Thermo Rocket Launcher

Flak Grenades

ABILITIES

Hover

Whirlwind

Ammo Beacon

Energon Sling

VEHICLE FORM

Tank

KILLSTREAKS

3 KILLS	5 KILLS	7 KILLS
Ammo Matrix	Electro Magnetic Pulse	Omega Missile

The Soldier is the damage dealer. This class prefers all-out, flak-filled brawls to measured, tactical fights.

ENERGON LEVEL:	8
MELEE WEAPON:	Energon Hammer

KILLSTREAKS

	NO. OF KILLS	REWARD	DESCRIPTION
	3 KILLS	Ammo Matrix	Lock your ammo clip for a short time and refill your team's ammo and grenades
	5 KILLS	Electromagnetic Pulse	Jams enemy team's use of abilities for a brief period
	7 KILLS	Omega Missile	Fires a guided missile capable of mass destruction

ABILITIES

HOVER

With increased damage while hovering, the Soldier can deal a deadly punch to opponents unlucky enough to be on this attack's receiving end. Not only can you use Hover as an offensive measure, but you can also use it to reach places higher than other robot forms can. Double-jumping and then using Hover at your jump's apex jump executes this extreme maneuver.

WHIRLWIND

Unleashing a slew of melee slams to eliminate multiple opponents can be very helpful to your team. Using this ability against a cluster of enemies is also very rewarding.

AMMO BEACON (UNLOCKS AT LEVEL 2)

Ammo Beacon offers defensive support and gives your teammates an offensive boost. This can be fatal to enemies lacking vigilance. Ammo Beacon replenishes your team's ammo supply and bestows increased damage potential. Use Ammo Beacon strategically when no enemies are present, as enemy fire can destroy it.

ENERGON SLING (UNLOCKS AT LEVEL 5)

One of the more powerful abilities in the Soldier's arsenal, the Energon Sling jams your opponent's abilities. This severely cripples your adversary's ability to execute special powers.

	P.O.K.E. ALPHA	Increase damage for Whirlwind	1
	SHARP SHOOTER	Reduce spread for all weapons	1
	DEATH FROM ABOVE	Increase damage of Hover	7
	GRENADE DISPENSER	Refill a grenade with Ammo Beacon	10
	HEAVY WEAPONS	Increased damage with Shotgun, Heavy MG, and Rocket Launcher	17
	PATH BLASTER	Spawn an Ion Displacer Turret with Ammo Beacon	23
	DEFENSIVE SKILLS TIER 2	**DESCRIPTION**	**LEVEL**
	FLAK ARMOR	Reduced explosion damage	3
	FLURRY OF BLOWS	Increase ground speed of Whirlwind	3
	SABOTEUR	Add time to Energon Sling	8
	FLIGHT PACK	Time added to Hover	13
	ENERGON ABSORBERS	Take reduced damage while performing Whirlwind	19
	IMPROVED HEATSINK	All weapons use Fast Reload	24
	GENERAL SKILLS TIER 3	**DESCRIPTION**	**LEVEL**
	WEAPON STABILIZER	Reduce recoil for all weapons	6
	NEMESIS MAKER	Increase damage radius of Flak Grenades	6
	BLASTER AMPLIFIER	2 more clips of reserve ammo added	9
	FIRST AID	Time decreased for health regen	15
	EXPLOSIVE CAPACITOR	Carry 1 extra Flak Grenade	21
	RAPID RECHARGE	Time between ability use decreased	25

SOLDIER TIPS

The primary offensive weapon for both factions, the Soldier has the most health of all. The Soldier can take a beating and still keep fighting. In robot form, its size hinders its movement speed. So, converting to vehicle form can be crucial for traversing areas as quickly as possible—something to consider when you attempt to support your teammates.

CODE OF POWER & COUNTDOWN TO EXTINCTION (AKA CTF & BOMBRUN)

If you're a carrier, these game modes are much harder for the Soldier class. Compared to the other classes, the Soldier has the slowest foot speed. But with the right escorts and support classes, and thanks to high maximum health, the Soldier can last quite some time. Just remember that, while you're carrying, you can use the Flag or Bomb to pack a punch to your opponents.

CONQUEST & POWER STRUGGLE

These game modes are the best fit for the Soldier class. With the ability to enter a zone and clear most of the enemies from it, the Soldier is a crucial class. Hover proves its worth in these matches. Quickly levitate above the ground and, with boosted damage, rain down terror, fully exploiting the Soldier class's ruthless attacks against your foes.

BERTH

This map is set within a small area of Iacon. The bridge is centrally located and contains an Overshield, which either team can attempt to take before the other grabs it. This bridge also offers elevation advantage. However, the bridge camper may also be subject to attack from below and from the sides, leaving him or her little choice but to run. The map's sides provide some small cubbies, which allow you to move around and take cover from incoming fire.

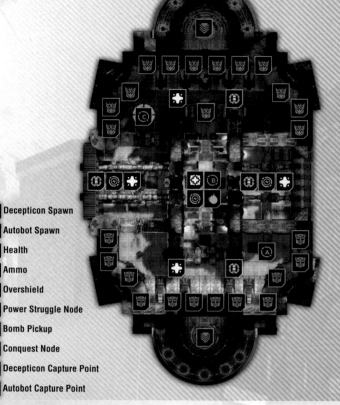

Decepticon Spawn	
Autobot Spawn	
Health	
Ammo	
Overshield	
Power Struggle Node	
Bomb Pickup	
Conquest Node	
Decepticon Capture Point	
Autobot Capture Point	

RUST

Rust and corrosion completely envelope an area that has been abandoned for over a millennia. Decepticons have since moved in, but a sole Autobot base stands defiant, prepared to ward off any Decepticons brave enough to try to take over this lonely area of Cybertron.

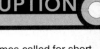

"Seed," as it is sometimes called for short, has seen the beginnings of a Decepticon invasion. A Decepticon War Machine has begun to take over this barren Iacon street.

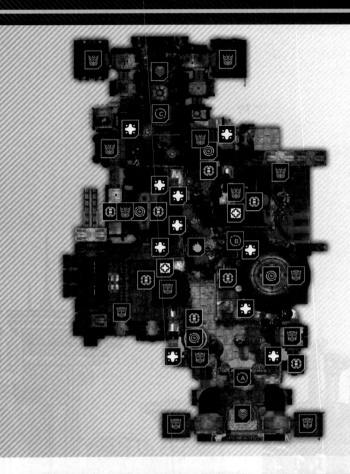

STREET

The aftermath of a Decepticon attack has ravaged this once thriving section of Cybertron. Now, a single Autobot base stands at the front of a newly established Decepticon base.

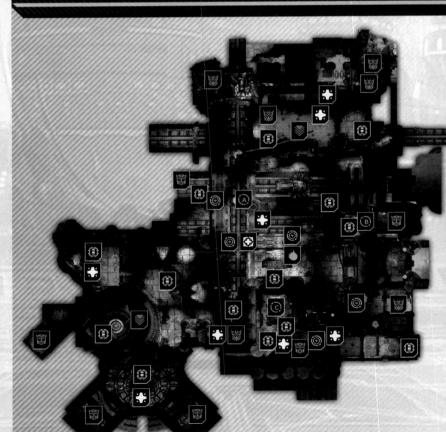

MOLTEN

A barren location of Cybertron is home to this Decepticon fortification. Covered in molten metal and debris, this map has seen the destructive force of war and its disfiguring wake.

- Decepticon Spawn
- Autobot Spawn
- Health
- Ammo
- Overshield
- Power Struggle Node
- Bomb Pickup
- Conquest Node
- Decepticon Capture Point
- Autobot Capture Point

DEBRIS

The floating remnants of an Autobot space station float partially intact in Cybertron's outer reaches. A Decepticon ship has recently crashed here, providing the Decepticons a way to overrun this Autobot-occupied territory and claim it for themselves.

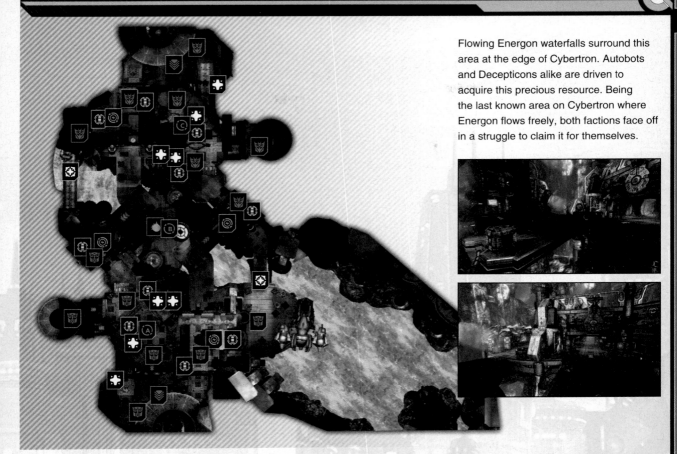

Flowing Energon waterfalls surround this area at the edge of Cybertron. Autobots and Decepticons alike are driven to acquire this precious resource. Being the last known area on Cybertron where Energon flows freely, both factions face off in a struggle to claim it for themselves.

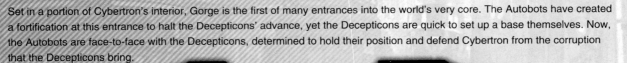

Set in a portion of Cybertron's interior, Gorge is the first of many entrances into the world's very core. The Autobots have created a fortification at this entrance to halt the Decepticons' advance, yet the Decepticons are quick to set up a base themselves. Now, the Autobots are face-to-face with the Decepticons, determined to hold their position and defend Cybertron from the corruption that the Decepticons bring.

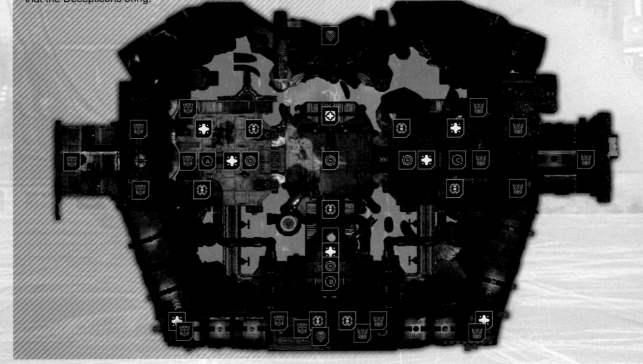

CHALLENGES

Multiplayer challenges offer loads of goals to accomplish during online gameplay. Basic challenges are accessible to all classes, while class-specific challenges emphasize the unique talents and abilities of a given class. You can view completed challenges in the post-game lobby or online at the website.

Basic Challenges

BONUS XP

CHALLENGE	DESCRIPTION	XP REWARD
TRAINEE I	Survive 30 seconds in a multiplayer match without being killed	25
TRAINEE II	Survive 60 seconds in a multiplayer match without being killed	50
TRAINEE III	Survive 90 seconds in a multiplayer match without being killed	100
DARK HORSE I	Kill 5 players who are at a higher level than you are	25
DARK HORSE II	Kill 10 players who are at a higher level than you are	50
DARK HORSE III	Kill 15 players who are at a higher level than you are	100
POWER SURGE I	Use an active ability 5 times	25
POWER SURGE II	Use an active ability 10 times	50
POWER SURGE III	Use an active ability 15 times	100
FIRST BLOOD I	Score the first kill in a multiplayer match 3 times	25
FIRST BLOOD II	Score the first kill in a multiplayer match 5 times	50
FIRST BLOOD III	Score the first kill in a multiplayer match 7 times	100
SACRIFICE I	Be the first one eliminated in a multiplayer match 3 times	25
SACRIFICE II	Be the first one eliminated in a multiplayer match 5 times	50
SACRIFICE III	Be the first one eliminated in a multiplayer match 7 times	100
KILL ASSIST I	Get 5 kill assists during a multiplayer match	25
KILL ASSIST II	Get 10 kill assists during a multiplayer match	50
KILL ASSIST III	Get 15 kill assists during a multiplayer match	100
SPRAY N PRAY I	Destroy 5 opponents without using fine aim	25
SPRAY N PRAY II	Destroy 10 opponents without using fine aim	50
SPRAY N PRAY III	Destroy 15 opponents without using fine aim	100
EAGLE EYE I	Destroy 5 opponents using fine aim	25
EAGLE EYE II	Destroy 10 opponents using fine aim	50
EAGLE EYE III	Destroy 15 opponents using fine aim	100
GEAR HEAD I	Clock 300 seconds in vehicle form	25
GEAR HEAD II	Clock 600 seconds in vehicle form	50
GEAR HEAD III	Clock 900 seconds in vehicle form	100
INITIATION I	Destroy a total of 25 enemies	25
INITIATION II	Destroy a total of 50 enemies	50
INITIATION III	Destroy a total of 75 enemies	100
ROAD KILL I	Destroy 5 enemies while in vehicle form	25
ROAD KILL II	Destroy 10 enemies while in vehicle form	50
ROAD KILL III	Destroy 15 enemies while in vehicle form	100

BASICS

CHARACTERS

WEAPONS

WALKTHROUGH

o1

o2

o3

o4

o5

o6

o7

o8

o9

10

MULTIPLAYER

ACHIEVEMENTS

Game Mode XP Events

CHALLENGE	DESCRIPTION	XP REWARD
CODE OF POWER		
IN THE BAG	Grab the Code of Power and return it to your base	200
THAT'S MINE	Successfully return the Code of Power after an enemy carrier has dropped it	50
DROP IT	Kill the enemy flag carrier	20
COUNTDOWN TO EXTINCTION		
SET US UP THE BOMB	Plant the bomb in the enemy base	50
NICK OF TIME	Defuse a bomb that has been planted in your base	20
DYNAMITE GOES BOOM	Bomb successfully detonates after you plant it	50
LINEBACKER	Kill the enemy bomb carrier	50
POWER STRUGGLE		
IT'S MY ISLAND	Kill an enemy while he/she is contesting a zone	20
TOURIST	You score points in an active power struggle zone	100
PLACES TO GO	You score more than 10 points in an active power struggle zone	200
AND I HELPED	You score more than 20 points in an active power struggle zone	300
SQUATTER	You score more than 30 points in an active power struggle zone	400
QUEEN OF THE HILL	You score more than 40 points in an active power struggle zone	500
KING OF THE HILL	You score more than 50 points in an active power struggle zone	600
CONQUEST		
CONQUISTADOR	Capture a Conquest Point	150
GET OUT OF HERE	Kill an enemy while he/she is trying to take your point	100

Scout Challenges

SCOUT WEAPON CHALLENGES

CHALLENGE	DESCRIPTION	XP REWARD
ENERGON BATTLE PISTOL		
FRONTLINE SCOUT I	As a Scout, eliminate 25 opponents with the Energon Battle Pistol	250
FRONTLINE SCOUT II	As a Scout, eliminate 50 opponents with the Energon Battle Pistol	500
FRONTLINE SCOUT III	As a Scout, eliminate 100 opponents with the Energon Battle Pistol	1000
TAG AND BAG 'EM I	As a Scout, eliminate 25 opponents with the Energon Battle Pistol after marking them	500
TAG AND BAG 'EM II	As a Scout, eliminate 50 opponents with the Energon Battle Pistol after marking them	1000
TAG AND BAG 'EM III	As a Scout, eliminate 100 opponents with the Energon Battle Pistol after marking them	1500
STUN AND GUN I	As a Scout, eliminate 25 opponents with the Energon Battle Pistol while they are stunned by your decoy trap	1000
STUN AND GUN II	As a Scout, eliminate 50 opponents with the Energon Battle Pistol while they are stunned by your decoy trap	1500
STUN AND GUN III	As a Scout, eliminate 100 opponents with the Energon Battle Pistol while they are stunned by your decoy trap	2000
SCATTER BLASTER		
SCOUT RAIDER I	As a Scout, eliminate 25 opponents with the Scatter Blaster	250
SCOUT RAIDER II	As a Scout, eliminate 50 opponents with the Scatter Blaster	500
SCOUT RAIDER III	As a Scout, eliminate 100 opponents with the Scatter Blaster	1000
DIDN'T SEE THAT COMIN'! I	As a Scout, eliminate 10 opponents with a single blast from the Scatter Blaster while coming out of cloak	500
DIDN'T SEE THAT COMIN'! II	As a Scout, eliminate 25 opponents with a single blast from the Scatter Blaster while coming out of cloak	1000
DIDN'T SEE THAT COMIN'! III	As a Scout, eliminate 50 opponents with a single blast from the Scatter Blaster while coming out of cloak	1500
INSTA-GIB I	As a Scout, Destroy 5 opposing Scouts while they are cloaked with a single blast from the Scatter Blaster	1000
INSTA-GIB II	As a Scout, Destroy 10 opposing Scouts while they are cloaked with a single blast from the Scatter Blaster	1500
INSTA-GIB III	As a Scout, Destroy 20 opposing Scouts while they are cloaked with a single blast from the Scatter Blaster	2000
PLASMA CANNON		
HEATMONGER! I	As a Scout, eliminate 25 opponents with the Plasma Cannon	250
HEATMONGER! II	As a Scout, eliminate 50 opponents with the Plasma Cannon	500
HEATMONGER! III	As a Scout, eliminate 100 opponents with the Plasma Cannon	1000
TANK BUSTER I	As a Scout, destroy 10 tanks with the Plasma Cannon	500
TANK BUSTER II	As a Scout, destroy 25 tanks with the Plasma Cannon	1000
TANK BUSTER IIII	As a Scout, destroy 50 tanks with the Plasma Cannon	1500
BUG ZAPPER I	As a Scout, destroy 5 planes with the Plasma Cannon after marking them	1000
BUG ZAPPER II	As a Scout, destroy 10 planes with the plasma Cannon after marking them	1500
BUG ZAPPER III	As a Scout, Destroy 20 planes with the plasma Cannon after marking them	2000
NULL RAY		
NULL RAY MARKSMAN I	As a Scout, eliminate 25 opponents with the Null Ray	250
NULL RAY MARKSMAN II	As a Scout, eliminate 50 opponents with the Null Ray	500
NULL RAY MARKSMAN III	As a Scout, eliminate100 opponents with the Null Ray	1000
NULL RAY EXPERT I	As a Scout, get 25 headshots with the Null Ray	500
NULL RAY EXPERT II	As a Scout, get 50 headshots with the Null Ray	1000
NULL RAY EXPERT III	As a Scout, get 100 headshots with the Null Ray	1500
BIRD HUNTER I	As a Scout, snipe 25 enemy jets out of the air with the Null Ray	1000
BIRD HUNTER II	As a Scout, snipe 50 enemy jets out of the air with the Null Ray	1500
BIRD HUNTER III	As a Scout, snipe 100 enemy jets out of the air with the Null Ray	2000

BASICS
CHARACTERS
WEAPONS
WALKTHROUGH
01
02
03
04
05
06
07
08
09
10

MULTIPLAYER

ACHIEVEMENTS

Scout Class Challenges

CHALLENGE	DESCRIPTION	XP REWARD
SKILLS		
NINJA I	Eliminate 50 opponents while using the Surprise Attack ability	250
NINJA II	Eliminate 125 opponents while using the Surprise Attack ability	500
NINJA III	Eliminate 300 opponents while using the Surprise Attack ability	1000
ASSASSIN I	Deliver the final blow on 50 enemies using the Backstab ability	250
ASSASSIN II	Deliver the final blow on 125 enemies using the Backstab ability	500
ASSASSIN III	Deliver the final blow on 300 enemies using the Backstab ability	1000
LOOK MA, NO WHEELS I	Dash 100,000 meters in multiplayer	100
LOOK MA, NO WHEELS II	Dash 250,000 meters in multiplayer	250
LOOK MA, NO WHEELS III	Dash 500,000 meters in multiplayer	500
HUNTER I	Deliver the final blow on 50 enemies after marking them with the Mark Target skill	250
HUNTER II	Deliver the final blow on 125 enemies after marking them with the Mark Target skill	500
HUNTER III	Deliver the final blow on 300 enemies after marking them with the Mark Target skill	1000
IT'S A TRAP I	Eliminate 50 enemies after stunning them with a decoy trap	500
IT'S A TRAP II	Eliminate 125 enemies after stunning them with a decoy trap	1000
IT'S A TRAP III	Eliminate 300 enemies after stunning them with a decoy trap	1500
MELEE		
SAMURAI I	Eliminate 50 opponents with the Energon Sword	250
SAMURAI II	Eliminate 125 opponents with the Energon Sword	500
SAMURAI III	Eliminate 300 opponents with the Energon Sword	1000
SPECIAL		
EMP GRENADE EXPERT I	Eliminate 25 opponents while they are stunned by your own EMP Grenade	250
EMP GRENADE EXPERT II	Eliminate 50 opponents while they are stunned by your own EMP Grenade	500
EMP GRENADE EXPERT III	Eliminate 100 opponents while they are stunned by your EMP Grenade	1000

Scout Vehicle Challenges

CHALLENGE	DESCRIPTION	XP REWARD
DEATH ON WHEELS I	Eliminate 25 enemies using car weaponry	250
DEATH ON WHEELS II	Eliminate 50 enemies using car weaponry	500
DEATH ON WHEELS III	Eliminate 100 enemies using car weaponry	1000
ROAD TRIP I	Drive a total of 100 miles (accumulated)	250
ROAD TRIP II	Drive a total of 500 miles (accumulated)	500
ROAD TRIP III	Drive a total of 1000 miles (accumulated)	1000
UNDERDOG I	Destroy 25 Tanks while in car form	500
UNDERDOG II	Destroy 50 Tanks while in car form	1000
UNDERDOG III	Destroy 100 Tanks while in car form	1500

Leader Challenges

LEADER WEAPON CHALLENGES

CHALLENGE	DESCRIPTION	XP REWARD
ENERGON BATTLE PISTOL		
BATTLE PISTOL MARKSMAN I	As a Leader, eliminate 25 opponents with the Energon Battle Pistol	250
BATTLE PISTOL MARKSMAN II	As a Leader, eliminate 50 opponents with the Energon Battle Pistol	500
BATTLE PISTOL MARKSMAN III	As a Leader, eliminate 100 opponents with the Energon Battle Pistol	1000
BATTLE PISTOL EXPERT I	As a Leader, get 25 headshots with the Energon Battle Pistol	500
BATTLE PISTOL EXPERT II	As a Leader, get 50 headshots with the Energon Battle Pistol	1000
BATTLE PISTOL EXPERT III	As a Leader, get 100 headshots with the Energon Battle Pistol	1500
DISRUPTOR I	As a Leader, take out 5 tanks with the Energon Battle Pistol after using the Transform Disruptor on a Soldier	1000
DISRUPTOR II	As a Leader, take out 10 tanks with the Energon Battle Pistol after using the Transform Disruptor on a Soldier	1500
DISRUPTOR III	As a Leader, take out 20 tanks with the Energon Battle Pistol after using the Transform Disruptor on a Soldier	2000
ION BLASTER		
PLATOON LEADER I	As a Leader, eliminate 25 opponents with the Ion Blaster	250
PLATOON LEADER II	As a Leader, eliminate 50 opponents with the Ion Blaster	500
PLATOON LEADER III	As a Leader, eliminate 100 opponents with the Ion Blaster	1000
ADRENALINE RUSH I	As a Leader, eliminate 10 opponents with the Ion Blaster while under the effects of your Warcry	500
ADRENALINE RUSH II	As a Leader, eliminate 25 opponents with the Ion Blaster while under the effects of your Warcry	1000
ADRENALINE RUSH III	As a Leader, eliminate 50 opponents with the Ion Blaster while under the effects of your Warcry	1500
WRECKING MACHINE I	As a Leader, take out 5 Scouts with Ion Blaster after slowing them down with the Moleculon Bomb	1000
WRECKING MACHINE II	As a Leader, take out 10 Scouts with Ion Blaster after slowing them down with the Moleculon Bomb	1500
WRECKING MACHINE III	As a Leader, take out 20 Scouts with Ion Blaster after slowing them down with the Moleculon Bomb	2000
FUSION CANNON		
FUSION CANNON EXPERT I	As a Leader, eliminate 25 opponents with the Fusion Cannon	250
FUSION CANNON EXPERT II	As a Leader, eliminate 50 opponents with the Fusion Cannon	500
FUSION CANNON EXPERT III	As a Leader, eliminate 100 opponents with the Fusion Cannon	1000
HAMMER OF JUSTICE I	As a Leader, eliminate 10 opposing Leaders with the Fusion Cannon	500
HAMMER OF JUSTICE II	As a Leader, eliminate 25 opposing Leaders with the Fusion Cannon	1000
HAMMER OF JUSTICE III	As a Leader, eliminate 50 opposing Leaders with the Fusion Cannon	1500
NO FLY ZONE I	As a Leader, take down 5 planes with the Fusion Cannon	1000
NO FLY ZONE II	Take down 10 planes with the Fusion Cannon	1500
NO FLY ZONE III	Take down 20 planes with the Fusion Cannon	2000
MAGMA FRAG LAUNCHER		
S.W.A.T. LEADER I	As a Leader, eliminate 25 opponents with the Magma Frag Launcher	250
S.W.A.T. LEADER II	As a Leader, eliminate 50 opponents with the Magma Frag Launcher	500
S.W.A.T. LEADER III	As a Leader, eliminate 100 opponents with the Magma Frag Launcher	1000
TOUGH LUCK I	As a Leader, destroy 10 tanks with the Magma Frag Launcher	500
TOUGH LUCK II	As a Leader, destroy 25 tanks with the Magma Frag Launcher	1000
TOUGH LUCK III	As a Leader, destroy 50 tanks with the Magma Frag Launcher	1500
OVERPOWER I	As a Leader, eliminate 5 Scientists with the Magma Frag Launcher after using the Transform Disruptor	1000
OVERPOWER II	As a Leader, eliminate 10 Scientists with the Magma Frag Launcher after using the Transform Disruptor	1500
OVERPOWER III	As a Leader, eliminate 20 Scientists with the Magma Frag Launcher after using the Transform Disruptor	2000

Leader Class Challenges

CHALLENGE	DESCRIPTION	XP REWARD
KILLS		
ROBOTOPOSSUM! I	Eliminate 3 enemies while downed and on Reserve Power Cells	250
ROBOTOPOSSUM! II	Eliminate 5 enemies while downed and on Reserve Power Cells	500
ROBOTOPOSSUM! III	Eliminate 7 enemies while downed and on Reserve Power Cells	1000
MORALE BOOSTER I	Eliminate 25 enemies while under the affect of Warcry	250
MORALE BOOSTER II	Eliminate 75 enemies while under the affect of Warcry	500
MORALE BOOSTER III	Eliminate 150 enemies while under the affect of Warcry	1000
SLOW MOTION I	Eliminate 25 enemies after affecting them with the Moleculon Bomb	250
SLOW MOTION II	Eliminate 50 enemies after affecting them with the Moleculon Bomb	500
SLOW MOTION III	Eliminate 100 enemies after affecting them with the Moleculon Bomb	1000
PUPPET MASTER I	Eliminate 10 enemies while they are affected by your Disruption	250
PUPPET MASTER II	Eliminate 25 enemies while they are affected by your Disruption	500
PUPPET MASTER III	Eliminate 50 enemies while they are affected by your Disruption	1000
MELEE		
WARRIOR I	Eliminate 50 opponents with the Energon Axe	250
WARRIOR II	Eliminate 125 opponents with the Energon Axe	500
WARRIOR II	Eliminate 300 opponents with the Energon Axe	1000
SPECIAL		
THERMO MINE EXPERT I	Eliminate 25 opponents with a Thermo Mine	250
THERMO MINE EXPERT II	Eliminate 50 opponents with a Thermo Mine	500
THERMO MINE EXPERT III	Eliminate 100 opponents with a Thermo Mine	1000

Leader Vehicle Challenges

CHALLENGE	DESCRIPTION	XP REWARD
KEEP ON TRUCKIN! I	Eliminate 25 enemies using truck weaponry	250
KEEP ON TRUCKIN! II	Eliminate 50 enemies using truck weaponry	500
KEEP ON TRUCKIN! III	Eliminate 100 enemies using truck weaponry	1000
ANTI-AIR EXPERT I	Take down 5 jets using truck weaponry	250
ANTI-AIR EXPERT II	Take down 10 jets using truck weaponry	500
ANTI-AIR EXPERT III	Take down 20 jets using truck weaponry	1000
FREIGHT TRAIN I	Destroy 5 cars by ramming them	250
FREIGHT TRAIN II	Destroy 10 cars by ramming them	500

Soldier Challenges
SOLDIER WEAPON CHALLENGES

CHALLENGE	DESCRIPTION	XP REWARD
NEUTRON ASSAULT RIFLE		
INFANTRY I	As a Soldier, eliminate 25 opponents with the Neutron Assault Rifle	250
INFANTRY II	As a Soldier, eliminate 50 opponents with the Neutron Assault Rifle	500
INFANTRY III	As a Soldier, eliminate 100 opponents with the Neutron Assault Rifle	1000
DEAD EYE I	As a Soldier, get 10 headshots with the Neutron Assault Rifle	500
DEAD EYE II	As a Soldier, get 25 headshots with the Neutron Assault Rifle	1000
DEAD EYE III	As a Soldier, get 50 headshots with the Neutron Assault Rifle	1500
VERTIGO I	As a Soldier, deliver the final blow to 5 enemies with the Neutron Assault Rifle after damaging them with the Whirlwind ability	1000
VERTIGO II	As a Soldier, deliver the final blow to 10 enemies with the Neutron Assault Rifle after damaging them with the Whirlwind ability	1500
VERTIGO III	As a Soldier, deliver the final blow to 20 enemies with the Neutron Assault Rifle after damaging them with the Whirlwind ability	2000
X12 SCRAPMAKER		
X12 MARKSMAN I	As a Soldier, eliminate 25 opponents with the X12 Scrapmaker	250
X12 MARKSMAN II	As a Soldier, eliminate 50 opponents with the X12 Scrapmaker	500
X12 MARKSMAN III	As a Soldier, eliminate 100 opponents with the X12 Scrapmaker	1000
X12 EXPERT I	As a Soldier, get 5 headshots with the X12 Scrapmaker	500
X12 EXPERT II	As a Soldier, get 10 headshots with the X12 Scrapmaker	1000
X12 EXPERT III	As a Soldier, get 20 headshots with the X12 Scrapmaker	1500
JUNKYARD DOG I	As a Soldier, eliminate 5 Leaders with the X12 Scrapmaker while you are hovering	1000
JUNKYARD DOG II	As a Soldier, eliminate 10 Leaders with the X12 Scrapmaker while you are hovering	1500
JUNKYARD DOG III	As a Soldier, eliminate 20 Leaders with the X12 Scrapmaker while you are hovering	2000
EMP SHOTGUN		
TRENCH GUNNER I	As a Soldier, eliminate 25 opponents with the EMP Shotgun	250
TRENCH GUNNER II	As a Soldier, eliminate 50 opponents with the EMP Shotgun	500
TRENCH GUNNER III	As a Soldier, eliminate 100 opponents with the EMP Shotgun	1000
NO GUTS, NO GLORY I	As a Soldier, get 5 headshots with the EMP Shotgun	500
NO GUTS, NO GLORY II	As a Soldier, get 10 headshots with the EMP Shotgun	1000
NO GUTS, NO GLORY III	As a Soldier, get 20 headshots with the EMP Shotgun	1500
THE REST WILL FALL I	As a Soldier, eliminate 5 enemy Leaders with the EMP Shotgun	1000
THE REST WILL FALL II	As a Soldier, eliminate 10 enemy Leaders with the EMP Shotgun	1500
THE REST WILL FALL III	As a Soldier, eliminate 20 enemy Leaders with the EMP Shotgun	2000
THERMO ROCKET LAUNCHER		
HOMING ROCKET EXPERT I	As a Soldier, eliminate 25 opponents with the Thermo Rocket Launcher	250
HOMING ROCKET EXPERT II	As a Soldier, eliminate 50 opponents with the Thermo Rocket Launcher	500
HOMING ROCKET EXPERT III	As a Soldier, eliminate 100 opponents with the Thermo Rocket Launcher	1000
ARCH ENEMY I	As a Soldier, eliminate 10 opposing Scientists with the Thermo Rocket Launcher	500
ARCH ENEMY II	As a Soldier, eliminate 25 opposing Scientists with the Thermo Rocket Launcher	1000
ARCH ENEMY III	As a Soldier, eliminate 50 opposing Scientists with the Thermo Rocket Launcher	1500
WHO NEEDS LOCK ON?	As a Soldier, eliminate 5 enemy Scouts with the Thermo Rocket Launcher while they are cloaked	1000
WHO NEEDS LOCK ON?	As a Soldier, eliminate 10 enemy Scouts with the Thermo Rocket Launcher while they are cloaked	1500
WHO NEEDS LOCK ON?	As a Soldier, eliminate 20 enemy Scouts with the Thermo Rocket Launcher while they are cloaked	2000

BASICS
CHARACTERS
WEAPONS
WALKTHROUGH

01
02
03
04
05
06
07
08
09
10

MULTIPLAYER

ACHIEVEMENTS

Soldier Class Challenges

CHALLENGE	DESCRIPTION	XP REWARD
SKILLS		
JAM IT! I	Eliminate 5 enemies after jamming their abilities with the Energon Sling	250
JAM IT! II	Eliminate 10 enemies after jamming their abilities with the Energon Sling	500
JAM IT! III	Eliminate 20 enemies after jamming their abilities with the Energon Sling	1000
MOTHER LODE I	Deliver 25 ammo crates	250
MOTHER LODE II	Deliver 50 ammo crates	500
MOTHER LODE III	Deliver 100 ammo crates	1000
AIRBORNE I	Eliminate 25 opponents while hovering	250
AIRBORNE II	Eliminate 50 opponents while hovering	500
AIRBORNE III	Eliminate 100 opponents while hovering	1000
SLICE 'N' DICE I	Eliminate 25 opponents with the Whirlwind	250
SLICE 'N' DICE II	Eliminate 50 opponents with the Whirlwind	500
SLICE 'N' DICE III	Eliminate 100 opponents with the Whirlwind	1000
MELEE		
PALADIN I	Eliminate 50 opponents with the Energon Hammer	250
PALADIN II	Eliminate 125 opponents with the Energon Hammer	500
PALADIN III	Eliminate 300 opponents with the Energon Hammer	1000
SPECIAL		
GRENADE EXPERT I	Eliminate 25 opponents with the Flak Grenade	250
GRENADE EXPERT II	Eliminate 50 opponents with the Flak Grenade	500
GRENADE EXPERT III	Eliminate 100 opponents with the Flak Grenade	1000

Soldier Vehicle Challenges

CHALLENGE	DESCRIPTION	XP REWARD
TANK COMMANDER I	Destroy 25 enemies with the tank cannon	250
TANK COMMANDER II	Destroy 50 enemies with the tank cannon	500
TANK COMMANDER IIII	Destroy 100 enemies with the tank cannon	1000
ANTI AIR I	Destroy 5 enemy planes with the tank cannon	250
ANTI AIR II	Destroy 10 enemy planes with the tank cannon	500
ANTI AIR III	Destroy 20 enemy planes with the tank cannon	1000
BATTALION LEADER I	Deliver the final blow on 5 enemy tanks with the tank cannon	250
BATTALION LEADER II	Deliver the final blow on 10 enemy tanks with the tank cannon	500
BATTALION LEADER III	Deliver the final blow on 20 enemy tanks with the tank cannon	1000

Scientist Challenges

SCIENTIST WEAPON CHALLENGES

CHALLENGE	DESCRIPTION	XP REWARD
NEUTRON ASSAULT RIFLE		
HACKJOB I	As a Scientist, eliminate 25 opponents with the Neutron Assault Rifle	250
HACKJOB II	As a Scientist eliminate 50 opponents with the Neutron Assault Rifle	500
HACKJOB III	As a Scientist, eliminate 100 opponents with the Neutron Assault Rifle	1000
LOBOTOMY I	As a Scientist, get 10 headshots with the Neutron Assault Rifle	500
LOBOTOMY II	As a Scientist, get 25 headshots with the Neutron Assault Rifle	1000
LOBOTOMY III	As a Scientist, get 50 headshots with the Neutron Assault Rifle	1500
MAD SCIENTIST I	As a Scientist, deliver the final blow to 5 enemies with the Neutron Assault Rifle after knocking them back with the Shockwave ability	1000
MAD SCIENTIST II	As a Scientist, deliver the final blow to 10 enemies with the Neutron Assault Rifle after knocking them back with the Shockwave ability	1500
MAD SCIENTIST III	As a Scientist, deliver the final blow to 20 enemies with the Neutron Assault Rifle after knocking them back with the Shockwave ability	2000
EMP SHOTGUN		
CQC EXPERT I	As a Scientist, eliminate 25 opponents with the EMP Shotgun	250
CQC EXPERT II	As a Scientist, eliminate 50 opponents with the EMP Shotgun	500
CQC EXPERT III	As a Scientist, eliminate 100 opponents with the EMP Shotgun	1000
NO CONTEST I	As a Scientist, eliminate 10 opponents with the EMP Shotgun while using your Drain ability	500
NO CONTEST II	As a Scientist, eliminate 25 opponents with the EMP Shotgun while using your Drain ability	1000
NO CONTEST III	As a Scientist, eliminate 50 opponents with the EMP Shotgun while using your Drain ability	1500
NOBODY'S FOOL I	As a Scientist, eliminate 5 disguised enemies with the EMP Shotgun	1000
NOBODY'S FOOL II	As a Scientist, eliminate 10 disguised enemies with the EMP Shotgun	1500
NOBODY'S FOOL III	As a Scientist, eliminate 20 disguised enemies with the EMP Shotgun	2000
PHOTON BURST RIFLE		
BURST RIFLE MARKSMAN I	As a Scientist, eliminate 25 opponents with the Photon Burst Rifle	250
BURST RIFLE MARKSMAN II	As a Scientist, eliminate 50 opponents with the Photon Burst Rifle	500
BURST RIFLE MARKSMAN III	As a Scientist, eliminate100 opponents with the Photon Burst Rifle	1000
BURST RIFLE EXPERT I	As a Scientist, get 10 headshots with the Photon Burst Rifle	500
BURST RIFLE EXPERT II	As a Scientist, get 25 headshots with the Photon Burst Rifle	1000
BURST RIFLE EXPERT III	As a Scientist, get 50 headshots with the Photon Burst Rifle	1500
BULL'S EYE I	As a Scientist, eliminate 5 opponents with the Photon Burst Rifle after a Scout has marked them	1000
BULL'S EYE II	As a Scientist, eliminate 10 opponents with the Photon Burst Rifle after a Scout has marked them	1500
BULL'S EYE III	As a Scientist, eliminate 20 opponents with the Photon Burst Rifle after a Scout has marked them	2000
ENERGON REPAIR RAY		
REPAIR RAY EXPERT I	As a Scientist, eliminate 10 opponents with the Energon Repair Ray	250
REPAIR RAY EXPERT II	As a Scientist, eliminate 25 opponents with the Energon Repair Ray	500
REPAIR RAY EXPERT III	As a Scientist, eliminate 50 opponents with the Energon Repair Ray	1000

BASICS
CHARACTERS
WEAPONS
WALKTHROUGH
01
02
03
04
05
06
07
08
09
10

MULTIPLAYER
ACHIEVEMENTS

Scientist Class Challenges

CHALLENGE	DESCRIPTION	XP REWARD
SKILLS		
TSUNAMI I	Eliminate 10 enemies with the Shockwave ability	250
TSUNAMI II	Eliminate 25 enemies with the Shockwave ability	500
TSUNAMI III	Eliminate 50 enemies with the Shockwave ability	1000
PLAGUE BEARER I	Eliminate 25 enemies using the Drain ability	250
PLAGUE BEARER II	Eliminate 50 enemies using the Drain ability	500
PLAGUE BEARER III	Eliminate 100 enemies using the Drain ability	1000
SPY I	Eliminate 5 enemies while disguised	250
SPY II	Eliminate 10 enemies while disguised	500
SPY III	Eliminate 25 enemies while disguised	1000
DEFENDER I	Eliminate 10 enemies with a deployed Sentry Turret	250
DEFENDER II	Eliminate 15 enemies with a deployed Sentry Turret	500
DEFENDER III	Eliminate 25 enemies with a deployed Sentry Turret	1000
MELEE		
SLUGGER I	Eliminate 50 opponents with the Energon Club	250
SLUGGER II	Eliminate 125 opponents with the Energon Club	500
SLUGGER III	Eliminate 300 opponents with the Energon Club	1000
SPECIAL		
FIRST AID I	Heal 1000 total accumulated health with a Heal Grenade	250
FIRST AID II	Heal 2500 total accumulated health with a Heal Grenade	500
FIRST AID III	Heal 5000 total accumulated health with a Heal Grenade	1000
COMBAT MEDIC I	Heal 1000 total accumulated health with the Energon Repair Ray	250
COMBAT MEDIC II	Heal 2500 total accumulated health with the Energon Repair Ray	500
COMBAT MEDIC III	Heal 5000 total accumulated health with the Energon Repair Ray	1000
LIFE FLIGHT I	Heal 1000 total accumulated with a spawned Repair Sentry	250
LIFE FLIGHT II	Heal 2500 total accumulated with a spawned Repair Sentry	500
LIFE FLIGHT III	Heal 5000 total accumulated with a spawned Repair Sentry	1000

Scientist Vehicle Challenges

CHALLENGE	DESCRIPTION	XP REWARD
DEADLY SKIES I	Destroy 25 enemies while in jet form	250
DEADLY SKIES II	Destroy 50 enemies while in jet form	500
DEADLY SKIES III	Destroy 100 enemies while in jet form	1000
DIVE BOMBER I	Destroy 5 tanks while in jet form	250
DIVE BOMBER II	Destroy 10 tanks while in jet form	500
DIVE BOMBER III	Destroy 20 tanks while in jet form	1000
THE RED BARRON I	Shoot down 5 planes while also being in jet form	250
THE RED BARRON I	Shoot down 10 planes while also being in jet form	500
THE RED BARRON II	Shoot down 20 planes while also being in jet form	1000

EXPERIENCE & LEVELING UP

You earn experience points that are equal to your match score in every multiplayer match you play, even if you lose. Earn points by completing objectives, getting kills, and making sure your team performs well. That score equates directly to experience points (XP) for the character class you are playing.

You can create three custom builds for each class, for a total of twelve. Each of these is available on a custom Autobot or Decepticon chassis, yielding a grand total of twenty-four custom builds.

You earn XP for all your custom builds in the specific class you are playing. Thus, when you earn enough XP, all your characters in that class level up. You can choose new skills for your characters after you level up their class. Classes level up independently. For example, you may have a Leader at level 5, while a Scientist might be level 2. Every character that you create in the same class levels up together, not just the last one you played. This encourages two things: trying out several different robot builds to fit unique situations; and leveling each class up to the max.

XP NEEDED PER LEVEL

Level	XP Required	Level	XP Required
1	500	14	80000
2	1500	15	95000
3	3000	16	112000
4	5000	17	131000
5	7500	18	152000
6	11000	19	175000
7	15500	20	200000
8	21000	21	227000
9	27500	22	256000
10	35000	23	287000
11	44000	24	320000
12	54500	25	355000
13	66500		

XP REWARDS

Following are examples of in-game events that award XP.

EVENT	DESCRIPTION	XP REWARD
KILLS		
DM KILL	Deliver the final blow to an enemy in deathmatch	10
TEAM GAME KILL	Deliver the final blow to an enemy in a team game	20
DM ASSIST	Assist in a kill in a deathmatch game	5
TEAM GAME ASSIST	Assist in a kill in a team game	20
3 KILL STREAK	3 Kill Streak	20
5 KILL STREAK	5 kill Streak	50
7 KILL STREAK	7 kill streak	100
FUNKILLER	End an enemy's Kill Streak	20
JUST A FLESH WOUND	Kill enemy while low on health	60
BREAK FREE	Kill an enemy that is dominating you	40
DOMED	Kill an enemy with a headshot	50
BEAT DOWN	Kill the same enemy 2 times in a row	20
HUMILIATION	Kill the same enemy 3 times in a row	40
SCRAP-MAKER	Kill the same enemy 4 times in a row	60
NOBODY'S FOOL	Kill an enemy while he/she is disguised	50
SITTING DUCK	Kill an enemy while he/she is hovering	30
SILENCE	Kill an enemy that has the Warcry effect on him/her	30
TRICKSTER	Kill an enemy while blinded	50
FAR AND AWAY	Killed an enemy at long range	20
SCOUT		
ENJOY THE GIFT	Kill an enemy after he/she is stunned by your decoy trap	50
TAG YOU'RE IT	Kill an enemy after marking him/her	50
ROGUE	Kill an enemy with Backstab	50
LIGHTS OUT	Kill an enemy after blinding him/her with a flash-bang	50
BOO	Kill an enemy using the Surprise Attack ability	30
KNIGHTED	Kill an enemy in melee with a sword	30

EVENT	DESCRIPTION	XP REWARD
LEADER		
VAMPIRE	Kill an enemy while draining them	30
NO MERCY	Kill an enemy while you are downed	20
BOWLED OVER	Kill an enemy after slowing him/her down with the Moleculon Bomb	20
ROADKILL	Kill an enemy while ramming	50
WHIPLASH	Kill an enemy after disrupting him/her	50
TIIIIIMBER	Kill an enemy in melee with an axe	30
SOLDIER		
HIGH AND MIGHTY	Kill an enemy while you are hovering	30
DIZZY KILL	Kill an enemy with the Whirlwind ability	20
JAMMED	Kill an enemy after jamming his/her abilities	50
TEST YOUR STRENGTH	Kill an enemy in melee with a hammer	30
SCIENTIST		
DOUBLE AGENT	Kill an enemy while you are disguised	20
SONIC PAIN WAVE	Kill an enemy with a Shockwave	20
BUBBLE BOY	Heal 3 or more team members with a single heal grenade	50
FROM THE BRINK	Heal a teammate with less than one Energon Cube	20
WARRIOR OF THE ANCIENTS	Kill an enemy in melee with a club	30

PRIME MODE

If you're a hardcore player and reach the max level in all classes, you can trade in all your XP/skills/weapons/unlockables and downgrade to level 0 to enter Prime Mode.

In Prime Mode, you have the suffix "Prime" tagged behind all of your characters in your online stats. Also, all other gamers can see this "Prime" tag during gameplay.

PRIME MODE CHALLENGES

An additional layer of challenges is available when you play in Prime Mode.

CHALLENGE	DESCRIPTION	XP REWARD
PRIME CHALLENGES		
UNSTOPPABLE I	Eliminate 15 enemies in row without dying	1000
UNSTOPPABLE II	Eliminate 20 enemies in row without dying	1500
UNSTOPPABLE III	Eliminate 25 enemies in row without dying	2000
SCOUT		
YOU CAN'T HIDE I	Activate the Orbital Beacon 3 times in a single match	500
YOU CAN'T HIDE II	Activate the Orbital Beacon 4 times in a single match	1000
YOU CAN'T HIDE III	Activate the Orbital Beacon 5 times in a single match	1500
ADRENALINE I	Activate Energon Recharger 2 times in a single match	1000
ADRENALINE II	Activate Energon Recharger 3 times in a single match	1500
ADRENALINE III	Activate Energon Recharger 4 times in a single match	2000
OMNIPOTENT I	Activate the Orbital Beacon 2.0 2 times in a single match	1500
OMNIPOTENT II	Activate the Orbital Beacon 2.0 3 times in a single match	2000
OMNIPOTENT III	Activate the Orbital Beacon 2.0 4 times in a single match	2500
ALL SEEING EYE I	Activate the Orbital Beacon a total of 25 times	500
ALL SEEING EYE II	Activate the Orbital Beacon a total of 50 times	1000
ALL SEEING EYE III	Activate the Orbital Beacon a total of 100 times	1500
REGEN JUNKIE	Activate the Energon Recharger a total of 10 times	1000
REGEN JUNKIE	Activate the Energon Recharger a total of 25 times	1500
REGEN JUNKIE	Activate the Energon Recharger a total of 50 times	2000
X-RAY VISION I	Activate the Orbital Beacon 2.0 a total of 5 times	1500
X-RAY VISION II	Activate the Orbital Beacon 2.0 a total of 15 times	2000
X-RAY VISION III	Activate the Orbital Beacon 2.0 a total of 25 times	2500

BASICS
CHARACTERS
WEAPONS
WALKTHROUGH
01
02
03
04
05
06
07
08
09
10
MULTIPLAYER
ACHIEVEMENTS

CHALLENGE	DESCRIPTION	XP REWARD
SOLDIER		
DROP THE ZERO I	Activate the Ammo Matrix 3 times in a single match	500
DROP THE ZERO II	Activate the Ammo Matrix 4 times in a single match	1000
DROP THE ZERO III	Activate the Ammo Matrix 5 times in a single match	1500
BAMBOOZLED I	Activate the Omega Missile 2 times in a single match	1000
BAMBOOZLED II	Activate the Omega Missile 3 times in a single match	1500
BAMBOOZLED III	Activate the Omega Missile 4 times in a single match	2000
BLACK OUT I	Activate the Electromagnetic Pulse 2 times in a single match	1500
BLACK OUT II	Activate the Electromagnetic Pulse 3 times in a single match	2000
BLACK OUT III	Activate the Electromagnetic Pulse 4 times in a single match	2500
COOL AS ICE I	Activate the Ammo Matrix a total of 25 times	500
COOL AS ICE II	Activate the Ammo Matrix a total of 50 times	1000
COOL AS ICE III	Activate the Ammo Matrix a total of 100 times	1500
NO MORE MR. NICE GUY I	Activate the Omega Missile a total of 10 times	1000
NO MORE MR. NICE GUY II	Activate the Omega Missile a total of 25 times	1500
NO MORE MR. NICE GUY III	Activate the Omega Missile a total of 50 times	2000
SHORT CIRCUIT I	Activate the Electromagnetic Pulse a total of 5 times	1500
SHORT CIRCUIT II	Activate the Electromagnetic Pulse a total of 15 times	2000
SHORT CIRCUIT III	Activate the Electromagnetic Pulse a total of 25 times	2500
LEADER		
REALLY? I	Activate the P.o.K.E. 2.0 a total of 3 times in a single match	500
REALLY? II	Activate the P.o.K.E. 2.0 a total of 4 times in a single match	1000
REALLY? III	Activate the P.o.K.E. 2.0 a total of 5 times in a single match	1500
MINE ALL MINE I	Activate the Thermo Mine Re-spawner 2 times in a single match	1000
MINE ALL MINE II	Activate the Thermo Mine Re-spawner 3 times in a single match	1500
MINE ALL MINE III	Activate the Thermo Mine Re-spawner 4 times in a single match	2000
WHAMBULANCE I	Activate the Intercooler 2 times in a single match	1500
WHAMBULANCE II	Activate the Intercooler 3 times in a single match	2000
WHAMBULANCE III	Activate the Intercooler 4 times in a single match	2500
STOKED I	Activate the P.o.K.E. 2.0 a total of 25 times	500
STOKED II	Activate the P.o.K.E. 2.0 a total of 50 times	1000
STOKED III	Activate the P.o.K.E. 2.0 a total of 100 times	1500
SEEK AND DESTROY I	Activate the Thermo Mine Re-spawner a total of 10 times	1000
SEEK AND DESTROY II	Activate the Thermo Mine Re-spawner a total of 25 times	1500
SEEK AND DESTROY III	Activate the Thermo Mine Re-spawner a total of 50 times	2000
PAINKILLER I	Activate the Intercooler a total of 5 times	1500
PAINKILLER II	Activate the Intercooler a total of 15 times	2000
PAINKILLER III	Activate the Intercooler a total of 25 times	2500
SCIENTIST		
BANDOLEER I	Activate the Health Matrix 2.0 3 times in a single match	500
BANDOLEER II	Activate the Health Matrix 2.0 4 times in a single match	1000
BANDOLEER III	Activate the Health Matrix 2.0 5 times in a single match	1500
GUARDIAN ANGEL I	Activate the Oversheild Matrix 2 Times in a single match	1000
GUARDIAN ANGEL II	Activate the Oversheild Matrix 3 Times in a single match	1500
GUARDIAN ANGEL III	Activate the Oversheild Matrix 4 Times in a single match	2000
PHOENIX RISING I	Activate the Nucleon Shock Cannon 2 times in a single match	1500
PHOENIX RISING II	Activate the Nucleon Shock Cannon 3 times in a single match	2000
PHOENIX RISING III	Activate the Nucleon Shock Cannon 4 times in a single match	2500
JACKPOT I	Activate the Health Matrix 2.0 a total of 25 times	500
JACKPOT II	Activate the Health Matrix 2.0 a total of 50 times	1000
JACKPOT III	Activate the Health Matrix 2.0 a total of 100 times	1500
DIVINE PROTECTION I	Activate the Oversheild Matrix a total of 10 times	1000
DIVINE PROTECTION II	Activate the Oversheild Matrix a total of 25 times	1500
DIVINE PROTECTION III	Activate the Oversheild Matrix a total of 50 times	2000
MAKE IT RAIN I	Activate the Nucleon Shock Cannon a total of 5 times	1500
MAKE IT RAIN II	Activate the Nucleon Shock Cannon a total of 15 times	2000
MAKE IT RAIN III	Activate the Nucleon Shock Cannon a total of 25 times	2500

GENERAL MULTIPLAYER TIPS

- Kill streak rewards are powerful additions to your arsenal. You can employ multiple kill streaks at the same time to crush your enemies. You do not lose your kill streak *reward* when you die, but you do lose your streak. So, time their use wisely, but be careful not to lose your kill streak count.

- Each vehicle form and robot form has its strengths and weaknesses against others. Learning these strengths and weakness helps you as you level up your character.

- Depending on your skill, you can navigate the maps with relative ease once you master the timing of changes between robot and vehicle. Try different combos of vehicle/robot/double-jump to gain more height or distance.

- Play your classes appropriately, and support your teammates with your abilities. Scouts are very good at hit-and-run tactics from flanked positions, but they are not good at charging through the front line. Leave the charging to the heavier classes, like Leader and Soldier, while you attack from the side. The opponent usually focuses on the front line, allowing you to unleash a devastating attack from the rear.

- Each class has a specific grenade type to support the class. Use them accordingly to deliver brutal attacks or offer defensive support for your teammates.

- Combine different Killstreak Rewards to level up faster.

- If a Soldier has the Path Blaster upgrade equipped with the Ammo Beacon ability, he or she receives an Ion Displacer in a multiplayer match.

- Killing groups of enemies results in more XP than killing them individually.

- Using a sentry gun on your base is a good defensive way to detect cloaked opponents.

- You can mix upgrades in order to increase the advantage of an ability.

- The Omega Missile kill streak for a Soldier can be remotely detonated by pressing the Fire or Fine Aim button in multiplayer.

- Use a Soldier with the Grenade Dispenser upgrade, and the Ammo Beacon ability allows each team member to refill his or her grenades.

- The Seeker upgrade increases the search radius of the Leader's mines, including mines dropped by Martyrdom.

- Place traps (like mines or decoys) near healing items to limit your opponents' options.

- A fully charged Plasma Cannon inflicts major damage with its huge splash damage radius. This is even more potent with the Surprise Attack upgrade. Just keep in mind that the charged energy means other players can see you if you're cloaked.

- Pick up enemy weapons. You might be surprised by what one class's upgrades and abilities can do to another class's weaponry.

- Keep your teams mixed up. While four Scouts can be scary, one good Leader or Soldier can devastate them all.

- Every team can use a Scientist. Always.

- You can use abilities while holding a bomb or the Code of Power.

- Soldiers can use Whirlwind when holding a bomb or the Code of Power. Combine this with the Flurry of Blows upgrade for a dangerous and fast carrier.

- Scouts can use Cloak when holding a bomb or the Code of Power. Use this with Dash to make your carrier very fast and hard to hit.

- The bomb and the Code of Power are one-hit kills when melee attack is used.

- Smaller Scout models are harder to see when they're cloaked.

ESCALATION

Escalation is a cooperative game mode in which players team up to fight against waves of enemies. Each successive wave increases in difficulty as numbers and types of enemies become increasingly difficult. There is no win scenario in Escalation, you will go down eventually; it's just a matter of how long you can survive. Don't count yourself out when you are eliminated during a round. If your remaining friends clear the current wave, you'll respawn when the next wave begins. Be aware that you lose any weapons that you purchased before dying, so you have to reacquire them when you return.

POWER

As you destroy enemies, you earn power, which can then be used at various machines placed throughout the map. You can acquire more ammo, purchase health, and upgrade to new and more powerful weapons. The amount of power you get from a kill depends on the enemy. Destroying stronger enemies gives you more power. Your total score is calculated by the total amount of power you collect. You can view this score on the scoreboard.

POWER VALUES

Enemy Type	Power Earned	Enemy Type	Power Earned
Decepticon Spiders	10	Jet Soldiers	60
Holo-Brutes	25	Shotgunners with Overshields	75
Machine Gun Soldiers	25	Brutes	100
Rocket Soldiers	30	Titans	100
CQC Cloakers	40	Tank Soldiers	300

MAPS

BROKEN HOPE

Broken hope is set in a Decepticon-controlled section of Iacon. You are assigned the impossible task of clearing the Decepticons from the area. This map is fairly open, giving you free reign to move about. For the most part, you should explore the space, open doors, and discover where all the machines are.

Generally, you should take cover in one of the building interiors. The openness of the streets and courtyard can leave you vulnerable to heavy fire. Each building has a stairwell that you can access by opening the doors. They provide excellent chokepoints to lure the enemies to you. You need to be cautious when you do this; each upper floor contains a sealed door that enemies can blow through at any given moment, so watch your back.

Your best bet is to begin by taking cover in building #1 near the health machine. As soon as you and your teammates have enough power, open the door leading upstairs. There you find an ammo machine. You can hold out for a few waves in this building. Around wave five or six, you may consider opening the door leading to the room with the Overshields—they come in handy when you fight the Shotgunners. Another option is to head over to building #3 and try to

SB Scatter Blaster	**RL** Therno Rocket Launcher	**RR** Repair Ray	**Overshield**
HP Heavy Pistol	**PL** Plasma Cannon	**Frag Grenades**	**Kamikazi Mines**
eSG EMP Shotgun	**Sn** Sniper Rifle	**Heal Grenades**	**Health**
GL Grenade Launcher	**SC** Turret Shock Cannon	**EMP Grenades**	**Ammo**
HMG Heavy Machinegun	**ID** Turret Ion Displacer		

get the Energon Repair Ray on the second floor. Whichever order you choose, you want access to these two items before the Brutes descend on you in the eighth wave. From there, you can head over to the main base in building #4 and acquire the heavier weapons.

Beware of exploding canisters placed in the map's open area; they explode from enemy fire as well as from your own attacks.

WAVE COMPOSITION

Following is a list of the enemy types and the wave in which they are introduced:

ENEMY TYPES	WAVE #
DECEPTICON SPIDERS	Wave 1
DECEPTICON SOLDIERS	Wave 1
DECEPTICON ROCKET SOLDIERS	Wave 2
DECEPTICON CQC CLOAKERS	Wave 4
DECEPTICON JET SOLDIERS	Wave 5
DECEPTICON SHOTGUNNERS	Wave 7
DECEPTICON BRUTES	Wave 8
DECEPETICON TITANS	Wave 10
DECEPTICON TANK SOLDIER	Wave 15

REMNANT

Remnant is an abandoned spaceport now used as supply depot for the Autobot war effort. Your mission is to take over the port and cut off the Autobot supply chain. However, Zeta Prime is well aware of the Decepticon plan and has set up an ambush. Unlike Broken Hope, Remnant focuses more on close-quarter combat. You have to develop an appropriate strategy to progress through the higher waves.

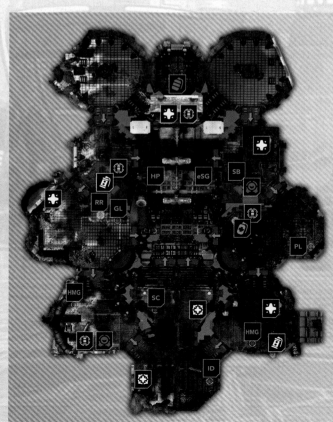

You begin within the station's main landing bay. At the bay's front-most part, you can find both a health and an ammo machine. Cautiously fight your way forward through the first enemy wave or two to reach these machines. From this point, there are two path choices: you can head up to the room on the right or to the room on the left. Both feature doors that lead you up through a series of rooms. Each side has its unique advantages, so it's up to you and your team to decide which way to go. Once you are familiar with the map, choose a path based on the items you want to acquire.

Whichever path you select, it's best to stick to that choice instead of turning back. Open the door, hold off your enemies, and then open the next door leading further into the base. You eventually wind up in the station's uppermost room. If you follow it all the way to the back, you'll find a doorway that leads back down into the landing bay. Hold up in the upper room as long as you can. If you get into trouble, you can escape by jumping out the back and heading back down into the hangar. Look before you jump; if you miss the ramp, you'll fall into the abyss of deep space.

WAVE COMPOSITION

Following is a list of the enemy types and the wave in which they are introduced:

ENEMY TYPES	WAVE #
ZETA PRIME'S HOLO BRUTES	Wave 1
AUTOBOT SOLDIERS	Wave 1
AUTOBOT ROCKET SOLDIERS	Wave 3
AUTOBOT CQC CLOAKERS	Wave 5
AUTOBOT SHOTGUNNERS	Wave 7
AUTOBOT TITANS	Wave 8
AUTOBOT BRUTES	Wave 10

GENERAL ESCALATION TIPS

- Open areas can be dangerous; you are exposed to multidirectional fire. Try to find cover and hold off your enemies from grounded positions rather than running around looking for them.

- Pay close attention to each player's character choice and abilities. Your choices from the beginning can make a big difference in your success or failure. Anticipate the role each player takes, and choose your characters wisely.

- If you separate, you become weaker and go down much faster. It also takes longer for a friend to reach you and revive you. Stick together.

- This is a cooperative mode, so you will get much further if you work together as a team. Develop a plan of attack, and work together to get the items you need. Communication is key to your success.

- Develop a strategy as a team. Coordinate your efforts on timing: when to open doors, when to go for the Energon Repair Ray, and so forth. Knowing where you want to go and when is the key to reaching the higher waves.

- Get a secondary weapon fairly early for better ammo management.

- The Overshields help immensely as you get into the higher waves. It should be one of the first items you locate.

- You should designate one person on your team to become the healer and plan on getting the Energon Repair Ray.

- Use time between waves wisely. You have a few seconds of safety. This is a good time to restock on ammo and health, open doors, or collect Energon Shards floating around from the previous wave.

- To make the most of your energy, plan weapon purchases and door unlocks with teammates ahead of time.

- Switch between main handheld weapons and vehicle weapons to stretch out your ammo supply.

- Don't waste ammo on Spiderbots. Instead, use melee attacks.

ACHIEVEMENTS & TROPHIES

ACHIEVEMENT TITLE	TASK	XBOX 360 PTS	PS3 TR
GOLD TROPHIES			
A PRIME PROBLEM	Complete Defend Iacon on any difficulty	10	15
THE LAST PRIME	Complete Kaon Prison Break on any difficulty	10	15
YOU GOT THE TOUCH	Complete To the Core on any difficulty	10	15
THE WAR WITHIN	Complete Aerial Assault on any difficulty	10	15
THE HARDER THEY FALL	Complete One Shall Stand on any difficulty	10	15
PAGING RATCHET	Revive 5 Autobot soldiers in Defend Iacon	15	15
BEAK BREAKER	Shoot the 3 Hidden Laserbeaks throughout Kaon Prison Break	15	15
SLUGFEST	Destroy the enemy attacking the giant slug by shooting a stalactite to crush the enemy	15	15
POWERGLIDE PERFORMER	Fly through the coolant tunnels in 23 seconds in Aerial Assault	15	15
FIRST WE CRACK THE SHELL...	Get smashed by Trypticon's hand as he falls into the Energon goo in One Shall Stand	15	15

BASICS
CHARACTERS
WEAPONS
WALKTHROUGH
01
02
03
04
05
06
07
08
09
10
MULTIPLAYER
ACHIEVEMENTS

ACHIEVEMENT TITLE	TASK	XBOX 360 PTS	PS3 TROPHY
GOLD TROPHIES			
AUTOBOT RECRUIT	Autobot Campaign Complete (Easy)	15	15
AUTOBOT COMMANDER	Autobot Campaign Complete (Normal)	30	30
AUTOBOT PRIME	Autobot Campaign Complete (Hard)	45	30
SILVER TROPHIES			
DARK AWAKENING	Complete Dark Energon on any difficulty	10	15
STARSCREAM'S BRIGADE	Complete Fuel of War on any difficulty	10	15
THE FALL OF IACON	Complete Iacon in Ruins on any difficulty	10	15
THE SECRET OF OMEGA SUPREME	Complete Death of Hope on any difficulty	10	15
VICTORY IS MINE	Complete The Final Guardian on any difficulty	10	15
YOUR LUCKY DAY	Kill all but 1 of the neutral prisoners in Dark Energon	15	15
THIEF IN THE NIGHT	Find and disable all security tripwire switches in Fuel of War	15	15
CHAOS BRINGER	Destroy the planets in the Stellar Galleries in Iacon in Ruins	15	15
MOTORMASTER!	Race across the Chasm Bridge in 33 seconds in Death of Hope	15	15
DEVASTATOR!	Destroy all cover in the arena in The Final Guardian	15	15
DECEPTICON GRUNT	Decepticon Campaign Complete (Easy)	15	15
DECEPTICON SEEKER	Decepticon Campaign Complete (Normal)	30	30
DECEPTICON WARLORD	Decepticon Campaign Complete (Hard)	45	30
BRONZE TROPHIES			
TILL ALL ARE ONE	Complete both Campaigns (any difficulty)	30	30
BRUTE-A-KISS!	Ignite a Brute's back 5 times in Campaign or Escalation	15	15
FOOTLOOSE AND FANCY FREE	Destroy a Jet Soldier's foot thruster 5 times in Campaign or Escalation	15	15
THAT'S NO MIRAGE	Headshot a Cloaker when it is invisible in Campaign or Escalation	15	15
TARGETMASTER!	Kill 2 Snipers in 5 seconds in Campaign	15	15
THERE ARE PARTS EVERYWHERE	Multi-Kill 3 Car Soldiers at once using an explosive weapon in Campaign or Escalation	15	15
BLAST-ARACHNIA!	Destroy 100 Spiderbots in Campaign or Escalation	15	15
FIRE IN THE SKY	Melee kill a jet vehicle in the air in Campaign or Escalation	15	15
FRIENDS TO THE END	Finish any level in Co-Op	15	15
UNLIKELY ALLIES	Finish any level in Competitive Co-Op	15	15
MORE THAN MEETS THE EYE	Earn a 1st Place MVP award in Multiplayer	15	15
YOU GOT SPARK, KID	Reach level 5 in any single class in Multiplayer	5	15
SPIKE'S BFF	Reach level 25 in any single class in Multiplayer	15	15
THE KUP'S HALF FULL	Reach a combined class level of 50 in Multiplayer	25	30
ONLY THE STRONG SURVIVE	Reach a combined class level of 75 in Multiplayer	50	30
TOP OF THE SCRAP HEAP	Reach a combined class level of 100 in Multiplayer	75	30
PRIME DIRECTIVE	Unlock Prime Mode	30	30
POWERMASTER!	Spend 25,000 Power in Escalation	30	15
HEAVY METAL WAR	Reach the 25th wave in Escalation	50	90
SCAVENGER WOULD BE PROUD!	Destroy all 25 hidden Autobot emblems in the Decepticon Campaign	25	15
GRIMLOCK, SMASH!	Destroy all 25 hidden Decepticon emblems in the Autobot Campaign	25	15
ACTION MASTER	Get 10 kills with a single detached turret in any mode	15	15
WAIT! I STILL FUNCTION!	Get 3 kills while downed before being revived in any mode	30	30
RAMHORN	Ram-kill a player who is stunned by an EMP Grenade in Campaign or Multiplayer	15	15
PLATINUM TROPHY			
VECTOR SIGMA VICTORY	Unlock all Achievements/Trophies	1000	975

OFFICIAL STRATEGY GUIDE

Written by Tim Bogenn and Kartal Peel

ISBN-10: 0-7440-1217-1

Printing Code: The rightmost double-digit number is the year of the book's printing; the rightmost single-digit number is the number of the book's printing. For example, 10-1 shows that the first printing of the book occurred in 2010.

13   12   11   10   4   3   2   1

Printed in the USA.

ACKNOWLEDGMENTS

BradyGAMES sincerely thanks everyone at Activision and High Moon Studios for their truly exceptional support throughout this project. Very special thanks to Jeremy Kopman, Letam Biira, Chris Pasetto, Aaron Gray, Tim Tran, and Lalie Fisher for all your help in creating this guide and making it the best it can be—we truly appreciate it!

CREDITS

TITLE MANAGER
Tim Fitzpatrick

BOOK DESIGNER
Dan Caparo

PRODUCTION DESIGNER
Tracy Wehmeyer

BRADYGAMES STAFF

PUBLISHER
David Waybright

EDITOR-IN-CHIEF
H. Leigh Davis

LICENSING DIRECTOR
Mike Degler

INTERNATIONAL TRANSLATIONS
Brian Saliba

HIGH MOON STUDIOS

MANAGEMENT
Matt Tieger
Chuck Yager
Matt Krystek
Ivan Power
Danny Taylor

ART
Charles Bradbury
Damon Wilson-Hart
Katie Choi
Mike Snight
Rich Zagala
RJ Biglang-awa
Tyler Wanlass
Yun Kim

DESIGN
Chris Pasetto
Adam Poulos
David Ruiz
Gabe Sheets
Jared Ellott
Jeff Cole
Keith Evans
Matt Bettelman
Mike Nuthals
Terry Spier
Travis Hoffstetter
Travis Wiglesworth

ACTIVISION

BUSINESS DEVELOPMENT
Letam Biira

BRAND TEAM
Andrew Conti

LEGAL TEAM
Kate Ogosta
Chris Scaglione

PRODUCTION MANAGEMENT
Rob Loftus
Doug Pearson
Jason Ades
Aaron Gray
Jason Potter
James Bonti
Tim Tran
Jeremy Kopman

QA
Dan Grant
Robert Tai
Ivan Arzate
Mark Simons
Jonah Evans
Mike Spragg